Eda LeShan
on
LIVING
YOUR LIFE

BOOKS BY EDA LeSHAN

For Adults

EDA LeSHAN ON LIVING YOUR LIFE

WINNING THE LOSING BATTLE

IN SEARCH OF MYSELF AND OTHER CHILDREN

THE WONDERFUL CRISIS OF MIDDLE AGE

NATURAL PARENTHOOD

SEX AND YOUR TEENAGER

THE CONSPIRACY AGAINST CHILDHOOD

HOW TO SURVIVE PARENTHOOD

For Children

THE ROOTS OF CRIME

WHAT'S GOING TO HAPPEN TO ME? WHEN PARENTS SEPARATE AND DIVORCE

LEARNING TO SAY GOOD-BYE WHEN A PARENT DIES

YOU AND YOUR FEELINGS

WHAT MAKES ME FEEL THIS WAY?

Eda LeShan
on
LIVING
YOUR LIFE

Based on the CBS Radio Network Series
"GETTING ALONG"

1817

HARPER & ROW, PUBLISHERS, New York

Cambridge, Philadelphia, San Francisco, London,
Mexico City, São Paulo, Sydney

FIRST EDITION

Designer: Ruth Bornschlegel

Library of Congress Cataloging in Publication Data
LeShan, Eda J.
    Eda LeShan on living your life.
    Includes index.
    1. Conduct of life — Addresses, essays, lectures.
I. Getting along (Radio program) II. Title.
BJ1581.2.L47 1982   158   81-47791
ISBN 0-06-014958-2   AACR2

82 83 84 85   10 9 8 7 6 5 4 3 2 1

for Larry,
who makes living my life worthwhile

Contents

Acknowledgments   **xiii**

A Prefatory Note   **xiv**

New Year's Resolutions — and How to Use Them   **1**
Dieting   **2**
Making Mistakes   **3**
How to Have a Happy Birthday   **5**
Marriage: How Much Togetherness?   **6**
Loafing Is Food for the Soul   **7**
Taking Charge of Your Life   **9**
Fear of Facing a Depression   **10**
Depression: Not Beating Out Your Own Music   **11**
Computer Games   **12**
Heroes: Martin Luther King, Jr., Day   **14**
Adult Siblings   **15**
What's So Great About Being Intelligent?   **16**
Testing, Testing   **17**
Stress   **19**
Fulfilling Yourself: What It Doesn't Mean   **20**
When It's Time to Act — to Protect a Child   **21**
St. Valentine's Day   **23**
What Therapy Is For   **24**
How to Choose a Therapist   **25**
Honesty: Washington's Birthday   **26**
What's the Difference Between Marriage and Living Together?   **28**
Babies Are in Bloom Again   **29**
The Two-Income Family   **30**
What to Do in an Airport When the Plane Is Delayed   **32**
The New Sexual Guilt   **33**
Joy and Pain   **34**

Forgetting Details 35

Dating at a Later Age 37

Shyness Is a Talent 38

Book Burning, I: The Fear of Words 39

Book Burning, II: The Fear of Ideas 41

The Human Mystery 42

Humor 43

On Blowing One's Top 45

A Living Will 46

Home Pride 47

Can a Sixty-Year-Old Male Chauvinist Change His Ways? 48

The Martyr Score 50

Homosexuality, I 51

Homosexuality, II 53

The Generation Gap 54

Privacy and Sharing 55

Income Taxes 56

The Gift of Tears 58

Agnosticism 59

Play 61

Realistic Feelings of Depression 62

Grief and Mourning 63

Widows and Widowers Living Alone 64

Grandparents 66

Old Age and Dying 67

Group and Family Therapy 68

Holding Grudges 70

Hugging 71

Childhood Shadows 72

Spring and Nature 74

Mother's Day 75

How to Have a Really Cheap Vacation 76

Everybody's Fat 77

An Exhaustion unto Madness 79

The Right to Life 80

How Family Members Speak to Each Other 81

Marriage and Taking Vacations 83

Born-Again Human Beings **84**
Loneliness **85**
Sex Education **86**
The Love Industry **88**
Communication Between Partners **89**
Family **90**
Single Parenthood: The Need For a Support System **92**
The Two-Career Marriage **93**
Marriage: When Relatives Are Prejudiced **94**
A Birthday Present: The Lobster Story **96**
Middle Age **97**
Denial and Celebration: Anne Frank's Birthday **98**
The Tyranny of the Weak **100**
What Should I Do with My Son-in-Law? **101**
Jealousy **102**
Failure **104**
Lying Is a Necessary Art **105**
Drugs **107**
Marriage: When Parents Are Critical **108**
The Right to Love **109**
Education for Citizenship **111**
Father's Day **112**
If Your Kids Are Off to Camp **114**
The Preoccupation with Externals — The Youth Cult **115**
When It's Too Late to Be Sorry **116**
Car Drivers: Dr. Jekyll and Mr. Hyde **118**
Accident Proneness **119**
In the Swim of Things **120**
Inflation and the Preoccupation with *Things* **121**
On Losing One's Job **123**
Life Has Calories **124**
The Traveling Man **125**
The Immoral Minority **126**
Once the War Is Over **128**
You Never Can Tell . . . **129**
Men's Liberation **130**
Human Liberation **132**

Bisexuality   **133**

Insomnia   **134**

The Search for Unconditional Love   **135**

Dreams to Grow On, I   **137**

Dreams to Grow On, II   **138**

Dreams to Grow On, III   **139**

The Most Endangered Species   **141**

The Extended Family   **142**

Retirement   **143**

Sex in Old Age   **144**

Betrayed by the Working Woman   **146**

Talking Can Be Highly Overrated   **147**

Divorce and Mourning   **148**

When People Leave Therapy Too Soon   **149**

Young Adults and Their Parents   **151**

Pure Fun   **152**

Imagination   **153**

"Is There Life After Children?"   **154**

Meditation   **156**

Searching for an Adopted Child   **157**

Adopting Older Children   **158**

How to Prepare for a Trip to the Hospital   **160**

Parent Kidnappers   **161**

How to Comfort People in Distress   **162**

Feelings of Ambivalence   **163**

Tips for Divorced Daddies   **165**

Tips for Divorced Parents, I   **166**

Tips for Divorced Parents, II   **167**

Tips for Divorced Parents, III   **168**

Tips for Stepparents   **170**

Labor Day   **171**

Great Teachers   **173**

Ages and Stages for Grownups   **174**

The Central Theme of All Growing   **175**

The Importance of Saying No   **176**

Caught in the Middle   **177**

Middle-Aged Men   **179**

Autumn — and Aging   **180**
The Lost and the Found   **181**
Taking Risks: Columbus Day   **182**
Bigger Is *Not* Better   **183**
How to Choose a Day-Care Center or a Nursery School   **185**
The Drama of the Nursery Years   **186**
The Real Meaning of Discipline   **187**
Parapsychology   **189**
Psychic Healing   **190**
Working Mothers, I   **191**
Working Mothers, II   **193**
The Creative Art of Homemaking   **194**
Prescription for Recovery from Traumas   **195**
What *Psychosomatic* Really Means   **197**
The Healthy Aspects of Anxiety   **198**
Getting Along Black   **199**
The Tragic Nature of Life   **201**
I Love You   **202**
Do It Now   **204**
Election Day   **205**
Senility Is Remembering   **206**
Friendship   **208**
The Limits of Friendship   **209**
When a Friendship Wears Out   **210**
When Children Take Over from Elderly Parents   **211**
Selecting a Nursing Home   **213**
What Is a Woman?   **214**
Thanksgiving: Preparations   **215**
Thanksgiving: The Macy Parade   **216**
Windowless Offices   **218**
Laying a Trip on a Trip   **219**
Envy   **220**
Holiday Dieting: Forget It!   **221**
Lending Money   **223**
Oh, My Aching Back!   **224**
Men Who Are Allergic to Commitment   **225**
Battered Wives, Husbands, and Children   **227**

Old-Age Homes   **228**

Taking Pictures on Trips   **229**

Holiday Depression   **230**

Will You Leave a Hole in the World?   **232**

Christmas Letters   **233**

Reflections on Thirty-seven Years of Marriage   **234**

Games the Unconscious Plays   **235**

Christmas Presents   **237**

A Lifetime of Patchwork   **238**

The Birth of a Baby: Christmas   **239**

Stuffed Animals   **240**

New Year's Eve   **242**

One-Year Anniversary: A Summation   **243**

Index   **245**

Acknowledgments

THIS BOOK, MORE THAN MANY of my others, represents the cooperative efforts of many people, to whom I am exceedingly grateful: Geraldine Rhoads, for her faith in recommending me to the CBS Radio Network; Dick Brescia and Frank Miller, for making me feel so comfortable, and for their patience with the new kid in town; Barbara Malinowski, for doing her best to make cuts palatable; Ida Gianetta, who helped me to feel at home in a studio; Ann Harris, that rare editor who believes in author's rights; Phyllis Wender, who always thinks I'm worth more than I ever think I am; and Fran O'Leary and Connie Flynn, who somehow survived typing and organizing nearly two hundred commentaries with humor and good will. My love and thanks to all.

A Prefatory Note

IN THE COURSE of the past year I have been presenting daily commentaries on the CBS Radio Network. The title of my segment is "Getting Along," which has left me free to wander wherever I wanted to go along the general waterfront of those issues having to do with how to cope with being human.

I must have been doing something right, because there have been many requests for transcripts of my broadcasts—and this collection is the result of those requests.

I think that what I was doing right was expressing an opinion that is rarely heard these days, when so many people seem to want so desperately to be given simple answers to complicated questions. This opinion is that *nothing* about being alive and human is simple. It is the opinion that a solution that might be helpful to me might be terrible for you—and that something that we might find useful at one stage of our lives could be a disaster at some other time. It is the opinion that, rather than trying to find some nice, easy formula to help us solve our daily problems, what we have to do is to develop our inner human skills, and bring whatever growth and maturity we can muster to each situation.

I suspect—I hope—that the response to "Getting Along" has occurred because many people are tired of answers which work for a short period of time, but which are too simple and superficial for any long-term changes. We are sick and tired of books which tell us how to fight, how to love, how to raise children, how to live through a divorce, in twelve easy lessons. We are sick of an approach to life which expresses a kind of "cosmetology," gives us lesson plans and tricks for changing our behavior without ever dealing with important underlying causes. Simple solutions to difficult problems are like treating a child's rash with cold cream when he has the measles!

I have never been able to deal with my own life problems in this fashion, and what I have tried to do in these commentaries is to share with you my experiences and some of the things I have learned which have helped me grow and change. I don't often (almost never!) solve a problem completely, but I rarely make the same mistake twice! I don't know all the answers, but I have been searching for ways to live more fully, more decently, more creatively all during my adult years.

When our daughter was a child, people used to ask us what effect it had on her to be the child of two people working in the field of psychology. When she grew up, she told us the answer. She said, "You made a lot of mistakes and you were pretty crazy sometimes, but there was one thing I always knew; you were *trying* to grow and to change and to be more tomorrow than you were today."

That is all I have ever been able to promise my readers — my companionship in having the courage to go on discovering, taking risks, experimenting — seeing life as an adventure which gives us the chance to become more and better until our last breath.

I have no solutions to life's problems, but I am sure about this: Solving problems effectively depends on the degree to which we work at understanding ourselves and caring for our own lives. Until we have a sense of our own lovability, we cannot really help anyone else. Until we are eager to search for our fullest growth, we can never be as sensitive or compassionate or creative as we may want to be.

And I am absolutely convinced, after well over a half century of living, that learning to ask the right questions is a far more productive activity than looking for easy answers.

You will not find the full two hundred sixty commentaries of my broadcasts in these pages; about seventy have been omitted because they now seem dated or were repetitious or are less appropriate to the written than the spoken word. I have included all those for which there have been the most requests for transcripts.

Eda LeShan
on
LIVING
YOUR LIFE

New Year's Resolutions—and How to Use Them

HOW ARE YOU DOING with those New Year's resolutions you made with such optimism? Well, don't get discouraged—there are more important things to do with them than keep them.

I have never met anyone who managed to keep his or her New Year's resolutions, and it suddenly occurred to me, somewhere about midnight on December thirty-first, that we don't have to make resolutions in order to keep them; we can use them to learn more about ourselves. What we are really doing, as the horns blow and the streamers fly, is giving ourselves a chance to make new *choices*. We ought to make the most of that.

Let me explain what I mean, by taking a hypothetical couple as an example. Her New Year's resolutions are: not to scream at the kids, never to eat cake and ice cream, to make an appointment with the doctor about her headaches, and to have the living room cleaned up when her husband comes home from work.

If I never met the lady, I would know a lot about her. She's full of self-punishments for not measuring up to the image she thinks she should have, of perfect mother and wife. She's eating a lot of cake and ice cream because she feels so guilty about not being overjoyed every minute while cooped up with two little kids all day. What I could not know, unless I met her, is that she gets headaches every day just before her mother calls to complain about being neglected. The New Year's resolution she probably *felt* like making was to take a fast trip to the Greyhound bus terminal on January first and buy a one-way ticket to anywhere.

Her husband's resolutions were: not to scream at his wife about the mess in the living room, to take the kids all day every Saturday, and to try to find a job in accounting and quit teaching high-school math.

If I'd never met him, I could tell that he's feeling guilty, too, and that he has a pretty clear image of his wife's restlessness, but feels frus-

1

trated about what he can do about it. What I would need to be told, to get the whole picture, is that he loves teaching, but feels that more money would make life easier. Chances are that if *he* could make the New Year's resolution he'd really like to make, he'd probably meet his wife at the bus station.

They seem to care a lot about each other, but not enough about themselves. She has a right to some new life choices, and he has a right to stick to teaching. Instead of trying to follow through on their resolutions, they need to read them over carefully, and then sit down and talk to each other about their real needs and their necessary dreams for the future. Changing one's life is more important than keeping one's resolutions.

Dieting

CHANCES ARE THAT with all the festivities you've been through from December twenty-fifth to January first, you have gained some weight, and one of your resolutions was to go on a diet. There's a secret ingredient to doing that, which I happen to know a lot about.

Having lived a long life in the company of an inordinate supply of fat cells, I have learned a great deal not only about dieting, but the much harder task of keeping the weight off. What I have discovered is that, among the many causes and cures of being overweight, one factor seems to stand out from all the others — and that is anger, not at other people but at yourself.

Right now, it probably goes something like this: You could *kill* yourself for eating all those canapés at the office party. You could *kill* yourself for eating stuffing and sweet potatoes and pumpkin pie on Christmas Day. You could *kill* yourself for drinking too much on New Year's Eve — and now, when you haul yourself up on the bathroom scale, you could *kill* yourself because you've gained seven pounds you didn't need at all.

That's a lot of violent thought to be heaping on one poor slob!

Unless you can change your attitude considerably, in a week or two it will likely be ten to fifteen pounds of extra weight instead of less. I never met anyone who could become a better person by being hated. I never saw a child or an adult who improved by threats or punishment. The truth is that the only force in the world that helps us to better ourselves is love and approval.

Chances are you really know that, and you operate on that principle with everyone but yourself. And that's the catch.

Let us change the scenario to a very different monologue. You say to yourself, "Poor, poor me! What a terrible, tempting life I lead! It's a wonder that, with all that pressure, I didn't gain fifteen pounds! What self-control it took not to eat any more canapés or a second portion of stuffing and sweet potatoes! What a noble soul I am for refusing to take some pie home! It was so difficult not to hurt my hostess's feelings — she would have been mortified if I'd turned everything down, after she slaved over that meal. Come to think of it, there's some underlying hostility there — she knows I have a weight problem. Well, I guess I should be more assertive, but I'm not really sorry I was kind. I'm a nice person — and life is full of too many awful temptations."

Having had that conversation with yourself, you should now feel a wave of sympathy and understanding flowing through you, and you will be ready to endure the miseries of dieting. Guilt and self-hatred are a direct line to a hot-fudge sundae. A lot of tender loving care for your poor self is the only road to melba toast and cottage cheese.

Making Mistakes

THERE WAS A TIME when people made fewer mistakes than they do today. They never had the chance. That was because they didn't do much *choosing*. It was a lot easier never to do anything wrong when some person, or some powerful institution like the church or the school or the family or the town you lived in, made all your decisions for you. It also must have been a whole lot more boring than life is today, and my guess is that fewer people ever got to be as complicated and interesting as most of us are right now!

Oh, there were always some exceptions — people like Socrates and Galileo, who decided to make choices despite the rules — but by and large most people grew up never doubting that they had to do what they were told to do.

As far as I know, there has never been a time when people had as many options as they do today. We have to make personal decisions about almost everything. If we go to the opera, we can wear blue jeans or street clothes or a costume from the eighteenth century or formal attire; we can choose an assortment of occupations stretching all the way from itinerant carpenter to astronaut; we can get married or live with a friend or join a commune; we can choose whether or not we want to have any children; we can leave school at sixteen or go on studying until we die. The choices are almost limitless. Therefore the possibility of making a mistake, or making wrong choices which may be quite disastrous, has also become almost limitless. That's probably what makes a lot of us feel so depressed so much of the time — we're going crazy trying to handle all that freedom!

I don't know about you, but as far back as I can remember, I have learned far more from my mistakes than I ever learned from the decisions that went smoothly. It seems to me that most genuine maturation — the deepest growing of mind and soul — occurs at times of crisis and uncertainty, and in the search for alternatives to whatever it is that we have done to get ourselves in trouble.

With so many choices to make, it is probably helpful if we follow a few important rules. It helps to try to examine our motivation for making a decision. It's a good idea to explore all the alternatives open to us. We need to weigh the positive and the negative aspects of each choice, and once we have made a choice we ought to give it a fair trial. If we conclude we have made a mistake, we ought to move on — without wasting a lot of time on remorse, guilt, regrets, or self-condemnation — and spend our energy on creatively getting ourselves extricated. But the most important thing about choices is that we must *never* stop making them. Mistakes are the price we pay for becoming most fully ourselves, for realizing our human possibilities. The price is right.

How to Have a Happy Birthday

I'VE NEVER MET anyone over the age of thirty who wasn't upset by his or her birthday. By that age we're usually over our childhood preoccupation with presents and more concerned with a growing sense of time passing. If today happens to be such a birthday for you, I hope you'll read this carefully. And if it isn't yours today, you'd better read it anyway.

There are several things you can do so that no matter how old you get, you can enjoy your birthday. Of course the first and most obvious thing to congratulate yourself about is that you are *alive.* There is nothing whatever we can do about being mortal, but there are lots of things we can do about celebrating as many birthdays as possible. In that category I would include such things as sensible exercise and a nutritionally sound diet — and, most important of all, the capacity to recognize what a very large part your mind plays in protecting your body from illness. If you get sick a lot, it's probably a good idea to check things out with a shrink after having a thorough physical checkup, to see why your natural powers of immunization and self-healing are out of whack. Having *healthy* birthdays is the first step to feeling reasonably cheerful about the passage of time.

The second important clue to a pleasant celebration is that very awareness of the passage of time. You *need* to have birthdays just to remind you how important it is to live every moment as fully as possible. Look upon your birthday as an essential message to yourself that there is not a moment to waste in reordering your life if the reason your birthdays depress you is because you aren't living fully enough.

Another opportunity that a birthday presents you with is the chance to check out something quite essential. It may well be a whole lot more fun to celebrate your birthday with people you love, but could you endure to spend it alone? Could you give yourself a birthday party? If the answer is no, then you have exactly 364 days in which to see to it that you become the kind of person you can appreciate.

Most important of all, I hope you will believe me that something new and exciting *is going to happen* between this and next year's birthday.

You may remember that this past Christmas was one of the coldest on record along the eastern seaboard. I happened to be at Cape Cod, and the day after Christmas I went to take a look at the ocean and discovered, to my absolute astonishment, that *the ocean was frozen!* I shouted to my husband, "I'm fifty-eight years old and never before in my whole life did I ever see a frozen ocean!"

For those of you who are thirty-five or forty or fifty today, I'd like to tell you that I wrote the first of fifteen books at forty-three, had my own television show at forty-seven — and didn't show up on the CBS Radio Network until fifty-eight. I know an eighty-three-year-old woman who is going to college and has just joined a sorority. I know a man who learned to swim at sixty-three. A friend of mine became a lawyer at fifty-seven. I went to visit an elderly aunt of ninety-three in the hospital, and she must have been reading my mind. She said, "I guess you wonder what's keeping me alive when I'm so sick and old and miserable. Well, there's always another sunset."

Birthdays guarantee another sunset, so stop complaining. Happy Birthday!

Marriage: How Much Togetherness?

IN THE DAYS before women's lib men went out into the world to work, and women stayed home and raised children. Most men had six-day work weeks, and most women worked from dawn to dark on household tasks. Chances are that the lack of much togetherness is what kept some of these marriages from falling apart.

Betty and Bob had what everybody thought was the perfect marriage, for they seemed genuinely crazy about each other. Betty was extraordinarily bright and ambitious, and she became a college professor. Bob, more quiet and introverted, inherited a small store from his parents and ran it until he was able to sell it for enough money to retire — at the age of forty-two. What he loved best was playing golf and being with Betty. Because she loved him a lot, Betty gave up her job and retired with Bob to a small town next to a terrific golf course.

Three years later Betty died of cancer. Some of her friends (including me) thought she died of boredom and a broken heart for having given up her own identity. After her death Bob became so deeply depressed that he had to be hospitalized. In discussing this tragedy with me a very wise friend said, "They didn't have two lives—they only had one."

There was a time when most of us held the romantic illusion that one could measure the success of a relationship by the degree of togetherness. I think we are learning that probably the best way to enrich a marriage—or any relationship, for that matter—is the presence of two individuals who come together not because they are lonely and need help, but because life is so rich and exciting that it's nice to share one's personal fulfillment with somebody else.

I have often found myself thinking about the qualities necessary for a successful marriage when watching a beautiful pas de deux at the ballet. Each dancer is unique: Each has moments of exquisite achievement on the stage alone. And when the two dance together, their individual talents enhance every move they make toward each other. They separate with both reluctance and anticipation; they come together in a kind of ecstatic triumph, growing out of what each has achieved separately.

One life is never enough for two people. But two people fully expressing their uniqueness can create one marriage that is a work of art.

Loafing Is Food for the Soul

I CAN'T PROVE IT, but I suspect that Newton was goofing off—just loafing—when he saw that apple fall from the tree and gave us gravity to think about, and Galileo must have been daydreaming—just loafing around—when he sat gazing at a lamp, swinging to and fro, and got the idea that this movement might be a means for measuring the passage of time. In one graduate school of special studies, where great minds are given a year or two for thinking brilliant new thoughts, each person is given the choice of having a desk face a window or a favorite painting of one's own selection. The hope is that the thinkers will daydream, goof off, loaf around. It's necessary food for the soul, and the source of most creativity.

To be very scientific about what loafing means, I'd call it subconscious cooking! It's letting ideas simmer on a back burner: It's waiting for the inner reservoirs of one's mind to refill. It is also, as far as I'm concerned, an absolute essential for a fulfilling and productive life.

Last summer, how many of you nagged and yelled and generally raised a whole lot of fuss when your children seemed to be doing nothing at all? The twelve-year-old may have been lying on the lawn, chewing a blade of grass; the sixteen-year-old might have been dozing in the hammock, with a radio going full blast; the five-year-old may have been spending four days in a row doing nothing but building a sand castle on the beach. You kept yelling, "Why don't you *do* something?" It's a scene every parent is familiar with. I'd like to suggest that, not even waiting for next summer, you give your kids and yourself plenty of room for loafing. It is not, I repeat *not,* a waste of valuable time. It is a source of renewal and rest and a way of showing respect for the needs of the mind and the body for plateaus, for the nourishing of inner quiet, inner peace.

My husband once went fishing for a whole week without putting a hook on his line. We were on a lake where all the other fishermen were catching an assortment of wonderful fish every day. They couldn't understand why my husband was so unlucky, and every day or two they'd give us one of their fish as consolation. My husband didn't want to fish for fish, he was fishing for ideas. That week of supposedly wasteful contemplation — pure loafing — led to many years of fruitful research. Loafing at regular intervals is just as important as working the rest of the time.

It makes me furious when a teacher tells a parent that a child is daydreaming, and both of them think this is a serious problem. All important progress made by the human race has its roots in daydreaming.

Taking Charge of Your Life

BECAUSE DEPRESSION IS an emotional problem of gigantic proportions for millions of people, I expect to be talking about it many times. Here I'd like to focus on the ways in which you can help *yourself* to come out of a depression. The theme is the importance of taking charge of your own life.

One of the many and complicated reasons why we get depressed is that we are not living our own lives: We are living somebody else's life — a person designed for us by parents or a spouse or other people who are sure they know what's best for us. They don't, and the sooner each of us recovers from that silly myth the better off we'll be.

One woman wrote me that she had been told by her doctor that she would have to have a radical mastectomy for cancer of the breast. "I was depressed enough about my condition, of course," she wrote, "but I think it got worse because I felt so helpless. But then my husband insisted that we investigate — do some research on our own. I went to the medical library every day for a week and took notes. I was then able to confront my doctor with the information that there was an overwhelming body of sound research indicating that chances for recovery were just as great from a partial mastectomy, and that I was going to get other consultations. Even though I had no medical background, I was taking charge of my own disease and treatment. I think that change in attitude is what accounts for my rapid recovery — seven years ago."

That's a very extreme example. For less dramatic periods of depression there are many alternatives. The other day a friend told me, "I marked the end of my feeling depressed recently with the day I decided I'd never give another dinner party for more than six people!" Another woman told me, "The day I learned to assert myself in a shoe store and not buy anything just to be agreeable, even if I tried on ten pairs of shoes, was a great step forward in dealing with my chronic depressions."

Long and chronic periods of depression may call for some long and serious reflections on the ways in which we are *not* taking charge of our own lives. We may have to start thinking about whether or not the things we are doing bear any relation to the things we *wish* we were doing. Depression is one of the healthiest signals we ever give ourselves. It is a cry for life. It is a cry we need to listen to. It is a call to action. There is no room for feeling depressed when we are fulfilling our authentic inner dreams and running our own show. Get a move on!

Fear of Facing a Depression

DEPRESSION IS ONE of the greatest emotional cripplers of our time, and has many and varied dimensions. What I'd like to emphasize here is the fear of facing a depression.

John was dying of cancer. There is a growing body of evidence that depression lowers the body's immune system, and John's doctor suggested that, in addition to chemotherapy treatments, John should see a psychotherapist. John had been divorced many years and had lived an isolated life since then; his children were a disappointment to him. A brilliant career had faltered badly just before the onset of the cancer. John's response to his doctor's suggestion was, "I'm too sick to look at all that garbage of my life." I believe that John preferred to die rather than examine the sources of his depression.

Barbara deals with a serious, chronic state of depression by developing a different set of symptoms of disease almost weekly. Dizziness and nausea one week, stomach pains the next, numbness in her arms and legs, and on and on — a never-ending parade of complaints for which no doctor over a five-year period, has been able to find any strictly physical cause. The only periods of relief are when her agitation to avoid acknowledging the underlying depression takes the form of managing to have a serious argument with someone. The state of constant agitation is a defense against facing the depression. What is so terribly sad about such situations is that depression need not be seen as so dangerous and frightening. One road to help may be through psychotherapy, and what any therapy patient can assure a novice is that facing one's past, one's fantasies and confusions, is *never* as terrible as dealing with serious psychological stress.

But what is even more to the point, nobody has to endure chronic, severe depression now, even without psychotherapy. While I am always very cautious and reluctant when it comes to taking drugs, there is at this time a wide assortment of relatively safe drugs which relieve many different kinds of depression, and there are neurologists and psychiatrists who specialize in finding the drug that will be most suitable, safe, and helpful in each individual case.

The severely depressed person tends to be someone who is quite out of touch with his or her deepest feelings, and it is that fractured state which makes a person feel something terrible will happen if he or she acknowledges the anguish and sadness of depression. I wish I could convince such people that the avoidance of facing the depression is a far worse experience, in every possible way, than getting the help one needs so desperately.

Depression: Not Beating Out Your Own Music

IT'S EASY TO KNOW you are depressed if you feel suicidal, or can't move out of bed, or eat your way through a five-pound box of candy during one afternoon. Sometimes, however, it is very hard to tell that you are depressed. The signs are sometimes very subtle.

Seth is thirty-five years old and a very successful young man — it says right here. He went to Harvard, has a law degree, and already makes over one hundred thousand dollars a year as counsel to a large industry. He has three interchangeable, gorgeous girlfriends. He's handsome and bright and very sophisticated. I knew him when he was a little boy. He was crazy about archeology and could spend twenty-four hours a day in museums of natural history — if you let him — but his father gave him two choices when it was time to go to college. Law or medicine. Anything else was "idealistic" or "childish or sissyish" — all expletives in daddy's terms. Seth capitulated, and everybody is impressed with his rapid rise to fortune. We met at a party and I asked if he was still interested in archeology. He smiled and then said, with the saddest eyes I've ever seen, "Yeah, funny you remember that. I never even get the magazines anymore. I guess I'm afraid to." I asked, "Why afraid?" And Seth said, "There are a lot of things I don't look at much, anymore. They remind me that I don't know why I'm alive, and it's all so meaningless." That, ladies and gentlemen, is a depression: gilded, but a depression just the same.

The most profound and chronic depressions are often well concealed behind a facade of success and well-being. Human beings have an unbelievable talent for covering up, for denying their real feelings. I'm sure that Seth was sorry he met me, because I stirred up something he had long since made a bargain with himself to forget. Unfortunately, depressed feelings which stem from not living the life you were meant to have a habit of reemerging in a number of different ways. Chronic, severe depressions can make you sick in body or mind or both, without interfering with your daily functioning. You go right on doing what you think you ought to do, with everyone else's approval.

But sooner or later the danger of not singing your own song tends to catch up with you, and illnesses tend to become critical, or relations with others more destructive — until all those wonderful things you do so well but hate so much begin to fall apart.

I wish Seth and a lot of other people would realize they are in serious trouble and do something about it. A depression is no way to waste a lifetime.

Computer Games

THERE IS A NEW DRUG on the market that makes me very nervous about the future mental health of this country. This drug is not taken internally. It is computer games.

It's all happened too quickly, and I guess I'm too old and set in my ways to make the necessary adjustment, but every time I see children or grown-ups bent over a little machine, with total concentration watching lights flash, listening to buzzing sounds, relating more intensely to a small screen than they do to other people, I get extremely uneasy. It even occurs to me that the rapid development of all the computer games might be a foreign plot to hold our attention while we are conquered and enslaved. Nobody would even notice.

If it were just young people who seem to be more enthralled with football and baseball by electrical impulse than by human activity, I would think it was just a problem of the generation gap, but I see grown men and women sitting fascinated for hours playing with machines, and I am nostalgic for a good game of checkers or "Monopoly."

It seems to me that this rage of popularity for computer games is just another of the many symptoms of a society that continues to accelerate in a drunken love affair with machinery and technology. I suspect it bears little relation to the kind of genuine fun and games that lead to feeling relaxed and refreshed. It seems to me to be one more way in which we focus attention on *things* in order to overlook all the human problems that beset us.

It scares me to death to think of children preferring to learn reading and arithmetic from a machine instead of a teacher. There is something wrong in the schoolroom if a machine is more patient and more entertaining than a human companion. It also scares me considerably to think of all the things people must *not* be doing while they fool around with computer games. Things like going on picnics in the country, or playing a real-live game of baseball, or reading some old-fashioned poetry printed on a page in a book, or watching a bird splash in a birdbath.

I expect to get a lot of hate mail; criticizing computer games these days comes pretty close to blaspheming about the Bible. But I suspect that when a game comes out (as it surely will) in which two dots representing a man and a woman appear on the screen, and their relationship to each other is controlled by pressing the buttons, a lot of other people may begin to agree with me that this whole thing has gone too far.

Heroes: Martin Luther King, Jr., Day

WHAT I REALLY HOPE is that, in celebrating the birthday of Martin Luther King, Jr., we can get through the day without having to hear some new exposé referring to some further human imperfection in the man. In this matter there is no question of discrimination. We seem to be bent on destroying *all* of our heroes these days. It's a sick kind of cynicism that disturbs me greatly.

I can understand the opinion that blind devotion to anyone is a dangerous thing. But I keep wondering if there isn't some way in which we can hold on to some of our heroes. There is a kind of compulsion these days to make sure that any illusions we may have about anyone's basic decency and value be destroyed. This has created an atmosphere of such cynicism that I think we and our children are suffering from a serious case of malnutrition of our ideals. Why do we have to search for every wart and examine it under a microscope?

It's not a simple problem. Worshiping a human being is surely a dangerous business; no one can live up to superhuman expectations, and the denial of human fraility makes for dangerous magic. But there must be some middle ground.

We are living through dangerous and terrifying times that have led to a kind of violence that leaves us feeling so much guilt and shame we cannot allow ourselves to believe in the capacity for good in people.

We share a hunger, a desperate need for beacons, people who act as guideposts, helping us lead more useful and ethical lives — inspiring us to be more tomorrow than we are today.

It is no accident that *Star Trek* became the phenomenon it did. Those were superheroes with a moral purpose. Underneath all the wild action, Superman, Wonder Woman, Flash Gordon also represent a basic morality, a concern with decency and good citizenship. But fantasy characters are not enough. What we need is the capacity to see beyond the inevitable warts of real human beings.

Washington had his ladies, and Lincoln had his depressions, and nobody is perfect. *So what!* The search for imperfections in Dr. King will never turn up anything that can rob him of the fact that he made us face up to some of *our* imperfections. We need desperately to believe there are exceptional people with vision and courage whom we can trust.

We ought to be able to celebrate a hero's larger meaning in our lives without having this obsession to follow him into the bathroom or the bedroom.

More people would volunteer for the job of hero if it weren't for this cynicism and shameless curiosity.

Adult Siblings

SOME BROTHERS AND SISTERS become the best of friends in adulthood; some never speak to each other. Whichever way the wind blows, we know one thing for sure: Grown-up sibling relations reflect old and sometimes unfinished business.

I know two sisters who haven't spoken to each other since the reading of their father's will. That was forty years ago. I know a sister and brother who go on competing with each other through the successes of their much-too-pressured children. And then I also know many siblings who discover that they greatly enjoy each other in spite of being related.

In the case of the two sisters, their father's will made it clear that he had every intention of continuing his discriminatory practices even after his death. He was, if we were to make a careful clinical diagnosis, a mean, crazy person!

The older daughter, Helen, stayed home to take care of daddy when her mother died. She was serious, devoted, and colorless. The younger sister, Betsy — vivacious, beautiful, and selfish — always adored by daddy, ran away at seventeen to get married and seldom returned to visit. Her husband and she ran a restaurant and became very wealthy, but never offered to help Helen, who was eventually supporting herself and her father on her secretary's salary. When daddy died, he left his house and all his insurance to his adored Betsy.

What seems to me to be so sad about the story is not so much a father who was so twisted in his relationship with his children, but the fact that two adult women remain victimized by this injustice. Neither could surmount past history.

The brother and sister who are pushing their kids so hard are also continuing to live out old business, of a lifetime of growing up in which they always saw themselves as competitors for parental approval, never as individuals of worth on their own.

Whether or not brothers and sisters grow up to be friends is, too often, dependent on the hidden agenda of childhood. There is no reason to suppose that all siblings everywhere should or could be crazy about each other in adulthood. There is more to loving than having lived together. Sometimes differences in personality and interests, as well as geographic distance, mean we have little reason to want to remain close to each other.

But I think we ought to have some conscious choice in the matter, and whether or not we stay close ought to depend on who we are *now,* not on the rivalries and complexities of when we were growing up. It's something worth talking about, together. It's not *necessary* to stay close, but brotherly love is still a worthy goal among civilized people.

What's So Great About Being Intelligent?

I WAS RECENTLY interviewed by a class of college psychology students, and while they put it more subtly than this, what they really wanted to know was whether or not, now that I was so old, I felt as if I had learned any fundamental and eternal truths. I think I have, and I gave them my list of several; and now I want to discuss one of my strongest beliefs — that intelligence is highly overrated in this country.

Recently there was a great furor because some of the answers on a standard aptitude test required by most colleges turned out to be wrong. I wasn't the least surprised, because I have felt for most of my life that *all* the answers on *all* tests were wrong: wrong in the sense that the tests always ask the wrong questions. They want to know how many facts a person has memorized, and I don't think that has anything to do with intelligence.

Why have we become so obsessed with intelligence anyhow? Where are the lessons of history? After World War II, it seemed perfectly clear to me, from the Nuremberg Trials, that, with rare exceptions, the Nazi hierarchy was made up of men with very high IQs. After all, there were medical doctors, who must have been smart enough to get into medical school, who had done just about the most bestial experiments on human beings ever heard of in human history. What's so great about a high IQ?

My husband and I have been noticing lately that young parents often seem quite obsessed with intellectual stimulation for their babies. I think it's wonderful to encourage any living creature to explore and play and become adventurous, but this preoccupation with colored flashing lights and mobiles and crib paraphernalia doesn't impress me in the least. Babies surrounded by attentive, loving, curious people will learn. Babies without that human contact won't learn even if every crib is equipped with constant computerized programming. My husband's comment as we left the home of one highly stimulated infant was, "I'll bet there weren't any mobiles on Einstein's crib!"

Does anyone really care to know some silly number for an IQ on Mozart or Michelangelo? Edison, Churchill, and even young Einstein himself were considered very dumb when they were young.

If we would concentrate more on such virtues as compassion and curiosity, and responsibility and imagination and a spirit of adventure, intelligence would take care of itself.

Testing, Testing

HAVING CONFESSED my indifference to the concept of intelligence, I should say that the reason I feel that way is that intelligence has gotten so tied up with testing; and it's really the testing that is the villain. The inventors of the IQ test, two nice French gentlemen, Simon and Binet, must be rolling in their graves; they never meant the test to be used for judging every poor little kid who ever went to school, but simply as a measure to help them understand problems of serious deviation — retardation. If they could have predicted all the miserable, unhappy, perfectly normal children and adults who would feel demeaned by some arbitrary number, I'm sure they would have stood in bed.

I had my first IQ test when I was five. My mother asked me about it when I came home, and I said it was pretty easy except for one question which I thought was very peculiar: The lady asked me to draw a lion between a chair and a pail in a picture. I knew I could never draw a lion, so I drew a daisy instead. My mother said, "But Eda, I'm sure they wanted you to draw a line," and my answer was, "Oh, but Mommy, that would have been too easy!" Can you imagine some psychologist trying to score that daisy?

My second encounter occurred several years later and involved the beginning of a lifelong battle with arithmetic. The question was "The fox ate the three little rabbits; the fox ate the four little rabbits; the fox ate the _____ little rabbits," the dash being the place where you were supposed to add them up and write the word seven. I wrote the word *poor*. And to this day, I know my answer was the right one.

If you, as an adult, are stuck with some foolish number that you were given on an IQ test, there is very little you can do about it, because try as you might, you'll never be able to forget it. What you have to do is think about your life, your work, your successes and failures, and try to judge actions rather than numbers. I'm lucky, because I got a different score every time I was tested, ranging from ninety to one hundred and thirty. That means that I am either just slightly retarded or a genius, neither of which tells me much of anything about myself, anyway.

One thing you can do, if you are a parent, is to absolutely refuse to let anyone force you to judge the mysterious wonders within your child by number labels. We know now that even people with serious and demonstrable retardation can become useful and effective people, and this is surely true of most of us who get smart at what we love and dumb at what we hate. Always look at your *child* and relish that special person. He or she needs to fulfill inner dreams, not mathematical expectations.

Stress

STRESS HAS GOTTEN a bad name by being misinterpreted. So says Dr. Hans Selye, the man who is most responsible for bringing the word to our attention.

It has been a source of considerable help to all of us to learn that mental stress can cause physical damage. People who get heart attacks or migraine headaches — almost any disease, for that matter — are, I hope, now aware that pills alone won't solve the problem, that attitudes, feelings, one's whole lifestyle must be examined if recovery is to be successfully accomplished.

However, stress has gotten a bad name because, in learning more about it, we have tended to become preoccupied with its malignant side.

The right kinds of stress are good for us. It all depends on how we take it and how we use it.

If a principal comes to work at a school in a slum and finds that chaos reigns, that teachers are suffering from burnout and children are suffering from malnutrition, lack of discipline, and feelings of rejection, her job is a highly stressful one. If she is unable to see any way out of this mess and feels hopeless and paralyzed by it, there may be a peptic ulcer on its way to her stomach. If, on the other hand, she knocks herself out trying to make the changes she sees are necessary, and relishes each small victory, she may be dead tired at the end of each day's struggles, but she's not going to be taking much sick leave.

A man who feels required to take over his father's factory even though he hates the pressures, the worries, the gambles involved in daily survival may well crack under the strain, while his father, a tough old bird who loved every minute of the battle, may have retired at seventy-five planning to play two hours of tennis every day.

Each of us must find our own rhythm. Are we happiest when we are challenged to the limit of our energy and talents, or are we the slow and steady type? Are we actively competitive, or do we prefer watching the game from the sidelines? Are we enraptured by the noise and excitement of a big city, or do we feel most at home in the world observing the changing seasons from the front porch of a house in Vermont? What we must search for is not the absence of stress, but the kinds of stress that suits us. Anything worth doing is stressful in some ways. Even that house in Vermont can get a leak in the roof or frozen pipes, but that's a good kind of stress for someone who sees it as a challenge! We need to remember that, if it weren't for the stressful nature of nature, this planet might still belong exclusively to the amoeba.

Fulfilling Yourself: What It Doesn't Mean

THERE IS AN insidious idea floating around these days that true happiness can be gained only by fulfilling oneself. It is one of those half-truths that can lead you down the garden path to selfish and insensitive indifference to the needs of others.

Jeff is forty-three years old. Last month, on his fifteenth wedding anniversary, he announced to his wife that he needed to go and find himself. He has disappeared, leaving devastation behind him as his wife and his two kids try to figure out how to survive without him.

Barbara, the mother of four children under the age of ten, decided a year ago that she'd made a terrible mistake. Motherhood was not "her thing"; it was time to get away and become a painter. She sends her children in St. Louis pretty little drawings from Los Angeles.

There has been, of late, a great deal of confusion as well as very deliberate misinterpretation of the perfectly valid idea that the more fulfilled and happy a human being is, the more he or she can give love and support to other people. That's a terrific idea and worthy of our most serious consideration—but there is nothing in that idea to suggest that self-fulfillment can be achieved by hurting other people and running away from one's responsibilities. Jeff is not going to find a "self" worth living with as long as his children feel rejected and neglected, and even if Barbara turns out to be a female Picasso, cruel and irresponsible behavior is still the name of her game.

I would be the first to say that an unhappy, frustrated adult, doing the wrong work in the wrong place, is of no help to anybody; but there are other options than simply copping out. If a marriage is clearly on the rocks, it is possible to prepare children for an eventual divorce in such a way that the shock is softened by tenderness and loving concern for the child's feelings. If you find yourself caught in a job you despise, it is possible to ask for the loving support of one's family for a period of transition. Henry became a househusband at the age of forty-eight, when he realized his job was a bore and his wife had talents crying to be used. Rachel took a full-time job, and the two teenage kids got part-time work after school, so that George could get a Master's in education and give up being an accountant in a business that was giving him a peptic ulcer.

Sometimes we have to compromise. Sometimes we have to delay a dream for a while. We should never give up the search for our fullest potential, but if the road to that achievement is paved with other people's misery, the goal is poisoned. A grown-up is a person who sees self-fulfillment as a necessary goal for *everyone* and is able to adjust to that larger ideal.

When It's Time to Act—to Protect a Child

I RECEIVED A LETTER from a grandmother that disturbed me very much and that I'd like to share because it seems to me to bring up a most crucial and serious matter. She wrote that on several occasions I had discussed the issue of whether or not a grandparent had a right to interfere in the lives of children and grandchildren, and she was being torn apart by a situation in which she felt interference was necessary to save the lives of her grandchildren.

Sara wrote that her daughter, Kim, had left home to live with a young man when she was nineteen. The couple went to live in a rural mountain area, where they became involved with a small, fanatic religious sect. They married, and had two children. The group they belonged to believed that the only salvation was to become separate from everything connected with the modern world. The sect members lived in small cabins they built themselves, with no running water or electricity. The only heat in winter was from a fireplace, and the family lived all the time in one room. They did not believe in sending children to school and taught them at home. Their diet was vegetarian, but not intelligently so; there was a serious lack of protein.

Sara wrote that for the first few years, when she went to visit her grandchildren, who were never permitted to visit her, she was concerned, but accepted the situation. Her grandchildren seemed bright and alert and were learning well, even though they had little companionship with other children. She sensed Kim was unstable and becoming increasingly remote, but she had always been somewhat shy and withdrawn, and while Sara felt a good deal of anxiety, she also felt she had to mind her own business.

Her grandchildren are now ten and seven. On a recent visit Sara found that her daughter was very strange and distant, that her husband had left, that the children were not being taught at all anymore. But worst of all, the children were listless and terrifyingly thin. When she hugged her granddaughter, the child didn't have the strength to hug her back. It seemed to her that both children were severely malnourished, and that this was affecting their growth very seriously.

My answer to her question whether interference is ever appropriate was a resounding *yes!* It sounds to me as if Kim is very seriously disturbed emotionally and has surely become an unfit mother. While it isn't up to grandma — or me, heaven knows — to make a final decision, it is certainly time to bring in some experts, both legal and psychological, to assess the situation and probably sue for custody.

Whether or not one is a relative, it is *never* appropriate to allow young children to suffer for the serious problems of those who seem unfit to care for them.

St. Valentine's Day

I COULDN'T BE HAPPIER about its being St. Valentine's Day tomorrow. It means I get to talk about my most favorite subject. Love is the message, but not necessarily someone else's love.

Actually, not a single Valentine's Day has gone by since I was about seven years old, without my feeling a twinge of pain. This goes back to an early trauma when the children in my second-grade class exchanged valentines, and I only got three, and the prettiest, cutest, most popular girl got twenty. Or the year in junior high when Carl, the boy I had a crush on, didn't send me one, and I ended up sending one to myself and signing his name. At the time I felt guilty about lying about the card and utterly crushed and miserable — sure that nobody would *ever* send me a valentine.

Now, looking back, I feel very proud of myself. I didn't know what I was doing at the time, but maybe that valentine to myself was a way of acknowledging the fact that self-love has to come first.

Tomorrow, when the focus will be on sending cards and candy to someone else and getting the same from others, I would like to suggest that for whatever may ail you emotionally, and however much others may or may not remember you, this is a *terrific* opportunity to send *yourself* a valentine. Pick out the best one you can find and write yourself a message of love and approval. If you can *really mean it,* you will not, I promise, spend the day feeling depressed and unloved because your husband forgot, or your grandchild forgot, or your girlfriend's card was a little cool.

When I was a child, we were very carefully taught a great deal about loving other people. I'm afraid there were a lot of duties in those lessons. We *should* be kind, we *should* be thoughtful, we *should* be generous. If, when you were young, anyone ever told you that the only way you could genuinely feel all those nice things about other people was if, first of all, you felt them about yourself, your parents were ahead of their time. Many of today's younger parents are, fortunately, providing just that message, and if enough of them do, chances are very good that kindness, caring, and generosity will spring forth spontaneously rather than have to be demanded.

But since most of us did not get this message when we were young, we need to learn it now. The only way to avoid counting how many valentines you get, and feeling bad about who forgot, is to see to it that the nicest and most loving one is from you to yourself.

What Therapy Is For

FOR MORE AND MORE people mere survival isn't enough. For those greedy individuals who want to do better than that, psychotherapy may be one of the tools for hammering out a richer life experience.

A frequent reaction of many people, when they hear that I have spent a good deal of time over the past thirty-odd years in therapy, is "But why in the world would you do that? You're not crazy!"

The fact that I don't appear to be psychotic has nothing whatever to do with the matter. What *is* significant is that I decided a very long time ago that life is much too precious and much too short for me to waste any of it, and the pursuit of self-understanding seemed to me to be one important way to make every minute count.

Psychotherapy is one form of education — a way to go on learning and growing as long as one lives. It is also an extremely valuable tool for dealing with the crises of life, such as divorce or the death of someone we love. Psychotherapy can, at its best, offer us ways of examining alternatives, ways of making choices in our lives that best suit our deepest needs.

But most of all, psychotherapy is a process by which we can disentangle ourselves from some of the more ridiculous ideas we have about ourselves. Very few of us grow up without getting loaded down with misconceptions: such notions as we are good only if we do what others tell us; or we are worthwhile only if we make a lot of money; or we owe it to others to be more concerned about their welfare than our own. Most of all, a great many people have long ago repressed feelings and ideas that they perceive as being bad, when such feelings are merely human.

I can understand why many people are frightened of therapy: It is because we are so afraid the truth about ourselves will be awful. The real truth is that the person we ultimately discover in ourselves is always someone worthy of love and compassion.

Chronic depression, psychosomatic illnesses, severe anxiety are some of the signals of distress by which we tell ourselves it's time for an inner exploration. But because it's a delicate matter which requires skillful and creative tour guides, the logical next question is "How do you find the right person or the right group?" Precisely what I will talk about next.

How to Choose a Therapist

IF YOU HAVE DECIDED to enrich your life by exploring it through psychotherapy, some guidelines about how to choose a therapist may be useful.

The single most important factor in choosing a therapist is to trust your own judgment. We feel quite free to choose our lawyer and our dentist not only for their professional integrity, but also according to whether we like them as people. In choosing a therapist it is far *more* important that it be a person you might well choose as a friend: someone you trust; someone with similar tastes, attitudes, philosophy of life.

Professional credentials are a must. Run, do not walk, away from some overnight wonder who used to be a cab driver but after three training encounter groups is now a "facilitator," the person who runs things. The reason you want someone with the right working papers is that knowledge and experience free a therapist to use his or her own judgment and to move on to individualized creativity in human relations. Ignorance and inexperience can never, ever provide your precious psyche with the necessary safeguards. A good therapist is familiar with all schools of therapy and can then choose his or her own unique way of relating. It does not matter whether you choose a psychiatrist, psychologist, social worker, or counselor, provided the person has good training. Each of those specialties includes idiots and angels, incompetents and experts.

After ascertaining credentials, the next step is entirely up to you. The very first feeling that can tell you what you need to know is this — after your first session, do you feel more inclined than ever before in your life to like yourself, to feel you are a lovable human being? After that, did you like the office? Did the furniture, paintings, and books make you feel at home? Was the therapist willing to answer all your questions directly and openly? Did you get the impression this person feels he or she has all the answers to every problem (in which case run like blazes), or did you get the feeling that he or she was interested in exploring with you, with no preconceived expectations of where you'd be going?

A psychotherapist ought to be a loving companion — a sensitive, wise, mature person who shares an adventure with you. A therapy group ought to be a place where you feel comfortable and stimulated, protected as well as encouraged to take risks. In either setting you ought to get the clear message that you are in charge of your life and that what you need is a companion, not a crutch.

You may have to see a number of people in order to find the person whom you can look forward to meeting each time. It's a little like falling in love: When the chemistry's right, anything seems possible. That attitude in itself is therapeutic.

Honesty: Washington's Birthday

WHEN I WAS A CHILD, the story about George Washington admitting he'd chopped down the cherry tree sounded quite noble. Things seemed much simpler then. Now, I often wonder if honesty is always the best policy.

A woman, recently separated from her husband, was suffering from a serious depression. A friend recommended that she attend a weekend marathon of an encounter group, and Jane was so desperate that she decided to go, despite some misgivings. In the course of those forty-eight hours she was encouraged to let go, to allow all her feelings to come out; being in a most vulnerable state, Jane was soon sobbing uncontrollably and pouring out ten years of personal hell to a group of total strangers. She held nothing back about her sex life, her relationship with her parents, her confusions and failures. It was like a volcanic eruption.

Ordinarily, Jane tended to be a very private person. At the end of the weekend the group members hugged her, trembling and exhausted, and the leader assured her that now that she'd been honest with herself, she would be able to pick up her life and move forward.

Sounds wonderful? There is just one problem with this magical weekend miracle. Jane got back to her apartment, began to realize how she had exposed herself and all the members of her family to scrutiny by a group of total strangers, and had a first-class nervous breakdown, involving many months of a slower and less dramatic therapy that helped her to find her *own* pace, her *own* best way of looking at her life.

We have been living through an era in which an idea took hold in the field of therapy and counseling — that facing the truth as quickly and as dramatically as possible was the road to personal salvation. If you feel your wife is a lousy lover, tell her; if your mother is a hypochondriac, tell her what a bore she's getting to be; if a friend's hairdo stinks, say so. The truth shall make us free!

No such luck. Self-revelations arrived at too quickly may leave permanent scars on the psyche, and hurting other people's feelings turns *off* communication instead of opening it up.

The ability to face ourselves and our life situations with honesty instead of denial is certainly a worthy goal. Denial is such a heavy load to carry. Wanting openness in human relationships rather than deceit is another great idea. But as with all good things, a certain realistic temperance is necessary. If you *honestly* respect your own uniqueness, and if you *honestly* care about other people, you will be wary of those who tell you the only road to happiness is telling it like it is. The problem is who really *knows* how it is?

What's the Difference Between Marriage and Living Together?

WITHIN A PERIOD of two weeks my husband and I were invited to two weddings. Each couple had been living together for some time — three years in one case, eight in the other. I pleaded with all four friends to please explain to me why they had decided to marry after living together for such a long time. What made the difference? Why marriage now? The only answer I got was "I don't know," so I had to try to figure it out myself.

Pam and Dave, who have lived together for eight years, have redecorated their apartment and have traveled extensively; his family is crazy about her, and her family is crazy about him. Pam is devoted to Dave's adult children from an earlier marriage. She was supportive and compassionate when Dave's business was in trouble. Dave has watched Pam climb to great success in her work — he's her greatest booster. When Pam had pneumonia, Dave canceled an important business trip in order to take care of her.

Phyllis and Martin, who have lived together for three years, are excitable, creative people who love each other a lot but who also need a great deal of freedom and independence. It's an explosive relationship, and you're never sure whether or not they will be speaking to each other at all, or glowing and boasting of each other's accomplishments. He's full of pride in her paintings, and she sent letters to all their friends describing the reception of his piano concerto at a concert in California.

The thing is that all four of these friends already seemed to me to have fulfilled the criteria for marriage. They take pleasure in each other's company, but lead fulfilling lives of their own. They fight and make up. Their dreams and hopes for each other are just as intense as their hopes and goals for themselves. They can sometimes say and do hurtful and damaging things to each other, but instead of turning away they all seem to have the capacity to communicate honestly and figure out what's happening. Supportive sometimes, they can be willful and self-centered at other times.

In the years we have known them, we have seen them stretch themselves, fly off in different directions, search for individual fulfillment, and then, after a while, come together again as inexorably as the tides coming in and going out.

For these two couples, I really couldn't for the life of me figure out what would be the difference between living together and getting married. What had made them decide to have big family weddings? And how come they were doing it up so royally in each case, with a religious ceremony, engraved invitations, and a catered affair? It was all very mysterious and puzzling, and then in a brilliant flash of insight I figured it out: I know exactly why they were getting married. It was because that's what they'd already *been,* all along!

Babies Are in Bloom Again

IN THE SUPERMARKET the other day, it suddenly occurred to me that I've been seeing a lot more young babies lately. For a while it had seemed to me that babies were just a figment of my aging imagination, but, admitting to a firm bias, I'm happy to report babies are in bloom again.

Some years ago, a young man, trying to explain the sharp drop in the birth rate, said to me "You see, Eda, babies are an *impediment.*" During those years I heard a lot of similar opinions. In the first flush of women's lib it appeared that one of the first freedoms was to be the freedom from motherhood. Our awareness of the very real hazards of the population explosion seemed to dampen some parental urges. More living together, more emphasis on women achieving their rightful personal fulfillment, the awful expense of raising a child today all played a part in the presence of fewer babies.

I had mixed emotions. I feel we could change civilization for the better in one generation if every single child conceived was desperately wanted by two mature adults ready and willing to commit themselves to the hardest and most important job in the world. I wish all children could be so chosen. But I also think grown-ups need children in their lives — their own or someone else's — in order to remain civilized, hopeful, creative people.

I recently went to visit a young couple with a new baby. Janet and Herbert are in their mid-thirties. Each has explored a number of different lifestyles. Five years ago neither had any intention of becoming a parent. Like many other young people, they began to have second thoughts as the time approached when it would be too late to be able to choose. The three of us stood together gazing down at Jason, just two months old. What a miracle a baby is! The ultimate renewal, the bravest commitment to the future. I felt overwhelmed by the wonder of what was unknowable about Jason. What talents, what new ideas, what capacities for living and loving already existed in that tiny person?

I'm glad babies are back in style, and also that they are being chosen with deliberate care. Being chosen is good for the babies, and their presence in our lives is good for us. There is no creation anywhere in the world more civilized than a tiny baby. He or she looks out toward life without prejudice or deceit or meanness, and all through a child's growing years we are given the most precious gift of all — a chance to feel like a child again ourselves.

Cheaper by the dozen is definitely *out,* if we are to avoid standing room only. But I'm glad for the renewed sense of wonder and awe and delight that the birth of each new human person can bring into our lives.

The Two-Income Family

ONE OF THE MANY consequences of rapid inflation has been the necessity for both husbands and wives to hold down jobs. The extra money relieves the *financial* pressure, but may lead to a variety of *psychological* problems.

Janet is the mother of two young children: Given a choice, she would like to devote the major part of her time and energy to her kids for a few more years, but the financial burden on her husband, Bill, has become too great, and she has had to get a job. In addition to the realities of a heavy and taxing schedule, she is carrying a burden of hidden anger and resentment because she's given up the role she wanted, and she now feels she's doing two fulltime jobs instead of one. If she keeps her growing resentment to herself, sooner or later this will do serious damage to her marriage. It will also not go unnoticed by her children and may well lead to some variety of psychosomatic illness — a substitute avenue for expressing angry feelings. A far better approach would be to sit down with her husband and let him know just how rotten she feels. The sooner she says the words, the quicker this will rekindle her sensitivity and compassion for her husband's feelings. Then the two of them can work out some kind of program for sharing the load and meeting their children's needs together.

Fred and Susan have no children, but she earns more than he does. In spite of all the liberalizing influences of the past few years, there is still, deep inside many of us who grew up under different social attitudes, an uncomfortable residue of signals that the man is supposed to earn more than the woman. If this hidden agenda isn't brought out in the open, it too can poison a relationship. It can lead to the attitude of "I earn more than you do, so it's my money" or "I'm not as valuable a person as you are because I earn less."

In any close and loving relationship, each partner ought to have some private money, no matter which person earns it. Beyond settling on the amount each can take out of the general income for personal needs, the rest of the money ought to be *ours,* not *his* or *hers.* And if and when problems arise, they ought to be communicated fairly quickly.

I chose the words *fairly quickly* quite deliberately. The first step in dealing with the emotional baggage of two incomes is to try to face your own mixed feelings. The second stage may be to let yourself feel abused, mistreated, and exploited and to allow your anger and self-pity plenty of room between you and yourself. After that period of private catharsis, you will be ready to discuss the realistic problems with concern for your partner as well as yourself.

We may need a whole lot of money to live these days, but we need a whole lot of mutual respect and compassion even more if we are to make living worthwhile.

What to Do in an Airport When the Plane Is Delayed

ARE THERE ANY among us who haven't had to sit and wait in an airport for a few hours? Isn't it *hell?* Our numbers are legion, and we need help.

In the beginning, airports used to be very pleasant places. There were soft chairs and no lines or confusion, because there weren't very many people around. I need hardly describe the chaos, the miserable plastic chairs, or the mile-and-a-half walks to the plane that identify today's flying conditions. What used to be an exhilarating adventure now has many of the characteristics of riding in a New York subway.

There may be better ways to deal with this particular stress than drinking too much, eating junk food, or smacking somebody who hits you with a suitcase!

Since I travel a lot more than I want to, I now save up some of my bills and letters and put them in a writing case with stamps, an address book, and stationery, and take care of my correspondence during long waiting periods. When I finally get on the plane, I feel relieved at what I've accomplished, instead of wanting to kill somebody.

I have also discovered that waiting in an airport is a great time to phone some friend or relation I rarely talk to. I go through my address book and find someone who lives as close to wherever I happen to be as possible. I charge the call to my home phone so I don't have to keep looking for change, and I'm instantly soothed by the surprise and pleasure at the other end of the line. I'm also comforted by the sympathy I get for being stuck in that damned airport. When I board the plane I feel refreshed by our shared memories and the new communication between us.

Sometimes I check my bags and *deliberately* walk to the farthest gates, to get some exercise before the long period of sitting. Once, I met a jogger who told me he always carried his running shoes along, for just such an opportunity.

A friend tells some official she feels faint, and is immediately directed to a nice, quiet cot for a little snooze. Another enterprising friend, facing a four-hour delay, hailed a taxi and told the driver to take him to the best restaurant in the area, where they both had dinner and enjoyed each other's company!

Taking charge of one's time is in itself therapeutic. It's being your own pilot until you get on board.

The New Sexual Guilt

MANY MEN AND WOMEN in my grandparents' generation were inclined to feel guilty if they enjoyed sexual relations. The big news is that nowadays people feel guilty if they don't enjoy it enough.

The psychiatrist Thomas Szasz recently published a book entitled *Sex by Prescription.* It is, I think, a sign that a wave of reaction against the sex technicians is setting in, and I, for one, am greatly relieved. What Dr. Szasz is concerned with is the idea held by many physicians and sex counselors of all kinds that sex is a question of health or illness and that people need training in order to be fulfilled sexually. What has happened in the past ten or fifteen years, with the encouragement of Kinsey and Masters and Johnson, is a sharper focus on technique rather than on relationships. Most of these experts would deny this charge; they would protest that all their concentration on sexual skills is to help people achieve closer relationships. There is some truth in that argument — but if, for example, in the name of improved sexuality, marriage partners are encouraged to have sex relations with a surrogate partner, nobody can convince me that love is being given a higher priority than positions.

There have been some brave voices crying in the wilderness, long before Dr. Szasz. Way back in 1966, the psychologist Dr. Rollo May wrote a prophetic article in *The Saturday Review* in which he pointed out that while the old-fashioned Victorian psychiatric patient suffered from a serious repression of sexual impulses, feelings, and drives, the modern patient suffered equally from feelings of loneliness, isolation, and an inability to experience feelings of love, tenderness, and commitment.

No one in his right mind would suggest that we return to the dark ages of ignorance and shame about sex, and certainly there are serious problems for which people may need help. But the sexual revolution,

e all revolutions, has brought us to extremes, and we now need to
turn to a more balanced view. What we need to remember is that
people who are deeply in love, and who are open and honest with
each other, are capable of ingenuity and a spirit of adventure in the
privacy of their own experience. Since this is so, it would seem to me
that, while all of us can benefit from some scientific information, the
most important issue is not information but attitudes.

Dr. May concludes in his article that the Victorian person sought to
have love without falling into sex, while the modern person seeks to
have sex without falling into love.

Now that we've had our sexual revolution, we may come to our
senses. Guilt and ignorance can surely cripple a love relationship, but
there is another truth — that loving, each in our own special way, is still
the best reason for sex.

Joy and Pain

THE TROUBLE WITH trying to avoid all painful feelings is that you will end
up experiencing very little joy.

Some time ago my husband and I went to see a play called *On
Golden Pond,* which is about an elderly couple becoming increasingly
aware that time is running out for them. The play is a celebration of
their love and an honest look at their anguish, and we laughed and
cried with them. When the play was over, we knew that we had
moved closer to understanding our own future and that we would be
stronger for this experience.

A woman sitting in front of us, however, beat a hasty retreat out of
the theater, muttering, "I can't *stand* plays that try to make me cry!" I
felt sorry for her. If she couldn't bear to look at the dying, she must
not have noticed all the living and the loving, which were present in
equal proportion.

To know the full dimensions of ourselves, we need to be able to
feel very deeply — and there is no way of doing that without experi-

encing some very intense pain. It *is* possible to skim the surface of life without being profoundly touched by anything, but that isn't much of a life. The death of someone we love can cause the most terrible grief, while at the same time we find ourselves more aware than ever before of how precious life is. The failure to get a job we wanted very much can lead to deep depression, but that experience makes the exultation of later successes more intense.

In order to feel deeply about anything, it is necessary to feel deeply about many things, both painful and pleasurable ones. It's a package deal. A young woman told me a close friend from her childhood died a week before she herself gave birth to her first child. She said that somehow the shock and grief of that death had made the birth of her daughter a more profound affirmation of life, the most exquisite joy she had ever experienced.

While nobody could ever wish tragedy and suffering on another human being, life itself provides a good deal of pain; and when we don't try to deny its presence in our lives and we use it for growing, it deepens our capacity to experience the joyous in life.

Another friend, widowed at the age of forty, refused the tranquilizers offered to her by her doctor. "No," she told him, "I want to experience my grief. If I walk around like a zombie, it would make my life with Steve seem very trivial."

I know a woman who never goes to sad movies because they might depress her. The irony is that I've never seen her really happy.

It takes a great deal of courage to weep for the tragic in life. But I don't know any other road to roaring laughter and piercing joy.

Forgetting Details

HAVE YOU RECENTLY met someone you've known most of your life whose name you couldn't remember? Did it make you feel embarrassed and anxious? Take heart. I have good news for you. You're *not* getting senile.

My husband and I were sitting in a restaurant when I noticed a woman sitting opposite me who reminded me of someone who had been my next-door neighbor until about fifteen years ago. She was a lovely, generous, kind lady, and we were terribly upset when she died a few years ago. The woman in the restaurant could have been her clone — but that wasn't the point. What was driving me crazy was that I couldn't remember my neighbor's name.

Even though I tend to carry on a lot when I forget things, I know perfectly well I don't really believe I'm losing my marbles. What I *do* believe — and many psychologists are now supporting my theory — is that I am just becoming more selective about what I remember!

When we were born, we didn't know any facts at all. We were just a mass of wonderful and terrible feelings, ranging from the ecstasy of being fed at the breast to the agony of being lonely and wet and hungry.

After that normal phase, we were catapulted into the world of facts. The only way human beings survive in the real world is by knowing a lot of things — like crossing only at green lights, buying a coat, cooking a meal without getting burned, running a computer at a bank, or reading the fine print on a contract.

By the time we reach middle age, we know *millions* of facts, and selecting the more *important* ones becomes necessary for survival. Unimportant facts lose their significance. As we get older what we want to remember is the *essence* of our experiences, not the minor details. Most of all, we want to remember love, for if we are lucky, we have discovered that love is what life is all about.

Our forgetfulness, I am happy to report, is not a disease, nor a form of natural decay, but a higher level of selectivity!

Instead of getting flustered and embarrassed when you meet someone with a familiar face but no name, you might experience far less stress and make the other person feel less rejected, if you can openly and honestly say, "I remember some of the most wonderful things about you, which I'll be glad to recount, but your name has flown out of my mind at the moment."

Her name was Marian. I remembered it a few hours later. What difference did it make? I have never forgotten the two of us talking to our flowers in the backyard, how she loved our daughter, and how kind and generous she always was. What's a name compared to remembering love?

Dating at a Later Age

A MAN I KNOW told me that he stayed in a painful and destructive marriage relationship far longer than he should have because he was terrified of returning to the dating game! That man has a lot of company!

A fifty-year-old widow wrote me that she felt caught between loneliness and a revolting alternative — regressing to acting like a fourteen-year-old, just starting to date.

Many adults who are widowed or divorced seem to find the return to the courting process very difficult, painful, and embarrassing. One thirty-five-year-old man told me he couldn't get over the change in women since he first married at twenty-two. "Their language really embarrasses me," he said, "and so many of them are so aggressively instructive on what I should do to turn them on that I get completely turned off!"

A forty-three-year-old woman told me that it was very disconcerting to be going through exactly the same struggles as her fifteen-year-old daughter: They had confided to each other that they didn't know what to do about the pressures being put on both of them to hop into bed on the first date!

It seems to me that some of the discomfort of starting to date again after many years of being out of practice arises from the mistaken assumption that men and women make that it's supposed to be the way it was when they were teenagers — that they must now go through the same process that they have been through before.

I think that's nonsense. They are *not* teenagers anymore, and I can't see any reason why they should have to go through an experience that was painful enough the first time around.

And that's exactly my point. People in their thirties, forties, and fifties — even seventies and eighties — ought to have some better notion about who they are, what they like and don't like; they ought to have found more words for directly and honestly communicating about their feelings. Dating a second time around is *not* at all the same as the first time, and you ought not to try to make it the same.

One friend, divorced at fifty, told me that the best thing about dating at her age is that she no longer pretends her feet don't hurt in high heels! Another woman told me, "The difference between when I was a kid and now is that when a man is still in mourning for his marriage, I can really listen and really help — something I certainly couldn't do when I was young."

Beginning to meet new people can be an exciting adventure and a pleasurable refreshment if you remember that you are a grown-up: that you have maturity, experience, and humor you never dreamed you could be capable of when you were young. You can be frank and open and direct because you are *not* a terrified and self-conscious thirteen-year-old.

Act your age and be yourself. Use all that you have become, and it won't be a second try at an *old* game, but the newest game in town.

Shyness Is a Talent

CHANCES ARE THAT if you are shy, you wish you could get over it. Before you try too hard to fight it, I would like to suggest that you consider the idea that shyness is a talent.

First of all, let me try to clear up the myth that the shy person is the one who walks into a room full of people, turns bright red, stammers a lot, sinks into a chair in a corner, and is never heard from again. The clown who is shouting dirty stories at the top of his lungs and slapping people on the back, oblivious to their annoyance, may actually be just as shy. What both people have in common is feeling *ashamed* of being shy.

First we have to consider beginnings. If, when we were children, our parents and other adults made us feel ashamed of being shy, one way we learned to deal with it was by denial. We didn't get rid of this quality, we only disguised it. Becoming a buffoon is one way. If you end up enjoying whatever it is you are doing, that's a lucky break for you, but if your bluff is hard work, that's bad. Most children accept the adult view of shyness as a curse and end up teaching each new generation the same thing.

It's all such a shame, because if we had been told the truth when we were children, we could be proud of being shy, and that pride might make us less the blushing violet or the loud-mouthed boor.

While it is true that some of us are born with an inclination toward shyness, it is also something we learn when we are very young. Shyness is the way children express their growing awareness of other people. It is a way of being sensitive about other people's feelings. By the time we are four or five years old, we realize that human relationships are very complicated. People sometimes misunderstand each other; people's feelings can be hurt. We begin to understand that there are social customs we have to learn — how to be polite, how to talk to someone on the telephone, how to talk to people who are older than we are: The more we care about other people, the more shy we may feel.

What all this comes down to is that shyness is a form of sensitivity, a self-consciousness about whether or not we are making a good impression and know how to show a concern for others. What's bad about that? Nothing whatever, if we accept this quality in ourselves with pride instead of anxiety and shame. We might relax and enjoy that roomful of people without shrinking or shouting.

Book Burning, I: The Fear of Words

THERE WAS A RECENT REPORT that *365 Days,* a book on the Vietnam War by Ronald Glasser, was being banned in a school library. The book is a graphic report, written by a physician who was there. It has been on the bookshelves of libraries all over the country for the last ten years without censorship. Situations such as this are far too frequent for my comfort, but this particular event seemed to me to symbolize very clearly what book burning is really all about. It is a psychological problem with terrifying political implications.

365 Days is about the awful price of war. The parent who started the action to have the book banned was quoted in a newspaper as saying that he had no objection to the accuracy or the theme of the book, but it contained too many four-letter words which he didn't want his children to read. To my knowledge there are no four-letter words which are not known to most children over the age of ten, but that doesn't seem to me to be the crucial issue — which is that four-letter words, however distasteful they may be to a great many people, seem somewhat insignificant when the subject under discussion is *war*. What is a four-letter word in comparison to the death of even one young man?

The real question is: Why do words have such magical power over people? Why is it that certain combinations of letters can so enrage a person that a terrible human issue like the horrors of war can become a secondary consideration?

I think I know the answer, and it comes from forty years of studying child development. As adults we do something to little kids that gives words a magical impact. Probably nothing that happens in a child's growth is more significant than learning to talk. When a baby first says, "Da da," everybody smiles with approval. The child feels that a sound can make people crazy about him. But when the same child at three says, "Ca ca," he may suddenly meet with disapproval, anger, embarrassment (if it's said in a bus or in front of a neighbor). Just changing one letter creates a whole new atmosphere! And when a child combines some other sounds, which come out, "No, I won't!" he or she discovers that words seem to have a tremendous effect on other people.

Washing a child's mouth out with soap, or any other punishment for saying certain words, confirms the child's feeling that words are magical and can change human relationships. We get stuck in that rut of misconception unless adults teach us that words are *not* the same as actions. They can be pleasing or unpleasant because of how other people have been brought up to feel about them, but words alone are never the same as an action — a vital distinction.

Next I'd like to discuss another aspect of the book-burning syndrome, the fear of *ideas*.

Book Burning, II: The Fear of Ideas

WHAT I'D LIKE to talk about now is the fear of *ideas* and how that plays a part in the ugly business of book burning.

I believe that the perception that words and thoughts are synonymous with actions stems from early childhood experiences, as children discover language. For example, suppose a four-year-old turns sweetly to his mother, while she is bathing the new baby sister, and says, "Let's take her back to the hospital." If mother gets enraged or hysterical and punishes big brother for saying such a terrible thing, he will be learning that thoughts and ideas inside one's head are just as bad as taking action, doing something. If, on the other hand, mother is wise enough to smile and say, "You know, I think all brothers and sisters get to feel angry and jealous sometimes, and it's okay to *think* about it, but mothers and fathers don't let children *do* anything to hurt each other," the lesson the child will learn is vital to his good mental health. The message is that *thoughts* inside one's head can never hurt anyone, only actions can hurt. It is a message which also says that it is normal to have a very broad range of feelings and there's nothing at all wrong with that. This frees a child to become an adult who can accept human frailty and who will also understand that ideas are never dangerous unless they are put into action.

If people behave destructively, that's the time to stop them — not while they are just thinking about it. The book *Mein Kampf* didn't kill anyone; only people deciding to *act* on its message could produce a holocaust. The ideas in the books burned as a result of those human actions did not turn to ashes at all, because there is no way ideas and thoughts can ever be eliminated. It is only actions that need to be controlled for the safety and well-being of society.

Feelings, ideas, thoughts *can* be repressed if the punishment is great enough, and that's really the only possible way to make a thought dangerous. If a child is beaten for thinking something angry, the anger can get so buried that he never feels it at all — until it suddenly explodes, out of control, and kills somebody. Putting people in prison for ideas we don't like may stop them from talking about what's on their minds, but now the idea has been given a dangerous new dimension. Repression or censorship of thoughts is what leads to dangerous acts. Allowing for full freedom of thought makes us much safer. Differentiating between thoughts and actions may be just about the most important thing we can teach our children.

The Human Mystery

SOME YEARS AGO, when my husband was giving a speech at a psychological convention, he started out by saying, "Having now worked in the field of psychology for forty years, I've learned one thing; I don't understand people!" He was only partially kidding. After just about a century of the scientific exploration of the human mystery, we know quite a few more details than ever before, but not much more than Euripides and Shakespeare were able to figure out. It's discouraging but understandable.

A very sad thing happened to psychology on the way to being born. This field of human study came along just at the time, at the turn of this century, when great progress was being made in the physical sciences. Physics and chemistry were developing what has come to be called "the scientific method." What we are finally beginning to understand is that there is no *one* scientific method, but that we have to find new methods for each field of study.

Because research in physics and chemistry was going along so swimmingly, psychologists tried to adapt the same methods to the study of people.

As far as I am concerned, it has been one big bust. I consider almost totally invalid such wonderful things brought to us by the wrong scientific method as intelligence tests, statistical studies and questionnaires, and making broad judgments of large groups of people. It just can't be done using tools that should have stayed in other fields. We have learned small and unimportant things about human beings because our methods of study could deal only with little pieces of the whole. For example, the first intelligence test was invented simply to get a rough estimate of the differences between a normal, generally intelligent person and someone who was feebleminded. Laboratory tests, multiple-choice questions, statistical studies — almost all designed to study pathology, which they do reasonably well — tell us little or nothing about the broad range of human potential, about the ways in which we grow and change, about the ways in which the environment enhances or crushes our talents.

The only real progress in the study of people has occurred where the scientist was also an artist, with a broader perspective. But we still know little or nothing about genius or creativity or love or the reasons for war — and those are the larger issues that could help us understand ourselves. We know next to nothing about humor, which I think could be a real key to unlocking the human mystery, but which is not susceptible to mechanistic investigations.

Humor

IF YOU'RE INTERESTED in the subject of why some people are funny and other people aren't, I can save you a lot of trouble. It will do you little good to search the psychological literature to learn more about humor, because there's almost nothing there.

At one time I thought it would be an interesting idea to do some research on the subject of humor in order to write an article about how we could develop a sense of humor in our children. It seemed to me that in the course of my lifetime, most of the people I've admired, such as Abraham Lincoln or Danny Kaye or Art Buchwald or Will Rogers, were very civilized people. Along with having a wry sense of themselves and others, they were basically decent, good human beings. The people I hated the most, like Adolf Hitler or Joseph Stalin, seemed quite humorless — and extremely bad human beings.

I tried hard to find some useful material on this subject, but aside from a few psychoanalytic attempts to figure it out that didn't make much sense to me, there was very little information to guide us in the quest for helping our children develop a sense of humor.

I think you too will get a sense of the social importance of humor if you make your own list of people who have it and people who don't, among your friends and relatives as well as public figures. I think you will find that you are drawn to people who look at life with a slightly jaundiced view and can laugh at themselves as well as at life in general.

It's important to distinguish between the kind of humor which helps us all laugh together about ourselves and the kind of sharp, mean humor which is designed to be hurtful. The kind of humor I find most intriguing is the kind that points up universal human foibles and makes us feel closer to each other. For example, Adlai Stevenson was a very witty man, and when he could join in our laughter over the photograph of himself with a hole in his shoe, for that moment we were joined together.

If you just take the list of presidents over the past half century, I think you will find that those with a rich sense of humor, like Harry Truman, were more in touch with the needs of ordinary people than those who made jokes, like Richard Nixon, but never really understood the funny side of life.

The only clue I've got about humor is that the best humorists laugh the hardest at themselves. That suggests that they are very secure people with a high level of self-confidence — otherwise they couldn't laugh at themselves. I think that humor is just one more of the many clues we have that liking oneself is the beginning of being civilized to others.

On Blowing One's Top

WITH ALL THE EXPERTS running around loose, it becomes increasingly difficult for parents to maintain a sense of humor about child raising. We
feel our inadequacies so deeply and spend so much of our time feeling
guilty that we rarely enjoy our children.

Because of these feelings of guilt, I cherish a story told to me by the
mother of two restless, noisy boys, aged seven and nine, who were
both home from school recovering from the mumps. Toys were
strewn all over the house; there were endless fights and whining and
demands for constant entertainment. By the third week, this mother
said she seemed to be screaming all her waking hours.

One morning she woke up with new determination. She was going
to be the perfect mother — patient, understanding, sympathetic, full of
lovely and constructive plans. She suggested a festive tea party with
lace mats and the best china — and despite some inner misgivings, she
even suggested the party be held in the dining room instead of the
kitchen, for added glamour. Just as she placed cups of cocoa and a
can of Reddi-wip on the table, the phone rang. She warned the boys
not to touch anything, and she made the conversation as brief as possible, but as all mothers reading this have now anticipated, the boys
did *not* wait for mom. When she returned, the Reddi-wip had been
squirted directly into the cocoa, which was now all over the lace table
mats, the upholstered chairs, and the beige rug. This mother told me
that it was as though she went into some kind of fugue state; the
weeks of imprisonment had finally caught up with her. "I went crazy,"
she said. "I took that can of Reddi-wip and I sprayed it on the children,
on the table, on myself, on the wall — everywhere!" Then she asked
me, "Do you think I damaged my children psychologically?" I was
really too busy enjoying the image of that apartment to care, but I
asked what happened next. She said that when she came to and realized what she was doing, she was horrified, but the two boys were
rolling on the floor howling with glee. They helped her clean up, they
put away their toys, and when daddy came home, they giggled so
much they could hardly tell him the story. Now, whenever their mother's voice get the least bit strident or desperate, they shout, "Reddi-
wip!" and run for cover!

It hardly sounded to me as though this had been a traumatic experience: quite the reverse. Whenever life gets to be too much for me, I love to recall that mother and her can of Reddi-wip getting rid of all the frustrations, the exhaustion, the impatience, that are a normal part of the human condition. Laughter is the greatest healer of all.

A Living Will

THERE ARE FEW subjects about which people get more emotional than writing their wills. I'd like to suggest that we start writing *living* wills instead of *dying* wills.

I received a letter from my daughter a few weeks ago in which she said she had never been happier in all her life — that fifteen ducks were coming to be fed almost daily, including the duck with the broken beak. I felt a piercing sense of joy and spent the day in a warm glow, which returns every time I think about what she said.

She and her husband are living in a house belonging to me and my husband, which we plan, if we possibly can, to give them while we are still alive. The house is on Cape Cod, on a lake, and it is a place where I, too, have been happier than any place I've ever lived. It has become too big a burden, as we get older, to take care of the house and to commute back and forth to New York, but we have put so much of ourselves into the house and the grounds that we cannot bear to sell it. That would be the sensible thing to do, but the wrench would be very painful. In my younger years, and when travel back and forth was far less expensive, I became a gardener and a bird-watcher there, and fell in love with the wild ducks, who became my playmates.

After I read my daughter's letter, I realized that if I had waited for her to inherit the house when I died, I would never have known that she would love it as much as I do and that she, too, would become a duck freak. I would have missed having the knowledge that something of profound value to me is of equal value to my descendants.

Death represents such a frightening and painful reality for many people that, in writing their wills, they sometimes try too hard to perpetuate all kinds of attitudes and feelings — as if that would keep them alive after death. Sometimes these messages are loving, but too often they are cruel, a way of paying back old hurts. We will think less about dying if our messages are given straightforwardly while we are very much alive. Angry feelings ought to be talked about and settled, so that we can then bestow on ourselves the pleasure of giving what we can while we are still around to enjoy the results.

I denied my mother that pleasure. Whenever she offered me family heirlooms or a piece of her jewelry, I always turned it down—I didn't need it. After she died how desperately I wished she could see my pleasure in having things that had been hers.

It isn't the worth of a gift that matters. As we get older we need much less, and even giving away kitchenware or blankets or lamps or paintings or a rug or a pin, and then being there to see the pleasure it gives, makes the moment of living far more important than the inevitability of dying.

When I think of my daughter glorying in a sunset over the lake, I am enjoying my immortality right now. I recommend this marvelous feeling.

Home Pride

SOMETIMES I wonder if there ever was an Aunt Millie who just happened to have such a way with spaghetti sauce that her family and friends insisted that she share her genius with the rest of us. Did somebody's momma really invent that pizza? What were the true beginnings of that bread that could get its special flavor only from a brick oven? I know from what I read in the newspapers that miracles *do* happen, that a workshop in a garage can produce a million-dollar product, and that anybody's middle-aged sister who now owns three houses, two motorboats, and six cars may very well have started selling plum jelly house-to-house. But I'd like to talk now about another miracle—a case of home pride that has stayed that way.

On a quiet street in a very New England village, there is a very tiny restaurant and bakery. The people who eat breakfast and lunch there have in many cases been doing that for fifteen or twenty years.

They — and those few tourists lucky enough to hear about or happen upon this special place — know a good thing when they find it.

A friend told me about the place about eight or nine years ago. She told me that the owner made the most mouth-watering pies she'd ever tasted. The fruit pies were extraordinary, but her chicken and clam pies were ambrosia fit for the gods.

My informant was entirely correct. Ambrosia doesn't even adequately describe the experience. The chicken pie with a special gravy is so sensational that I order twice as much as I know any group of human beings can possibly eat — and there is never a scrap left over.

Any number of well-meaning people have exhorted this lady to capitalize on her talents and go public. Her response to date is that she will make only as many pies as she can personally supervise from start to finish. I find this an even greater miracle than the people who have made millions because they could make a better brownie or a better jam or sauce or bread — or anything else that started in a kitchen.

I think it is almost unbelievable in this day and age to find anyone who is so proud of a personal accomplishment that he or she cannot be seduced into getting rich quick. The lesson to be learned by all of us who do something really well is that, even if we may never become household names, we are lucky. The personal joy and pride in knowing that what we do is the best we can possibly do is a great gift we can give ourselves — a gift we can have all our lives and that can give us a profound sense of personal joy. There's nothing else like it for a sense of well-being.

And no, I won't tell the world where they can find this special gustatory pleasure. For those who know the source, there is a special good fortune not to be tampered with. For the rest, I hope you will simply be inspired to do your own thing — and enjoy it.

Can a Sixty-Year-Old Chauvinist Change His Ways?

CAN A SIXTY-YEAR-OLD male chauvinist change his ways? I ask myself that question quite often, since I'm married to one.

Early one recent morning, while I was banging away at my typewriter, intensely involved with a new book I was just beginning, my husband appeared at the door of my office and asked if I'd like him to help me make the bed before he left for work. I said no, that I didn't want to interrupt my writing, and he said good-bye. I did a double take a few minutes later. Where is it written, I thought to myself, that *I'm* the only member of this family who can make the bed *alone?*

Actually, it's unfair to designate this man a chauvinist. He is one only about the minor domesticities. During thirty-six years of marriage he has encouraged me in every way to seek my own fulfillment, and has relished my successes and always provided a comforting shoulder for my failures. When I needed a year off to change careers, he saw to it that I got it. We've done that for each other, mutually respecting each other's gifts.

But I must admit that all the consciousness raising that's going on around me has made me more aware of the assumptions of the middle-aged — our old habits of thinking and doing — and I really don't believe that either the men or the women in my age group can manage to change our ways as completely as we might like to. Some do — but they seem to be the exception.

The problem is not lack of goodwill, but deeply ingrained attitudes some of us are too old to exorcise successfully. For example, my young son-in-law, because he is *always* participating in sharing the domestic chores, really knows in his gut how much time it takes to do the shopping and the cooking and the cleaning and the laundry. Because I did most of these things most of the time, it is hard for my husband to understand how much time I actually spend on such matters, for all he sees is a very smooth-running operation.

For example, one morning, again when he was about to leave, I asked him to take a bag of garbage to the incinerator, and he told me he had too much else to carry. He doesn't really know that I often have too much to carry when *I* go out, too, and that I make several trips.

The main problem in retraining a man with chauvinist tendencies is the *woman* who has chauvinist tendencies — which just about covers all of us who came to the revolution in middle age. The truth is that my feelings of guilt stand in the way of progress far more potently than any resistance on the part of my spouse. I feel *so guilty* when this brilliant scientist goes down into the basement to do the laundry that most of the time I'd rather do it myself.

Well — we do our best to join the new world in the making, but neither of us succeeds all the time. Fortunately, long before women's liberation, we loved and admired and respected each other, and that's still the name of the game.

The Martyr Score

I HEARD SOMETHING the other day which I think might save at least a few couples from an unnecessary divorce.

It seems to me that one of the most serious deterrents to a reasonably happy and stable marriage is the way in which men and women silently nurse their wounded feelings, their sense of injustice and betrayal — often about very minor matters. *He* walks around fuming because *her* mother insists on *his* driving her to her sister's every Saturday. *She* feels deeply hurt because *he* doesn't volunteer to go with her to buy a dress for *his* company's dinner-dance. *He's* furious because she knows how he hates such chores — and anyway, isn't he doing enough already, being nice to her mother? She can't see any reason for gratitude — after all *she* talks to *his* crazy uncle on the phone twice a week!

I could go on and on — as could any of you, I'm sure. Most of us are too inclined to wallow in martyrdom; I suspect we must enjoy it, or there would be less of it. Rather than nursing all our wounds and feelings of being misused, we'd have to come out and talk about it and settle the issues. Instead, too many couples walk around each other very stiffly because of the crosses they are carrying on their backs.

I think I may have found the answer to at least this hazard in married life. A friend of mine told me about a game she and her husband play called "The Martyr Score." They have been happily married for twenty-five years, and they feel this solution to the martyr complex has been an essential ingredient to their survival.

This is how it works. Each month they put up a new chart on the kitchen door. They decide together the number of points each of them is to get for a particular martyrdom. For example, Herb gets fifty points for talking to her mother on the phone; Ellie gets one hundred points for meeting Herb at the airport in a snowstorm at eleven o'clock at night; Herb gets twenty-five points for returning the theater tickets that Ellie bought by mistake, for a night when Herb has his bowling club. He would have gotten fifty points ordinarily, but they agree on twenty-five because he passes the theater on his way to work. Ellie gets seventy-five points for painting the porch floor. She got that many points because she thinks that's Herb's job; she didn't get any more points than that because Herb doesn't agree that it's his job.

In order to keep a martyr score, a couple really must talk to each other; that's the only way you can reach agreement on the proper score. What I suspect is that when two people take the time to explore each other's feelings in this way, and when they have the sense of humor to begin with to invent such a crazy scheme, they are already ahead of the game. I suppose keeping a martyr score could only help couples who have those qualities to begin with, but maybe a lot of people do, without knowing it. It's worth a try, anyway. This month my husband's score is higher than mine, and I'm pretty sore about that, so I get an extra forty points!

Homosexuality, I

I KNOW TWO YOUNG ADULTS who I believe have chosen to become psychotic rather than to face their own homosexual feelings and the anguish they feel their parents would suffer. That seems like a terrible choice.

Let me hasten to add that in such extreme cases, there must of course have been many other kinds of predisposition for serious mental illness, but the fact remains that if any part of an unconscious decision to escape from reality is related to such deep shame about a choice of one's own sex, that seems to me to be a very serious and shocking judgment of our society.

Homosexuals are not good people or bad people. All the label "homosexual" tells us is that this is a person with social, sexual, and emotional interests in people of the same sex. We still don't know anything about the kind of person this is, any more than we can make any valid judgments about a heterosexual just because he or she prefers the opposite sex. The sooner we use more useful criteria for judging people, the better off we will be.

Attitudes toward homosexuality have varied from one extreme to another, in the course of human history. The Greeks and Romans thought it was an ordinary fact of life. The Puritans saw it as the devil's damnation; the Victorians expressed shock and disapproval publicly, and privately did as they pleased. But the advent of psychoanalysis in the twentieth century put an end to such swings of the pendulum. The final word was in: Homosexuality was a disease brought on by psychological pathology in the early years of life.

Fortunately, this theory is now on its way out. We ran into some thorny problems—such as the fact that an awful lot of people with strong mothers and either very weak or violently aggressive fathers remained doggedly heterosexual. There was also the nasty fact, which wouldn't go away, that several cultures which did not look upon homosexuality as a disease produced such geniuses as Plato and Michelangelo.

The newer psychological approaches seem to me to be far more productive. Mental illness in its broadest sense, including all serious emotional maladjustments, is something which interferes with, or actively destroys, an individual's capacity to fulfill himself. Any personal characteristic would then be judged in relation to whether or not it worked for or against personal fulfillment and enhanced or impeded one's capacity for individual growth.

On that basis, whatever consenting adults may or may not do behind the bedroom door is irrelevant. What would matter would be the *quality* of one's human relationships.

Homosexuality, II

A PSYCHIATRIST, Dr. Martha Gassmann, once told me about a theory of mental health she'd recently heard. She said, "If a neurosis is sitting in front of your throat and choking you to death, that's bad. But if a neurosis is sitting in back of your neck and working like an outboard motor, that's good." This flexible approach to mental health seems to me to be appropriate to discussing homosexuality.

One of the great values of sex pioneers such as Dr. Alfred Kinsey was the information that if we were to judge the degree of psychological pathology by the sexually inventive and highly individual tastes and pleasures of married heterosexuals, we'd be in big trouble. Such relatively straight folks have just as many and varied sexual activities as even the most creative homosexual.

If one or both partners in a heterosexual relationship are unhappy or destructive, we might say that their sex life is *symptomatic* of their troubles, but we would hesitate to say that this was the *cause* of their problems. More important attitudes and feelings may be expressed through sexual relationships.

The newer breed of psychotherapist asks not whether his patient is homosexual or heterosexual but whether he has found successful avenues for expressing what is most special and valuable about himself as a human being. From such a point of view, one's sexual preferences become secondary to questions having to do with an individual's struggle to find his own identity, to be able to give and receive love, to continue to grow as a person.

One of the reasons why it has been easy to view homosexuality as a disease is that, because of social attitudes, homosexuals have more than their fair share of self-contempt and self-hatred. Anyone who grows up not liking himself is in trouble, and in our society that is the likely fate of many homosexuals.

However, the new militancy, accompanied by changing attitudes of the general public, seems very helpful to me. I am reminded of the very aristocratic woman who found out her son wanted to be a truck driver and who responded by saying, "Well, I hope you will be the *best* truck driver you can possibly be!" I think the day is upon us when a parent will be able to say, "Well, I hope you'll be the *best person* who is a homosexual that you can possibly be." It's a good goal for heterosexuals, too.

The Generation Gap

PEOPLE USUALLY SPEAK of the generation gap in connection with the relationship between teenagers and their parents. It seems to me there is an even wider gap in empathy and mutual understanding between young adults in their thirties and parents in their late fifties or early sixties.

A woman I know recently described a difficult visit to her married daughter. She said, "My daughter and I have a better relationship than most, but there are things about getting older that young people simply can't comprehend. My daughter can't seem to believe or accept the fact that I get more tired more quickly than I did ten years ago. She refuses to believe that there even *is* an aging process! If my back hurts or if the arthritis in my ankles makes me walk stiffly in the morning, she tells me it's all psychosomatic, the result of stress! I love to see her, but to tell you the truth, after a few days I can't wait to get back to my own friends, who are going through the same changes I am! How do you help a younger person understand the feelings of getting older?"

My answer is that, for the most part, you can't, and there's not much point in trying. It is always difficult to anticipate accurately a later stage in growing, and old age is the most difficult of all to imagine — even for those of us who are getting there fast.

When my mother was in her sixties, she often told me that her grandmother had said to her, "Wait until you're old, then you'll understand." Now my mother was experiencing and understanding what her grandmother had meant, and she was saying the same thing to me: "Wait until you're older and then you'll understand." When she told me that, I had no idea what she meant. I thought it was just nervousness that made her get up to go to the bathroom several times during the night. When she said the water was too cold for swimming in the middle of the summer, I called her a sissy. When she and her friends began comparing notes on their various physical complaints — mostly about the shortcomings of their digestive tracts — I said they were all hypochondriacs.

Now I wish my mother were still alive so I could tell her I'm there now, and I understand at last. Now it's my turn to tell my daughter that someday she'll understand.

Beyond all the very real physical changes we see ourselves going through, the hardest thing to communicate to grown children is our growing awareness of our mortality. We can try to sensitize our children to what we are going through, but it seems to me we ought not to expect to be very successful. The best solution is to spend a good deal of time with our contemporaries and accept, sadly, the fact that someday our children will themselves know only too well how we now feel.

Privacy and Sharing

AMONG THE MANY silly jokes going around about how many people does it take to change a light bulb is that in California it takes four people: one to change the light bulb and three to share the experience. The trouble is, that's not so funny.

I recently got a brochure inviting me to spend my vacation with Rick and Sue. Those are not their real names, but they wrote that they would like to share their marriage with me and my husband. Rick and Sue travel around the country leading sharing workshops. Frankly, they give me the creeps. I have this awful vision of their being so totally focused on sharing that this probably continues during the few hours when they are alone. I wonder if they share their feelings about cleaning their teeth or having indigestion or making their next plane reservation.

At one time when my husband had been invited to speak at Esalen, California's most famous growth center, I considered going along, but only if I could make myself a sandwich sign, on which would be emblazoned in large red letters, "Keep your cotton-pickin' hands off my authentic self!" It's a long time since California could claim dominance in the privacy-shattering business. There is hardly a community in the land that doesn't have some sort of workshops for people to share their feelings with each other.

This approach to mental health and improved human relations was not at all a bad idea. Too many people feel isolated and alone, ashamed and guilty. Life in big cities can make us feel lost and anonymous. We are inclined to wear too many masks, hiding our doubts and fears. There can be something very therapeutic in meeting with others in an atmosphere of openness, where we do not feel threatened, where we can get in touch with how we feel through sharing universal human experiences with others. A wonderful idea, and beautifully executed by many talented professional psychotherapists.

It is the extremes, the fanatics, that I find dangerous — the oversimplified idea that telling everything, especially about sex and anger, is a sure road to being a terrific person.

In the hands of inexperienced, untrained people, self-revelation can lead to serious problems. If you want to try this kind of short, intensive experience, be sure you check the credentials of the leaders.

I know a woman in her seventies who thought she'd try one of these encounter groups. Within the first five minutes she was told to find a male partner and "touch his body in a sensual way." She nearly had a stroke! The trouble with so many of these groups is that they overlook another equally valuable quality of growth and change — private thought and personal dignity.

Income Taxes

IT BEING THAT TIME of year, it might be a good idea to discuss some of the reasons — emotional, not financial — why paying our taxes can be a source of monumental stress.

Of course a feeling of imminent bankruptcy can cause anxiety, and fear is a natural consequence of wondering if the IRS is going to put you in jail for listing Aunt Martha's birthday party as a business expense. But I think there is a deeper cause for stress, which has to do with our feelings about what will happen to our money after we part with it — who will decide what to do with it.

I'm not too sure just how it would work, but one solution might be to let each of us designate where our money is to go. *I* would never again have to worry about contributing to the making of a nuclear missile. *You* might be happy to contribute to our national defense. *I* could sleep easier knowing that all my hard-earned money was going to be used for hungry children and bringing arts programs to poor people. *You* might feel safer if all your money was going to be used for helping the cities enlarge their police forces. Each of us could feel that we were really contributing to something that mattered to us very much.

I doubt the government is going to buy my idea, but I think that we will all feel less tense and unhappy if we try to examine some of the underlying feelings we have about the emotional aspects of taxation. I've been doing that a lot lately, and while it doesn't really change anything, I feel better able to live with my anxieties and frustrations.

As I analyze my personal problem, I realize that I would like to run the government finances the way I operate my own home. For example, if I have a child who breaks a leg, I don't ask if there is enough money in the budget to have it set — I just rush the poor kid to the hospital. I know such an emergency must be taken care of no matter how long it takes to pay for it. The same would be true if I had an elderly parent who didn't have enough money to pay for heating oil. Assuming I was living quite comfortably, I would get rid of luxuries — sell an antique or sailboat, or I'd quit eating in restaurants — in order to buy that oil. If I had a child who seemed to be deeply troubled and was stealing or hurting other people, I'd get help for that child, even if I had to put off buying a new rug or a sweater or chocolate cake, because I would know that if I didn't do something immediately, that child might end up in prison or be otherwise destroyed.

I think what causes my distress is that as a nation we seem to get confused about the difference between an investment and an expenditure. Preventing *future* problems by dealing with them *now* seems beyond our collective understanding. I was always terrible at math, and high finance is beyond me, but I keep having this feeling that something is wrong.

The Gift of Tears

MY FATHER'S LETTERS often make me cry. Other people report the same phenomenon, and we have all concluded that his letters make us cry because they are so beautiful and wise and move us so deeply. One day when I was discussing this with a friend, it occurred to me that there are many circumstances in which tears are a great gift.

One recent weekend a young woman came to visit us from another city. She came to visit some colleges, and we spent a good deal of time together. She happens to be the daughter of a close friend of ours who died about seven years ago. My husband and I marveled at what a lovely, sensitive, wise young woman Bob's daughter had grown up to be. We had a lot of fun together, but when I said good-bye at a bus stop, I suddenly burst into tears. First, because of the tragedy that Bob didn't live to see this lovely person, and second, because she couldn't know how much he would have adored her, and then, for myself and my terrible sense of loss. I realized, as I whipped out my sunglasses and walked through the park, that I hadn't cried for this loss for a long time, and that the great sadness had built up once again to the point where I needed my tears.

One of the best things I've seen happen in my lifetime is the changing attitude toward men and tears. It used to be that little boys were deprived of the comfort of tears by being told it was unmanly to cry. Many other men are profoundly crippled by this nonsense, but younger men, who have been learning that tears have no gender but are merely human, are having fuller, richer lives because the range of their emotions and the behavior allowed them has become much wider.

My husband and I knew that a friend we hadn't seen for a long time was having a very difficult time. His second marriage was breaking up, and his son had become a drug addict. One night my husband called and told John he'd been thinking about him. Could they get together? Would it help to talk to an old friend? John sounded embarrassed, said thank you, asked for a rain check, and hung up. Ten minutes later he called back and said, "I don't know why I turned you down; I'd love to see you." My husband later told me that the two of them met in front of a bar, embraced each other, and John wept. It seemed as if his tears were the gateway to his pain, and in now being able to share his suffering and his need for loving concern, John was able to begin the process of moving on toward rebuilding his shattered life.

There are, of course, some crybabies who drive us all crazy, who use tears as a way to manipulate others or who substitute tears for genuine sadness. But tears, in and of themselves, are really nature's way of helping us to understand the pain and the glory of being human — and that's a gift.

Agnosticism

WITH GOOD FRIDAY today, and both Easter and Passover being celebrated this coming Sunday, I thought at first that it would be appropriate to talk about some of the common bonds among the major religions — but then it suddenly occurred to me that perhaps this would be an even more appropriate time to talk about a religious minority in this country which is currently suffering from a good deal of misunderstanding, anger, and outright prejudice. I wonder if you can guess which group I'm talking about.

These days the word *agnostic* has become an epithet, and agnosticism is being viewed in many quarters as a terrible danger to the moral health of this country. As a card-carrying member of this minority, I'd like to suggest that we are not less religious than others and that we take our religion very seriously, even if we are mostly unorganized and nonjoiners.

I can't speak for all agnostics, but I can tell you what it means to me.

I have never been able to come to the conclusion that one religion is better than all others, but I have a profound respect for the human struggle to make sense out of life. I honor all the great mystics, wherever they have sprung to life, wherever they have taught that all men are brothers. In the last few years of my life I have worked hard to understand and practice the deep meditation which all the great mystics taught – often calling it prayer.

One of the reasons I think I was attracted to finding my own inner religious experience rather than joining any group is that I have always been appalled by the terribly cruel wars which have been fought in the name of religion. This was permanently symbolized for me in the story of a friend in the American Air Force during World War II who went to church in England early one morning and ended the day impaled on a church steeple in his parachute in Germany – passing from church to church, with the most terrible war in history in the middle.

Unlike an atheist, I am not sure I know any answers. I have a sense of wonder at the mysteries, I sense some profound order in the universe, but I am not prepared to say that I know what it is. I only know that there is beauty and terror, love and hate, serenity and panic, and that out of all the contradictions of life, there is only one thing I am sure about – that life on earth must mean something and that I must work to try to do whatever I can to make the world a better place to live for everyone. I am in awe of what I cannot fathom. But I am *not* confused at all about what I must do to be a good person. I share with all others in the celebration of spring, of birth and renewal; I honor those who remember enslavement and celebrate freedom. I deeply respect the holiness of the search for meaning and spiritual fulfillment; and for those of you who will be going to your churches and synagogues, I'd like to suggest that what we share with you is of far greater importance than what we don't share with you.

Play

A PSYCHOLOGIST, Max Wertheimer, described an adult as a *deteriorated* child. Can you figure out why?

Children know how to do something quite naturally that is absolutely essential to good mental health. Most of us have to relearn it, because when we were kids few people understood that we had a precious gift — the ability to *play.*

Nobody has to tell a child — or even a puppy, for that matter — how to play. It just comes naturally, as a way to learn about the world and oneself. It is also the most important avenue to creativity and a sense of well-being.

Play for a child is sitting in a sandbox, singing a little original song while making mud pies, climbing a tree, or taking apart a broken watch. It is doing what comes naturally. It is responding to curiosity, wonder, delight in just *being.* It is *not* trying to be the best pitcher on the Little League team or painting a picture by numbers.

It is daydreaming; it is doing something just for the sake of doing it, not to achieve anything.

When we adults feel depressed or tense, it may well be because we have forgotten how to play. It isn't really what you do, but the way that you do it. If you jog or play tennis or bridge just because it's fun, that's play. If it is only in order to beat somebody else or lose weight or stay young, that's not play, it's work.

I have never yet met a great scientist or artist, in whatever field of endeavor, who did not understand that the road to the fullest creativity and energy lay not in struggle and hard work, necessary though these are, but in being playful with ideas, with a research project, with starting to paint a new canvas, with writing a book. The people who achieve the most inner satisfaction in daily living are those who are the *least* grim and determined.

I know a man who started playing with clay because he saw how much fun his four-year-old was having. He's still doing it, although his daughter is now thirty, just because he has fun. I know a very learned scientist who flies kites every weekend, as a way of recovering from exhaustion, and a psychiatrist who plays the flute between patients.

One of the most important tasks we ought to set ourselves is to explore what play means to us. It can be cooking, needlepoint, chess, mountain climbing, camping, sailing, running, sketching, singing in a chorus, a thousand other things. Just *thinking* about giving yourself one playful activity a day will undoubtedly refresh your soul. We may need to work for physical survival; we need to play to make survival worthwhile.

Realistic Feelings of Depression

DEPRESSION IS CERTAINLY one of the most complicated of all human emotions, and I've been talking about many of its facets from time to time. When we feel deep depression, it is usually related to some part of our past and to some part of our present life, involving our personal growth and development and relationships with family and friends.

But there is another kind of depression which has nothing much to do with the past, though plenty to do with the present — but most of all, it has to do with the *future*. It's a realistic, sane, intelligent awareness that the world is in a terrible state and seems to be getting worse all the time! This is what we might call a social depression — a sense of impending doom.

In most periods of history, people have had this feeling to some degree. Imagine the feelings of the first man who realized what the combination of gunpowder and cannon could do to a stone fortress, or the terror about the future when it seemed as if everyone would be wiped out by the black plague. Well, *our* moments of terror seem more than a match for the past, and a feeling of depression seems a normal reaction to Love Canal and Three Mile Island or a recent report by a group of physicians that nobody would survive a nuclear war, so we better not have one!

There is reason to worry, but this is one kind of depression that we *can* overcome. Depressed feelings about the future stem partly from what's happening, but also from feeling paralyzed, feeling we can't do anything to change the future.

We can and we must. I've been reading a fascinating book called

Avenue of the Righteous, by Peter Hellman, in which he describes some of the suffering of the holocaust years and the miracle of heroism that stayed very much alive. He tells the stories of some of the ordinary human beings who became extraordinary for their bravery. And as I read these inspiring stories, it occurred to me that during the worst period of human history *I* know anything about, nobody talked about feeling depressed. People were miserable, hungry, bad, angry, terrified—but not depressed. I believe it was because they were too busy trying to fight for a future they still believed might be possible. I'm sure terrible depression may have come afterwards, in the loss of family, in the horror of revealed events, but taking action at a time of crisis is an antidote to depression.

Righteous indignation is the best medicine for social depression, followed immediately by large doses of personal commitment and action. At no time in human history has anyone ever been able to do more than his own best, and that's all any of us can do now. But are we doing it? If you are frightened by the future, what are you doing about it? The only way to stop worrying about the future is to be part of changing it.

Grief and Mourning

When I was a child, grown-ups thought it was a good idea to protect children from death as much as possible. We were not taken to funerals; we never saw our parents cry; we never said good-bye. As a result, many people my age and older are still in mourning for people whom we loved who died when we were young. There is no way to conquer grief except to live through it.

I recently received a letter from a woman who had become widowed after fifty-one years of a very happy marriage. She told me that shortly after her husband's death her children had talked her into taking a cruise. She wrote, "I know it's silly—you'd think the more people around the less lonely I'd be, but it's just the other way around. Well, you can't look back—you have to look forward."

The reason she wrote to me was because she felt guilty about her grief. The reason she wasn't overcoming it is that she was fighting so hard against it.

You can't talk yourself out of being grief-stricken — nor is there the slightest value in such distractions as a cruise until you have allowed your grief to live its life. The fact of our mortality gives a tragic cast to our lives; each life is infinitely precious, and the loss of someone we love is the most terrible thing we are forced to deal with. The work of mourning is a necessary human way to deal with genuine suffering. It can't be pushed aside without leaving an open wound forever.

When I was a child and the grandfather that I adored died, I was sent into another room when the family gathered. No one helped me to express my grief. I mourned his death silently, unconsciously, until I was in my mid-thirties and was able to deal with it in the course of psychotherapy, having nothing at all to do with that event.

When someone dies whom I love, I allow my grief all the room it needs. Great waves of pain wash over me. When it subsides, I let it go; when it suddenly erupts again, I don't try to shut it off. After a while the sharpest anguish softens, the waves of pain occur less frequently, and I go on with my life, never trying to deny the terrible hole left in my universe by my loss. Through this process of mourning, all the good memories begin to flow back and fill my life, and finally I find I'm a better person, doing more good in the world because that loved one is now part of me.

What that traveling widow needed desperately was a small, private place alone, without distraction, to pay homage to those fifty-one years. She'll be ready for a cruise when she has cried enough tears to let the good memories flow back into her life.

Widows and Widowers Living Alone

A FRIEND OF MINE has a widowed mother who is living alone in a nine-room house, which seems ridiculous. But *is* it?

Many of us have been or will be faced with helping a widowed parent make the painful and difficult choice between living alone and moving into some kind of group setting.

The most important issue is to help a widowed parent explore his or her real feelings by *really* listening. The second most important issue is to allow a lot of time to pass before the decision is made. One seventy-four-year-old widower looked around his apartment after his wife died and thought he simply couldn't bear to be surrounded by so many reminders of happier times. Much too abruptly he sold everything and moved into a hotel, and his grief and mourning increased a thousandfold. A widow I know who has continued to live in her own home, surrounded by the accumulated memories of a lifetime, has shut off a few rooms because of the heating crunch and has rented one part of her house to a young couple. That seems to be a workable compromise for many people, especially because adult children feel less guilty and worried if there's someone else close at hand.

We must try not to let practical considerations take precedence over the emotional needs of the person most involved. One middle-aged son told me, "My father needs to be in the place where he shared his life with my mother. If we talked him into moving in order to save money and not to have to take care of such a large place, I think he would die, too. He can't afford it, so now he goes around the neighborhood doing odd jobs for people — taking care of plants and pets when people go away, baby-sitting, painting a porch or a kitchen. At first I wanted to encourage him to move to a warmer climate and find a small apartment, but earning enough to maintain his home has seemed to give him a new lease on life."

Of course there are many things to be considered, such as the general health of a widowed parent, the resources available in making choices, and the pros and cons of two generations living together, if that's another alternative. I'll be talking about some of these issues later, but for the moment the most important thing to remember is that if we dig up roots too suddenly and arbitrarily we may kill the plant.

Grandparents

THERE IS A GROUP meeting in a suburban community center to discuss the problems of being grandparents in today's world. Once upon a time grandparents felt they knew exactly what was good for their grandchildren, but these days grandparents are experiencing the same kinds of upheaval, confusion, and uncertainty that their children and grandchildren feel.

About thirty grandparents were discussing what they felt their relationship should be to their grandchildren. A social worker was leading the discussion. What might once have been an unusual scene was one that is becoming more and more common. There has been such rapid social change that grandparents are no clearer about their role than anyone else and seem to find great comfort in each other's sympathetic counsel.

Ideas about child raising have changed so much and so often that many grandparents feel that their children have no respect for their opinions — that they are too old-fashioned to be listened to. At the other end of the scale, grandparents are healthier and more active and live longer than any previous generation, and many of them are too busy leading fascinating and fulfilling lives of their own to want to devote a great deal of time to baby-sitting. Grandparents are also having to face the problem of divorce among their children and the new extended families created by divorce. One grandma told me, "My son has been divorced and remarried twice. There are children from each marriage and two children by a previous marriage of his wife's. There are so many grandparents in this picture that we've had trouble figuring out enough different names for each of us!"

Like so many other groups in our society, grandparents are developing their own self-help organizations in order to manage all the changing conditions of life. For example, one grandmother has been seeking help from her support group about the fact that her former son-in-law has refused to let her see her grandchildren. He has full custody and has made contact of any kind impossible. Many grandparents are fighting this denial of their rights of grandparenthood, partly on the basis of their own needs, of course, but in addition because they believe so strongly that children need a sense of connection and continuity with family.

There are certain universal qualities of grandparenthood that never change. It is not a chance to be a parent again, but to give a very special kind of unconditional love. My favorite grandma story is a true one about a little boy who insisted his grandmother had to go to school with him the next day. When she arrived, the teacher was surprised and then laughed. She said, "I told the children to bring their favorite thing, but I was expecting stuffed animals and wind-up cars!" I can't imagine any higher goal for anyone than to be a child's special thing, and grandparents need to study that role and then insist on having it.

Old Age and Dying

WHETHER YOU HAPPEN to be twenty-five or forty or eighty, the facts of old age and death exist for all of us. If we try to deny them, we will never know the full sweetness of being alive. I was reminded of this by a beautiful movie called *Tell Me a Riddle*. It is a masterpiece — a sensitive, utterly human, profoundly spiritual look at the meaning of life and death, which probably explains why you may never have heard of it, in this age of horror and monster and disaster and pornographic movies.

The last scary movie I went to was *Jaws;* the last disaster movie was *The Poseidon Adventure*. I have never seen a horror movie, never plan to, and have happily avoided almost all violence, except where it was fully appropriate to teaching me something about what it means to be human. After this confession, you now know that in this area of experience I border on being un-American. But I consider myself very fortunate, for I can bear to cry real tears, and I don't bury my terror of death by having to get fake chills in movie theaters.

Tell Me a Riddle is one of just a handful of movies that helped me to grow as a person and inspired me to new depths of understanding; while I sobbed my heart out during most of it, I came out of the theater with a piercing sense of joy at being alive and far more aware of the things I must do with whatever is left of my life in order to make it all mean something.

It is the story of two people, long-married, long-lived, growing further and further apart mostly because they are old, but also because there is so much unfinished business in their relationship to each other. It is the story of what has to happen to two human beings in order for them to begin to understand their own lives.

One of the most interesting insights in the film is how much better old people are understood today by their grandchildren rather than their children. The children tend to be victims of an age too focused on having things and burying feelings; the young and the old seem to be discovering that feelings, hopes, memories, and loving are the things which make mortality bearable.

We need to face the fact that preparation is needed for dying as well as for living. We need to search our roots, remember our lives, sort out what has mattered, feel again the throbbing pulse of life in nature. There is a moment in the film when the old woman runs toward the pounding surf, so alive and powerful, and the memory of that scene will help me to remember I must reach toward life in order to accept the inevitability of my own death.

Group and Family Therapy

I'VE JUST BEEN TAKEN to task for apparently having given the impression that I thought all forms of group therapy were destructive. I was talking about weekend wonder-cure marathons, run by nonprofessional or semiprofessional leaders. Group therapy, carried on by people with good training and sound principles, is another matter entirely, and I am profoundly impressed by the ways in which group therapy can help people in trouble.

A nine-year-old boy, in trying to describe to the therapist what he had gotten out of a series of family therapy sessions, said, "You put my poor little shivering heart right out there on the table, and I thought it would kill me, but instead you made my family help me put my heart back inside as a happy heart." I can think of few professional descriptions that might be more accurate, and certainly none as poetic.

One of the most hopeful and helpful developments in group therapy has been the growth of family therapy. Virginia Satir, a highly respected pioneer in this field, said recently, "What we used to do when a family had problems was to pluck out the bad person, fix him up, put him back, and, lo and behold, he'd fall on his face again." This approach failed, she explained, for the same reason that a wart or a pimple doesn't grow by itself; the whole system is involved. A family is a place where nothing happens in isolation, and family therapy now offers new hope to many people in trouble.

I mentioned earlier that some psychotherapists are wonderful and some are terrible — just like people in any other profession. In the same way, group therapy can be a place in which to explore oneself in relation to others, and it can also be a place that is destructive and dangerous. I am opposed to any group which uses cruelty, screaming, or pressure of any kind to force people into angry or terrifying confrontations. It's all very exciting and dramatic, signifying nothing.

Some people feel more comfortable in a group than in a one-to-one therapy relationship. Group therapy is often used in conjunction with individual sessions — and in the current economic crunch, group therapy can lower the cost of treatment.

If you want to get a picture of just how remarkable and helpful family therapy, as one kind of group therapy, can be, I suggest you read a book called *The Family Crucible,* by Augustus Napier and Carl Whitaker. When therapists can help people reveal their "shivering" hearts to each other and come through the experience with new sensitivity, compassion, self-understanding, and a joy in each other's love, it is a creative art. But it never happens in a lasting way without a necessary period of growth — always longer than a weekend.

Holding Grudges

IN THESE DAYS of energy shortages, it seems to me that the least we could do is to stop holding grudges. It takes a lot of psychic energy to stay mad.

I was waiting in the lobby of a theater for a friend, when a woman came up and said hello. I hadn't seen her for about twenty-five years, but I did remember that I had met her through the person I was waiting for. When I commented on this coincidence, her face clouded, and she said, "Well, I better get into the theater before she comes!"

When my friend arrived, I didn't mention this encounter; the woman's behavior had seemed strangely inappropriate, since I could have no idea what it was all about. But on the way out of the theater, we met the same lady, who smiled at me and deliberately refused to acknowledge the greeting of my companion, who laughed out loud at the snub. Now *really* curious, I asked what this was all about, and my friend said, "I don't even *remember!* I haven't seen Kay in eighteen years, but I know we had an argument about something. How silly can you get?"

How silly, indeed. The lady certainly didn't have to gush, but a casual greeting would, it seems to me, have been just a bit more grown-up.

This episode reminded me of the far more painful experience of a friend. Her aunt and uncle, both of whom she loved, had a bitter fight about something that was obviously very distressing—so much so that they simply could not deal with it and proceeded not to speak to each other for about five years. At her mother's funeral, this sister and brother continued to ignore each other, leaving Joan with the shocking conclusion that even in confronting the fact of our *mortality,* we are still capable of holding old grudges.

With life such a short and precious span, I cannot imagine any wound worth all that effort. In the autumn of my life, it seems a terrible waste.

I find myself very eager to undo any hurt feelings that occur with people I really care about, and I find myself wondering what in the world gives a grudge such tenacity so often. I think it is that the hurt went very deep because it had to do with some very old business of childhood — some really sensitive and vulnerable psychological Achilles' heel, some place where more than likely we didn't consciously know we were hurting.

The only way to get over a grudge is to examine one's own hidden agenda, those old feelings that make the hurt go so deep.

And then to have the maturity and good sense to give it up and use all that energy in more productive pursuits.

Hugging

I'M VERY PARTIAL to both kissing and hugging as extremely pleasurable activities, but I suppose it is a clear sign of my advanced age that if I were forced to choose one or the other, I'd go for hugging. I hope I'll never have to make that awful choice, but I'd like to suggest that hugging is especially good for one's mental health.

I know I will never forget one poignant moment during the week of the American hostages' return from Iran. When their families were waiting for them at the Washington, D.C., airport, one little girl raced past the military guards and police, and literally *flew* into the arms of her brother. Watching that moment on the television screen gave me goose pimples. The impact of those two bodies against each other seemed to me to represent the ultimate miracle of what it can mean to be a human being.

There were many such moments during that emotionally charged week, and looking back, I have the feeling that above and beyond all the social and political aspects, what truly satisfied all of us was that we got to look at real-live people hugging each other with such intensity that there was no mistaking how desperately we need to feel close to those we care about.

The importance of hugging and touching first came to my attention, professionally, when in the 1940s two very wise and observant psychiatrists, Dr. Margaret Ribble and Dr. René Spitz, began noticing that foundlings — infants in hospitals — who were rarely picked up tended to die much too mysteriously and much too often. They both arrived at the conclusion that these babies were dying for lack of touching. From the moment of birth we desperately need a sense of connection to other human beings, but we make a serious mistake if we think hugging and touching are necessary only to children. I went to visit a friend who had been widowed for about two years. She lives in Chicago, and I live in New York, so we don't see each other very often. When she opened her door, I gave her a good, solid bear hug, and I was shocked by her reaction. She explained her teary condition by saying, "You can't imagine how good that felt. Aside from my grandchildren, whom I see only about twice a year, nobody has given me a really good hug like that since Al died."

In this age of sexual freedom, we too easily think of hugging and touching as having to do only with sexual drives. The truth is they have far more to do with the human craving for being loved and connected to others, and I am convinced that hugging is one of the greatest of all secret weapons against feeling lost and alone. Whom have *you* hugged lately?

Childhood Shadows

BEFORE SIGMUND FREUD, most people figured that however we turned out, it had to do almost entirely with our genes. After Freud and the psychoanalytic revolution, we seemed to forget heredity altogether for a time and assumed that childhood experiences were entirely responsible for the way we turned out. After a while, *that* theory developed some serious holes, because no two kids in any one family are ever exactly alike and children in similar circumstances turn out to be quite different from one another.

We now seem to have arrived at a sensible view that everything we are, and everything that happens to us, makes an imprint on our natures. Still, every once in a while something happens which reminds me once again of just how important childhood impressions can be.

My husband and I were standing in front of a store window where there was a miniature carousel — enchanting and beautiful in every detail, with horses that went up and down and people climbing on or riding. I was utterly transported, carousels being one of my weaknesses. Two young children were watching, as fascinated as we were, their eyes big with wonder and delight.

Our mutual revery was sharply interrupted when the mother of one of the children said, "Are you coming with me, or do you want to stay here by yourself?"

In the midst of childish delight, I suddenly felt a chill; the child being given this awful and impossible choice was about two or three years old. How could she stay by herself? Who would take care of her? It was as if a childhood shadow had suddenly crossed the sunlight, and I felt an ancient panic.

I've no doubt this was a nice, good-hearted mother, with the best of intentions, who knew perfectly well *she* didn't mean that such a choice was open to her daughter — but what she didn't realize was that little children do not understand the difference between the things grow-ups say which they mean and the things they say which they don't mean.

Whenever we feel unloved and lonely, full of a strange floating anxiety, it may very well be the residue of just such moments in childhood — when somebody we loved and needed desperately said something thoughtlessly that we took seriously — something like, "If you don't keep on walking, I'm going to leave you right here!" Try to remember how it felt — and don't say it to another generation. What's truer and far more necessary is the absolute assurance that little kids must never feel alone. Something like, "We have to go now, and you must come with me because we need each other."

Spring and Nature

IT IS PROBABLY A SIGN of my advanced age, but few things in life give me the lift that I get from seeing a bud open on a tree still scrawny with winter or from discovering a bird at the serious business of nest building. I don't know what it would be like to live in a climate that is balmy all year 'round, but here in the frozen north of the eastern seaboard, let me tell you, it's a pretty sensational time.

Wherever we may live, whatever the seasons, it seems to me that there never was a time in human history when it was as important to sensitize ourselves to the miracle of growth and change in living things. In a recent news broadcast I heard a reporter, with a sense of shock in his voice, saying, "Even *the computer* can't find the killer!" He was describing a massive search for a murderer, and I got the feeling it did not surprise him at all that no human being had solved the case, but he had certainly expected better of the machine!

That, I think, is a kind of metaphor for the state we are all in. We have become victims of such a massive technology that we rarely have any sense of being what we really are — the ultimate miracle of nature.

Somehow, when I watch a clumsy duck waddling up to get fed, quacking at me in that ridiculous tone of voice, or when I watch a mother bluebird putting food into the gaping beaks of her babies, or when I watch a bright yellow finch at the feeder, I calm down. I rediscover some quiet inner rhythm that makes me part of nature, part of a universe in which there are no screaming car horns, no clunking machines, no ear-shattering jackhammers, no poisoned wells, no leaking radiation. For a moment the terror of living in a world gone totally mad with technology is left behind, and I begin to hope for mankind's survival again.

It seems to me that we are truly lost if we ever lull ourselves into believing that electronic machinery is of a higher order of things than a rose bush or the first crocus or some baby geese.

It is certainly very convenient to have novocaine and penicillin and plastic bags for garbage and air conditioning and indoor plumbing — but if such remarkable inventions leave us with undrinkable water and unbreathable air, the price is not right.

My favorite television show is *Sunday,* with Charles Kuralt: If television had been invented just so I could watch that incredibly beautiful CBS magazine of the air, it would have been worth it. Each Sunday, at the end of the program there is a short segment in which we are allowed to refresh our souls with some lovely piece of nature — a swamp, a bird sanctuary, a forest, a waterfall — and I recently heard the senior executive producer, Robert Northshield, report that this segment is the most popular part of the program. That gives me hope that we still have our priorities in order.

Mother's Day

PEOPLE HAVE BEEN killed for less, but I can't help it — I hate Mother's Day. My daughter has known since she was old enough to talk that any mention of such a festivity would bring on the rolling thunder of my anger. I'll try to explain my un-American attitude. Let me add at once that I'm crazy about motherhood. I don't think that any other experience in my long life has helped me to grow and change and become more fully human than being a mother. And I miss my own mother as much today as I did when she died almost ten years ago. Maybe even more.

But what I hate is sentimentality at the cash register. Mother's Day was a Congressional concession to people who make cards and sell flowers and candy. What I hate is being told that we owe mothers some special deference that is somehow different from the love and respect we ought to have for every human being. I deeply resent being told on what day I ought to have told my mother I loved her.

I admit to a certain irrationality in my attitude; after all, I have never minded being told what day to remember the Pilgrims and Indians and to enjoy the harvest. I've been trying to figure out why I dutifully start basting a turkey at the right moment, but always hated having to buy my mother a present on Mother's Day.

Almost every therapist I have talked to on the subject has reported that more women are depressed the day after Mother's Day than any other day in the year. I think I know why — and it also explains me to myself! I think it's the same reason that a lot of little kids seem sad and are often naughty the day after Christmas. It's because in creating certain kinds of romantic myths, we have set up the most impossible expectations. In the case of Mother's Day, there is, for example, the myth that just becoming a mother makes a woman wise and patient and understanding and loving. There's the myth that every child who remembers to send a gift or a message on Mother's Day really wants to.

There are wonderful and terrible mother-child relationships. Mothers can be artistic parents, and they can fail. Most often parents and children end up really liking each other — and sometimes they don't. However, we really don't need romantic illusions to celebrate the lovely human satisfactions that can come with parenthood.

It seems to me that, instead of giving presents, a good way to celebrate Mother's Day would be to provide more health clinics and day-care centers and programs for parent education. Or to offer to volunteer for a Parents Anonymous phone service for parents who are abusing their kids. If we took all the money spent on gifts this one Sunday in the year and spent it all on day-care centers for working mothers, I'd be crazy about Mother's Day.

How to Have a Really Cheap Vacation

IF INFLATION HAS knocked out your vacation plans, there is an alternative to a cruise or a trip to Europe or going away at all. More and more people are trying it and liking it.

Ellen, aged twenty-six, was planning to go to a mountain resort for her two-week vacation, when two things happened: She broke up with the young man who was to accompany her, and she took a look at her bank account and realized that she couldn't do it on her own. "I *thought* of killing myself!" she told me, somewhat overdramatically, "but then," she added, "something wonderful happened by acci-dent." What happened was that Ellen, unable to do otherwise, went to bed for four days. She cried a lot, disconnected her phone, and lived on ice cream and soup. She watched a lot of television, read some magazines that had been lying around for months, and slept at odd hours of the day and night, whenever she felt like it.

On the fifth day she arose from her bed of pain and went for a walk in the park and fed the ducks at the lake. On the sixth day she cleaned out her closets, answered mail, paid bills, and finished an af-ghan she'd been working on for two years. For the rest of her vaca-tion she saw an old high-school friend for lunch, went to the movies and to two museums she'd never been to before, and walked four or five miles a day, exploring her city as if she were a foreigner.

She told me she had no idea why she felt terrific when she went back to work. I think I know why: Into each life some regression must fall, if we are to keep our sanity. There is no cheaper vacation than to allow oneself the opportunity to regress into helpless, passive self-indulgence in one's own home — and there are probably very few va-cation plans that offer a better prescription for good mental health. The pressures and the pace of daily living seem to become more in-tensified every day, and the only antidote is to cop out once in a while. If we do that occasionally, we are less likely to do it too much. For beyond the regression another reason such a vacation can be re-freshing is that we are giving in to our basic needs, following our in-stincts, allowing time to flow. When I was a child we used to put sticks into a rushing brook and watch them sail away, utterly without plan or purpose. People need that kind of trip, too, once in a while.

Everybody's Fat

IN CASE YOU WEREN'T aware of this fact, almost everybody in this coun-try is fat. I am not speaking here of the very considerable number of people who really may need to lose weight, but rather of all the *thin* people who *think* they are fat. Since it's all in their heads, I suppose we might call them fatheads.

I went to a wedding reception the other day, where I thought I might faint from the effort I had to make *not* to eat a piece of the most gorgeous chocolate cake I have ever seen — and I've seen them all. A young woman about five feet, three inches, tall, with a waist I could have spanned with my own fat hands, and who said she weighed one hundred pounds, was also offered a piece of the cake. She protested in horror, saying "Oh, no! I'm *much* too fat!"

I have had a lot of experience with people like that, and because I have always been either very fat or very hungry, I really hate their guts. But I'm beginning to understand them; and slowly but surely, I can feel compassion creeping through my cellulite.

What I have discovered, in the course of my own dramatic and heroic efforts to lose weight, is that how much a person weighs has little or nothing to do with feeling fat. A friend of mine, five feet seven and one hundred and twenty pounds, whom I was about to kill when I saw her eating a celery stalk and two tablespoons of cottage cheese for lunch one day, explained it to me. She said, "Eda, it has nothing to do with what I weigh or what you see; it has to do with hating myself." *That* I understood perfectly, since I have several advanced degrees in self-hatred. The thing is that the word *fat* has become synonymous in our culture with the word *ugly,* and ugly in our society means an assortment of things, all the way from stupid to rotten to hopeless. The word *fat* has become a kind of shorthand by which thin people let us know they have what we might call a low opinion of themselves, to put it mildly.

Human beings are very susceptible to the disease of trying to find simple answers to difficult problems. By constantly worrying about their weight and constantly dieting, thin self-haters manage to avoid the real task at hand, which is finding out why they see themselves as fat and ugly and no damned good. That takes real courage and a lot of hard work, and often involves getting some help from someone who knows a great deal about the subject of self-hatred.

I'm sure I will have a good deal more to say about those of us who spend our lives trying to lay siege to our fat cells. But for those lucky skinnies who feel fat, I suggest you get off that scale and start weighing your feelings.

An Exhaustion unto Madness

I WOULD LIKE to plead with all parents of young children under the age of five to make my life happier and less stressful. There is something you can all do right, which I did wrong when I was a young mother, and that is to understand what exhaustion can do to very small children. If you will follow my advice, I will cry less in public.

When I was a young mother, and got caught in a supermarket when it was my daughter's time for lunch and a nap, I had a fit when she'd start to whine, or pull cans off the shelves, or scream so loud that the other shoppers thought I was killing her. I got angry, and I was embarrassed and ashamed. I was rotten to my poor little kid, and I'm sure she thought it was all her fault that she was behaving badly.

There were other episodes that I hate to remember, such as refusing to carry her when she wanted me to pick her up and getting angry at the temper tantrum that followed. Thank God I never said I'd leave her behind if she didn't keep up with me — but I understand the feelings which produce such unkind behavior.

Long after my daughter was too old to benefit from my further growth and learning, I came to a point in my own psychotherapy where, for the first time, I was able to get in touch with a special kind of exhaustion that I can only describe as a sort of childhood psychosis. Do you sometimes get the feeling, after a long, hard day and a late night, that if you don't get to bed in the next two seconds you're going to start crying and kicking? It never goes away entirely, but children under the age of five frequently experience a sudden onset of fatigue, which makes them feel a little crazy. They have no control over what they do. They feel disoriented; they feel frightened and can become quite hysterical. There is nothing abnormal or dangerous happening. It is simply that young children do not know when they are getting a *little* tired. Fatigue doesn't hit them gradually, it comes on all at once like a kick in the head.

When a young child says, "I can't walk, carry me," he or she is not being ornery; it's really true. The child who suddenly starts screaming and squirming on a bus isn't a rotten kid — he just needs lunch and a nap. And my poor daughter wasn't trying to drive me crazy when she pushed a whole row of cans to the floor — she was just crazy-tired.

If I had a chance to do it over again, I'd sit down anywhere, including the floor, rock my child in my arms and comfort her, give her a banana or some raisins, and assure her I'd get her home and into her bed as fast as possible. Instead of getting mad, I'd tell her I understood exactly how she felt, and she shouldn't be scared, she was just tired. When we don't understand this exhaustion unto madness, our children feel terrified and guilty — *they* don't know why they are being difficult, and *we* have to tell them.

I sure plan to do a whole lot better with my grandchild!

The Right to Life

I FIND IT QUITE TERRIFYING that the question of abortion has become an inflammatory political issue, which may do more to fragment this country than inflation, war, and the pollution of the planet. The subject rightfully belongs within the conscience of each person and is a medical and psychological decision — a very serious one to be sure — but I have been trying to figure out why we are engulfed in such fury and hysteria. I think it is a way of denying how we *really* feel about children, how we really deal with them, and it reflects the fact that we do *not* have a genuine sense of the sacredness of human life. I know of no more dangerous psychological problem in our culture.

It would be wonderful if no unwanted child was ever conceived, but that is not the case. Even in this time of mass information about birth control, at least fifty percent of all pregnancies are not chosen. In many cases, of course, the pregnancy itself creates an attitude of loving expectation, but in many more cases these pregnancies lead to babies who, from the moment of conscious awareness, know they should never have been born. Their life experiences are brutal beyond the imagination of the people who are focusing all their concern on the unborn fetus — lives of beatings, unspeakable acts of violence, sexual molestation, hunger and malnutrition, misery and hopelessness.

As a nation we have been doing almost nothing for the unwanted children who are already born, and it is clear our government is planning to do even less about the health and the educational and the psychological problems of these children in the future.

The institutions and courts which eventually become the caretakers of many of them offer more rejection, not loving care and concern.

I do not hear passionate voices raised about the millions of children already alive whom nobody wants. I do not hear any screams of rage because none of us may have the right to much life when there is standing room only.

In a new book, *The Children of Jonestown,* Kenneth Wooden tells us that two hundred forty children under the age of sixteen died in Guyana, yet the House Foreign Affairs Committee report devotes only two paragraphs to this fact. Children under the California foster care system were turned over to Jones, and he received forty thousand dollars a month in public support funds. Two hundred ten of the children who died were never even identified. I recommend this book to those who think that concern for children is the issue in the current struggle about abortion. It is, instead, an evasion, drugging our senses so we can forget our sins against the living.

How Family Members Speak to Each Other

THE OTHER DAY, as I was walking along a street, I saw an older man standing at the corner. He seemed extremely agitated. Just as I got to the corner, a car pulled up. A young man was driving, and the older man began pounding on the window and screaming such epithets at the driver of the car that there isn't one single word he used which I want to set down on this page, though I'm sure you know all of them and need no blueprint. I assumed at once that this was a father-son relationship, and I'd like to tell you how I knew this.

I knew they were related because very few people would have been that rude to anyone but a close relative! Being a nosy eavesdropper, I gathered that the son was supposed to take his father to the doctor and had been delayed in very heavy traffic, due to an accident en route. They were still screaming at each other, now both in the car, when the traffic light changed and they moved on.

A mother told me that when she scolded her son for yelling at her, he replied, "If I can't yell *here,* where *can* I yell?" He had a point. We all have to let off steam somewhere, sometime, and home, with the family, ought to be a safer place than the office or school. If we can't show our human frailties at home, what's a family for?

But there is a catch. I don't think letting off steam necessarily means being cruel, unfair, or vulgar. The important thing about being yourself is that you get to show your real feelings — and that can be done in a variety of ways, which can make a real difference.

Let me describe what I mean through a hypothetical family. The father, Sam, was told at work that part of his job was going to be taken over by a younger man, and he is terrified what this might mean. Son Jimmy was beaten up in the school playground by the class bully, and wife Jean, who is a saleslady in a shoe store, had one customer who tried on twelve pairs of shoes and bought none. In one scenario Sam walks into the living room and starts screaming because he can't smell anything cooking in the kitchen. He describes his wife in a few charming words like "lazy slob" or "dumb pain in the neck."

Jean tells him he knows what he can do with his supper, in very colorful words, and Jimmy hits the dog.

Now all of that is quite human, and if it lasts for a minute or two, it may be inevitable. But the goal of love seems to me to be the right to express feelings, but in ways that are constructive and don't hurt others. Sam needs to tell about his fear and be comforted, Jean needs a sympathetic ear and some help in the kitchen, and Jimmy needs a lot of reassurance about the greater worth of people who *don't* hit other people.

Good manners doesn't mean bottling up our feelings, but rather letting people know our troubles and listening to theirs with respect and caring. That's what a family is for — and it's a lot easier on the family dog, as well!

Marriage and Taking Vacations

IF YOUR MARRIAGE is very shaky right now, if you and your spouse are so mad at each other you can't even talk about it, that is *not*—I repeat—*not* the best time to take a vacation together!

It seems to me that one of the factors that may well play a part in the ultimate separation or divorce of a couple is the attempt to patch things up by taking a vacation together. I think that's in the same dumb category as having a baby to patch things up.

If most of a couple's irritability has to do with fatigue, too many demands by other people, work problems, or a feeling of being exploited by other people's needs, then a vacation together may be helpful and soothing. But if there is real trouble brewing, a vacation in each other's exclusive company may well boil over into total disaster.

One psychologist, Dr. Florence Miale, told me that sometimes the most serious problems erupt on a vacation, even when a couple may not have consciously realized they were in trouble. She told me, ''There you are, alone on that quiet beach or sharing a stateroom on a ship, or having to face each other over three meals a day instead of the usual one or two—and after a while little irritations, little annoyances, related to being together almost twenty-four hours a day, begin to crop up—and before you know it, in the middle of a minor disagreement you are suddenly confronting each other with hidden angers, frustrations, and resentments that you'd been burying successfully because you were too busy to deal with them. Vacations are highly overrated as solutions to very serious problems.''

Before the travel agents stone me to death, I ought to add that once we give up our foolish illusions about what vacations *ought* to be, they can be wonderful, constructive, useful times together. Under the best of circumstances they can enhance a loving companionship, an awareness of mutually shared rhythms and interests, and a sense of adventure. But sometimes when things have reached a silent, stony impasse what is really needed is *two* vacations, taken separately, to help each person gain a sense of perspective, look inward, see what he or she is contributing to the cold war.

If unexpected crises develop during a vacation, we need to give up all the shoulds about what a vacation is *supposed* to be like and deal with whatever it is that has risen to the surface. You're darn lucky you happen to have the time alone to deal with it.

Sometimes "bon voyage" means taking an *inner* journey.

Born-Again Human Beings

THERE IS ONE ROAD toward a reasonably good state of mental health that is too often neglected, and that is becoming a born-again human being. It's a job open to anyone of any religious persuasion.

There's a small town in Pennsylvania where vandalism has been increasing at an alarming rate. The town has a large population of teenagers, who roam the streets at night and dare each other to do stupid and thoughtless things none of them would do on their own. They are not criminals, just bored and restless kids, but the townspeople have been putting increasing pressure on the police to arrest them for acts of vandalism.

A friend of mine recently moved to this town. She noticed an elegant but unoccupied community center — a new building with nobody in it. When she heard about the vandalism, she suggested there ought to be a club for teens in the community center. She was told that this had been tried and the kids loved it, but there were not enough adults in the community willing to volunteer to supervise the program — not even one evening a week.

In Michigan there is a group home for six mentally retarded young adults who are supervised twenty-four hours a day by trained workers. The home is in a middle-class neighborhood, and the people are up in arms and have been meeting to protest this awful presence in their midst. As a result of their hysteria, property values may go down, and their children may live in permanent terror of human beings who happen to be different.

I keep wondering, where have decent people gone? Is it possible there aren't twenty people in that whole Pennsylvania town who care enough about young people to want them to feel worthy of attention? In the whole neighborhood in that Michigan suburb, where is a woman who wants to say "welcome" to people who are less fortunate than she is and bring over a homemade cake? Where is a man who offers to teach carpentry? Why aren't the school children asking these people to come to their basketball games? And what is going on in the religious centers in this country if it is so easy to forget the most fundamental teachings of the great mystics?

The young people in Pennsylvania will grow up — some well, some not. The mentally retarded group will survive — their immediate caretakers are helping them to become the best they can be. The people *I* worry about are the people who are sitting on their hands and doing nothing. The angry or indifferent people are at least expressing an opinion. Somewhere, out there in our towns and cities and suburbs, there are too many people who are not doing what they could be doing for others. I worry about their mental health. Decency and compassion for others are ingredients as important to a satisfying life for oneself as anything I can think of.

Loneliness

THE POET MAY SARTON has written, "Loneliness is the poverty of self; solitude is the richness of self."

If you feel desperately lonely when you are alone, you are missing the companionship of a very special person: the only friend you can count on to be with you from birth to death. YOU.

A Japanese scholar was asked how he would describe the difference between American and Japanese attitudes. He said that if a Japanese person is working at a desk, people feel free to interrupt to ask a question. If, on the other hand, the same person is staring out a window or looking off into space, no one will interrupt because such moments of daydreaming are considered to be the time when the most important work is being done. Americans would hesitate to interrupt someone at work, but would feel free to interrupt anyone who was just sitting and thinking.

I am inclined toward the Japanese point of view, whether or not it is a valid distinction. An appreciation of solitary thought seems to me to be a prerequisite for the enjoyment of being alone.

One of the most disparaging things a teacher can tell a parent about a child is that he or she is a daydreamer: It is always reported as if this were a serious disease! It is *not*. If we allowed children to cultivate this fine art, we would have fewer lonely people.

A high-school English teacher asked his class to write a composition on something they would really hate to have to do. He was astounded by the number of students who said they would hate to be alone in a room without a radio or TV or a telephone. While we do very little to help young people delight in the companionship of their own thoughts, there have been heartening developments in adult attention to yoga and meditation and sensory awareness, which are ways of discovering the inner resources at our disposal when we are alone.

The deepest and most painful feelings of loneliness arise not only from atrophied daydreaming, but also from a profound inner sense of unworthiness — the feeling that we are boring, dumb, unlovable. No wonder we don't want to be alone with such a creep!

To reduce such loneliness we need to take some risks: We need to cultivate that inner companion. If we give ourselves half a chance, we will discover someone more than worthy of our full attention. One way to begin is to pretend you are taking a friend out to lunch or for a walk in the country. Observe this friend. Any interesting ideas crop up? Maybe a talent for noticing something lovely? The patience to stop and watch a squirrel with a nut, a wobbly baby taking a first step, a sunset? How about curiosity and a spirit of adventure? Slowly but surely you will begin to see that your companion is just the person you've been looking for to keep you from being lonely.

Sex Education

A FRIEND OF MINE is Dean of Women at a large university. One day she told me, "Whenever a girl comes in and tells me she's pregnant, I know that she knows nothing at all about sex except how to get pregnant." I'd like to talk further about the high correlation between ignorance and pregnancy.

Most experts agree that girls who find themselves in this situation almost never have had sex education from their parents — unless you include as sex education statements such as 'You better not get in trouble" or "Just stay away from boys."

The majority of young girls who become pregnant feel unable to tell their parents what has happened; many feel their parents will beat them — even kill them — if they find out. Even if such ideas may be somewhat exaggerated, they certainly make it clear that healthy communication about the sexual facts of life has not been prevalent.

Those who say that sex education in the schools is responsible for casual sex are dead wrong. Quite the opposite is true, if the sex education program is planned and executed by mature and responsible adults who believe that knowledge makes you free to make better choices. Although of course some pregnancies occur among young people who have had a close, honest, and open relationship with parents, this is the rare exception.

Since much-too-early pregnancies are becoming epidemic, what we need desperately is fewer people trying to shut off the subject of sex, and more educational programs for both parents and teachers on how to help young people understand their drives and feelings and how to make choices about the priorities in their lives.

In the course of working on a book called *The Roots of Crime,* I interviewed a number of prostitutes, ranging in age from fourteen to forty. Their ignorance of the most basic facts about the human body was astounding. They either had totally inaccurate ideas about the way it functions, or, underneath their bravado, they were scared and confused. A woman who'd been a hooker for seven years said that menstruation was caused by junk food; a fifteen-year-old newcomer to prostitution said that you couldn't get pregnant if you ate pineapple after intercourse. It is time to face the fact that ignorance destroys, knowledge gives choices.

The Love Industry

THERE HAVE BEEN dating agencies for a long time, but I gather they are now multiplying by geometric progression and even advertising on television. I have a theory about why this is happening.

My theory is that young people are getting fed up with all the freedom and anonymity of the singles bar. In fact, I think a lot of people are discovering that the sexual revolution has not often led to the joy of you-know-what, but rather to a whole lot of feelings like depression, loneliness, and anger. There doesn't seem to be any place where people can meet each other, knowing that others are greatly concerned about their welfare; and maybe that's essential for mutual feelings of self-worth. We don't live in small towns anymore, and parents and other relatives aren't around to supervise the dating and courting process, and everybody thought that this would be just dandy — and you know what? It isn't.

I think the reason for the burgeoning popularity of dating services is that a lot of people, of all ages, are looking for the people who used to help other people get acquainted with each other: the mother who sewed the dress for the prom; the father who checked out each boyfriend and gave a sermon about safe driving; the minister of the small-town church who helped widowed parishioners find each other; the busybody neighbor who served as either an official or an unofficial matchmaker.

Because so many relationships built on a whole lot of freedom have tended to fall apart, and because having no commitments has not turned out to be the road to nirvana, I think some people may be feeling nostalgic for some of the old ways in which people met each other, usually surrounded by other people who loved them and cared what happened to them. Maybe we need a setting for the kind of falling in love that can lead to genuine commitment and caring; maybe people need to be surrounded by affection and concern for their welfare.

At a singles weekend in the mountains, nobody you're with really cares what happens to you, except maybe the friend you brought along for moral support. You're really on your own, and it may be hard to remember to care for your own life and to make good choices. If, on the other hand, you go to a dating service, and some-body sits down and talks to you about your life and your interests, and shows some genuine respect for you as a person, it may give you that old-fashioned feeling that your life is important to others. What looks like a love industry may really be the means by which we reestablish those necessary connections which we've been missing a whole lot — like knowing there's a light under your parents' door and that they want to hear what happened. The lady at The Togetherness Club may be a substitute for the caring we thought we didn't need, but which begins to look better and better.

Communication Between Partners

THE OTHER DAY, when I wasn't feeling well, my husband left early in the morning and came home late. What I said to him was very intelligent, and I'd like to share the wisdom of a long relationship with you.

In the early years of our marriage — in those days there wasn't too much unmarried living together, but the same ideas still apply — if I felt neglected, unhappy, in need of attention and tender loving care, my attitude was that my husband owed all this to me. It was his job, I foolishly thought, to make me happy. I have since learned that life has been a whole lot better for both of us since we each took responsibil-ity for our own well-being.

In earlier days I would have spent the day building up steam, and when my husband walked in the door, I would have said something brilliant like "You should have stayed with me when I feel so miser-able!"

That greeting would usually lead to a guilty and angry silence on his part and would confirm my feelings of rejection.

The other day, after suffering with a sinus headache all day, in the aftermath of several very bad days of major disappointments, what I said when my husband walked in at ten o'clock at night was simply, "I missed you." All that did was express my *feelings,* without making any claims on him. And because there was neither a judgment nor a criticism in my attitude, I got some chicken soup and ice cream and a lot of hugging.

What I have had to learn the hard way, in over thirty-seven years of living with the same person, is that nobody owns anybody — that the only way two people can feel real compassion for each other is if neither expects it as a natural consequence of sharing the same home. If you are unhappy about your job, or if you need a vacation, or if you're not getting along with your parents, or if you think you should go on a diet, nobody can do anything about any of those issues except you. They are not the responsibility of the person you live with. And what is so absolutely sensational about learning this lesson is that the minute you believe it and live it, the other person in your life will *want* to help you.

The minute you really understand that you are responsible for your own life — when you stop hanging on and demanding help, when you give up bitter anger and resentment — you will discover you never have to be alone again.

Family

THERE WERE THREE regional White House conferences on the family during 1980. One of the things that interested me the most about the reports was the great struggle and controversy about settling on a definition of the family.

There are people who say the family is dead as a social institution. There are others who say the word *family* doesn't mean anything anymore — that it's been horribly corrupted by the new and different combinations of people who call themselves families.

I don't think the family is dying at all — but it *is* changing. With a kind of instinctive wisdom we see too rarely in human events, most people, I think, are adapting remarkably well to the rapid social changes of our times. I think two lesbian women who live together out of free choice and mutual devotion are a family. I agree with the courts that a single man and the two kids he's adopted are a family. A single parent raising children is the head of the family, and two widowed people in their seventies who live together but don't get married because of ridiculous Social Security and health insurance regulations are a family. Twenty assorted adults and children living in a commune are a family, and two eighteen-year-olds living together in a college dorm are a family.

Ah, you may be saying, those last two can't *possibly* be a family because chances of their staying together for any length of time are mighty slim. Not much more so than two young people who get married these days and divorce before the ink is dry on the marriage license.

I not only think family life is alive and well; I also believe that it is still a bulwark for morality, even in all this variety of forms. What I think we are seeing is simply new and different expressions of old needs that probably haven't changed since the dawn of man. There is a song about "people needing people," and that has always been and will, I think, always be the name of the game. Family is people loving each other — the most moral of all human ideas.

It is true that family life often seems to be more unstable these days than in the past. There is little question that the skyrocketing divorce rate has caused a variety of changing family groupings. But people who have children and who divorce each other don't suddenly *not* have a family. The old-style family unit gets spread out and eventually shifts. Seventy-five percent of divorced partners with children remarry within five years — hardly a statistic suggesting total discouragement with the idea of family.

I like my husband's definition of the family the best. He says, "The family is a group where if you don't come home, they'll go out looking for you." I rest my case.

Single Parenthood:
The Need for a Support System

I KNOW A LITTLE BOY who lives in San Francisco and has five uncles, nine aunts, and two grandmothers all living in his apartment building. He's a lucky kid to have all those loving people around him, and what's even more remarkable is that there isn't a blood relative in the whole lot.

If there is one message divorced single parents would probably like to broadcast to any novices who currently may be joining their ranks, it might be, "Get a support system going as soon as you can!"

It's hard enough to raise kids even when there are two parents around. A single parent is likely to be a person who has a constant new companion: *exhaustion*. But on the positive side, the greater informality and social ease among people of all ages provide more sources of help and encouragement.

Few families, married or divorced, live in the same place where they grew up. Aunts, uncles, grandparents often live hundreds if not thousands of miles away. Industries move people around at such a rate that many young families have a hard time establishing friendship relationships that last more than a few years.

As a kind of balance to these negatives, some wonderful things have been happening. We have begun to realize that common needs and mutual understanding can create an emotional support system on very short notice.

That lucky kid in San Francisco lives in a building in which there are a great many young families, many of them with single mothers and fathers. The landlady and her sister, widows who might have spent a lonely old age since all their own children and grandchildren have moved to other places, serve happily as substitute grandparents, while all the married and single parents share a common devotion to every child's needs. It is a kind of informal commune in which working parents share their resources in order to provide for their children's needs as well as their own.

"These days," one young woman told me, "all you have to do is go to the laundromat and introduce yourself around. In half an hour five people are helping you, and you're helping them." This kind of new instant family grows out of need, but I think it is a lifestyle that can stand on its own merits under any kind of circumstances. I have a vague feeling I've read about it somewhere — before it was called a support system, I think it was called the Golden Rule.

The Two-Career Marriage

WHEN I WAS A YOUNG BRIDE, back in the early 1940s, there was one problem I did *not* have. I never had to worry about getting a job someplace else than where my husband was, because it never occurred to me that that was a possibility. I assumed — and without any sense of frustration or unhappiness, as a matter of fact — that whither he went, I would go! It's not like that anymore, and a whole new set of problems has developed in two-career marriages.

Women's lib has wrought some complicated relationships. Mary works in Cleveland, and Joe works in Chicago; they meet weekends, taking turns on who does the traveling. There are no children, and they enjoy their work and their time together, and think this is a fine way of live. But both agree that if they ever want kids, they may be in trouble.

Sue and David have kids and live apart. Dave and two teenagers live in New York City with a housekeeper, and Sue lives in Washington, D.C., and is a weekend and vacation mom. Neither is really happy with this arrangement, but Sue earns a lot at a fascinating job that she just couldn't resist, and Dave teaches at a college where, if he leaves, he would lose a juicy pension and tenure. Life is becoming increasingly strained, and while the children were supportive at first, the glamour of a successful career mom has worn off, and they are growing petulant.

John is a labor lawyer and adores his job, in Boston. His wife is doing a medical internship in Detroit. John says the marriage was on the rocks three months into this experiment. His wife says, "I think we might have had a good marriage if we could have stayed together, but the separation was just too difficult, and neither of us was willing to give up what we were doing.''

There are no easy solutions to this dilemma, but one thing I am sure about — if careers are more important than the marriage, chances are pretty good the marriage will sooner or later shrivel up from lack of tender loving care. If two people who treasure their lives together find themselves in a situation where careers conflict, they need to sit down together and figure out what they are each willing to sacrifice for their marriage, and then make some tough choices and decisions. Sometimes these decisions may mean that one partner loses out for a while — he or she may move to where a spouse has a spectacular job, hoping that eventually new opportunities will appear. Sometimes a separation will seem the only solution, but is seen as temporary, until a couple can decide together which job is the more important one.

The only way such complicated relationships can survive is if each partner is totally committed to the other, and both want to safeguard their marriage above all else.

Marriage: When Relatives Are Prejudiced

I GOT A LETTER from a young man, recently married, who is very disturbed because his grandmother, with whom he has had a very close relationship all his life, would not come to his wedding and will not speak to him or his wife, the reason being that his wife is Mexican-American.

One of the many challenges of a changing society is the fear, the discomfort — even the outright prejudice — some parents and grandparents feel when a younger, liberated generation declares that loving has no boundaries related to race or religion or differences in background. Getting angry about such a situation won't help the young or the old. What is needed is compassion, understanding, and patience — and what I would tell this young man is that if he and his wife can respond with those necessary qualities, chances are that grandma will change. This point of view is not based on wishful thinking but on facts. In most cases the problem can be solved, and is, if there is loving concern for the feelings of older people, who were born into a different time and a different world, and who find it difficult to give up the beliefs and attitudes of a lifetime.

I suggested that, for the moment, this young man try at least to reestablish his own relationship with grandma. I think it is a mistake to take the attitude "If you love me, you have to love my spouse" right away. Chances are that grandma feels that somewhere along the line the family has failed in helping this young man accept the values by which it has lived. She needs to be reassured that this is not the case. Grandma needs to be loved and respected more than ever; she needs to hear her grandson say he loves her a lot, that he learned a great deal about loving while he was growing up. He needs to talk to grandma about the ways in which life has changed, as well as the ways in which it hasn't changed. He needs to try to help grandma understand that, while the appearance of things may change, he is just as responsible and caring and loving as he has ever been, and that his wife has just the qualities of decency and good sense and caring that have always been important in his family. If he's willing to see grandma alone for a while — if he does everything possible to keep the lines of communication open — grandma will be reassured of her importance and her value, and it is more than likely that in a few months it will be possible to invite her for Sunday dinner and have her accept.

Feeling respected and understood for one's life experiences is really the only avenue to reconciliation. Standing off in anger closes off the possibility for change, for modification of outworn attitudes.

Most young married people feel very insecure about themselves and their marriage, so the tendency is to take a stand together, to reinforce their own stability. It is a greater sign of strength to be forgiving.

And one thing we know for sure: Very few parents and grandparents are able to hold out when young marrieds become parents. The need to participate in the cycle of one's mortality is the cure for feelings that need to change in today's world.

A Birthday Present: The Lobster Story

TOMORROW WILL BE my fifty-ninth birthday, and, as usual, I am utterly astounded by the passing of the years. It seems to me that yesterday I was twenty-five and that the year before that I was about twelve. However surprising birthdays may become, I find them useful for one reason; they remind me that I must not waste a minute of my life. And that I must keep on growing and changing, in order to truly celebrate my birthdays. In that connection, I'm going to give *you* a present on my birthday. It's a story about lobsters. This is my crustacean tale.

A number of years ago, I wrote a book called *The Wonderful Crisis of Middle Age*. The reason I felt middle age could be called wonderful was that it seemed to me to be a chance for a second adolescence, during which I could make new and better decisions about the rest of my life.

At a dinner party, while I was writing a book, I met an oceanographer who asked me if I knew how it was possible for a lobster to grow bigger when its shell was so hard. I had to admit that this problem had never been very high on my list of priorities, but now that he had mentioned it, how in the world *could* a lobster grow?

A lobster grows by shedding its shell at regular intervals. Its body begins to feel pretty cramped inside a three-pound shell, so the lobster tries to find a reasonably safe spot in which to rest while the hard shell comes off, and the new pink membrane just inside the hard shell becomes the next shell, which will be big enough for a four-pound lobster to live in. But no matter where a lobster goes for this shedding process, it is in danger and very vulnerable. It can get tossed against a coral reef or eaten by a fish. In order to grow, a lobster has to risk its life.

I found myself very preoccupied with this story for days after first hearing it. I finally realized that it was a metaphor for the book I was writing. The lobster could teach us that the only way in which we can endure the passage of time and the limits of our mortality is if we take risks in order to change.

We know when our shells are getting too tight. We feel angry or depressed or frightened, because somehow life is no longer exciting or challenging.

Some of us continue to smother in old shells that are no longer useful or productive. At least that way we are safe — nothing can happen to us. Others of us know that even though we will be very vulnerable — that there will be dangers ahead — we have a kind of divine discontent and know we must take risks or suffocate.

On my birthday, I invite you to my party, where I take off this year's shell, no matter what the dangers, in order to get ready for new adventures.

Middle Age

A BATTLE-SCARRED MOTHER told me that one day when she and her daughter were screaming at each other, her daughter had said, "You shouldn't be so mean to me, because I'm a *teenager!*" Mother had shouted back, "And you shouldn't be so mean to me, because I'm a menopausal mother!"

Mother and daughter really had much more in common than they knew; they were both going through periods of adolescence, and if they could have understood that fact, perhaps neither would have been so mean to the other!

The first adolescence is a period of growth during which a young person needs to rebel against adults in order to become part of his or her own generation. It is a time for the search for one's identity, a time of making choices about the ways in which one can relate to others while still becoming more and more uniquely oneself.

If you are middle-aged, you have exactly the same task. Middle age is also a time of identity crisis, a time for rebellion.

Middle age can arrive anywhere from thirty-five to sixty years of age. The clearest symptom of its arrival is the sharp awakening to one's mortality — the fact that we will not live forever. Middle age is upon us when we realize we will never read all the books in the library, never visit all the cities of Europe, never fulfill all our dreams. It can be a time of despair, but it can also be the most exciting and rewarding turning point in one's life — an even better adolescence than the first one, when, even if we rebelled against adults, we were still stuck with trying to be well liked by our peers.

Once we face the fact that we will not live forever, our choices become far more important. Because we are adults and not as concerned with popularity, or as dependent on it, we can, perhaps for the first time in our lives, decide which friends and relatives we want to continue to cultivate and which ones bore us to death; we can decide whether or not to go on working at what we are currently doing or to make some new choices so that whatever is left of our lives can be a greater adventure.

Middle age ought to be a time for taking risks, for discovering our deepest needs, for exploring new possibilities. Up to this time we've probably used most of our energy measuring up to our parents' expectations and our children's demands. It's time to say, "*Everybody off!*" That declaration of independence can make the middle years the best years of our lives.

Denial and Celebration:
Anne Frank's Birthday

TODAY IS THE BIRTHDAY of Anne Frank, who wrote *The Diary of a Young Girl.* She would have been fifty-two — a startling thought. The day has a significance for me, and I'd like to tell you why.

My parents became friends of Otto Frank, Anne's father, and his second wife, Fritzi, after World War II. Mr. Frank came to New York about the time of the American publication of Anne's book. When I read her *Diary,* I could not imagine anyone surviving so much suffering and loss — being in hiding, going to the death camps, and then losing one's whole family. My mother invited my husband and me to a dinner party for Mr. Frank, and we went with our daughter, who was then three years old. I felt guilty and apprehensive — how could a man who had lost his whole family endure having dinner with a family in which there were parents and grown children — even a grandchild? What I learned that night was that the power of recovery is probably the most remarkable thing about the human race — that there are people who can grow beyond bitterness and rage and suffering, and still come out whole. Mr. Frank sat our daughter on his knee and enjoyed the pleasures that life still had to offer — and taught me a lesson I will never forget about courage.

In recent years, and in many countries, there have been people who have come to the conclusion that the holocaust never happened. That is carrying the psychological defense of denial to its ultimate irrationality — but that teaches me something, too. There are two ways of dealing with something that is unbearable — denying it exists and running away from it, or using it to enhance one's life and learn something from it.

Anne's *Diary* is a celebration of life, and her death did not destroy the only member of her family to survive. All through his life he corresponded with thousands of people in every country, encouraging, helping, offering his friendship. A man in Texas wrote him that Anne had saved his life. He'd lost his whole family in a fire and had been collecting sleeping pills in order to commit suicide. In a drugstore, waiting for the final prescription to be filled, he happened to pick up a copy of the *Diary,* began reading it, bought it, took it to the motel room with him, read it and wept, and wrote to Otto Frank, "Your daughter saved my life. She made me realize it is possible to have the courage to live."

There are literally thousands of such touching stories — especially about young people for whom the diary became a focus for their personal problems. In one case, shortly after the war, a fourteen-year-old Greek girl wrote to Otto Frank to tell him she had read the diary. At the age of twelve she had been raped by Greek soldiers and had lost the ability to speak. She and Mr. Frank began to correspond, and eventually he went to Greece to see her. At the airport, she ran into his arms, shouting, "Papa" — her first words in several years. She's now a middle-aged lady, and she has a daughter named Anna.

Otto Frank always responded — and celebrated life. Denial of pain and shock cheats us of feeling alive. Celebration of life is the only antidote for human suffering. So, it's a birthday: Let's blow out the candles and make a wish.

The Tyranny of the Weak

A YOUNG MAN I know just married a girl who is the exact opposite of his dear old mom. Tom confessed to me that his wife made him feel strong and masculine. "I've had my fill of strong, competent women," he told me. I think he's in for a few surprises.

Tom's mother is a friend of mine. She has a full-time job — has had one for as long as I've known her — has raised two kids with only minor participation by her husband in the daily routines of the household, and maintains an active social life. Her husband is something of an absent-minded professor, easygoing — or "laid back," as they say these days.

Tom's new wife says she has no desire to be a career woman, just wants to stay home and have babies. She likes the idea of having a man take care of her and looks up at Tom with adoring eyes.

Maybe it will work, but I'm reminded of something we are sometimes inclined to overlook — the tyranny of the weak! What Tom might discover is that dependence can be far more overpowering than assertiveness.

I'm thinking, for example, of an older woman who, having become fearful and anxious after her husband's death, has bound her son to her with heavy emotional shackles. Although she is in reasonably good health, she tells him she can't go anywhere unless he takes her. She refuses to see old friends and sits in lonely isolation, letting her son know that the only pleasurable hours in her life are when he comes to see her. Her son says, "I couldn't feel any more overwhelmed with guilt and imprisoned by her power than if she stood over me with a whip."

Kathy is in her mid-thirties and seems to be terrified of life. She's insecure with people she doesn't know well and retreats from situations in which she might be uneasy. Her husband, John, works for a large corporation in which it is important to attend social events and to do some entertaining. Every time he asks Kathy to go to a dinner with him, she gets a terrible headache, and he has to go alone; when he suggests entertaining in their home, she becomes so panic-stricken that he drops the subject. He says he found her dependency charming for a couple of years, but now feels that he can't really hope to progress in his job or enjoy a social life.

Pete is a charming fellow who loudly approves of women's lib. He thinks it's just great that his wife is competent and ambitious, and when he speaks of her accomplishments, what I notice is how exhausted his wife looks because she carries most of the financial and domestic burdens of their lives.

It's easy to recognize power in the powerful; but the mask of weakness and dependency may sometimes represent an even greater force.

What Should I Do with My Son-in-Law?

I'VE HAD A PLAINTIVE LETTER: "Would you please tell me what I should do with my son-in-law? I think he's a terrible person and I worry all the time about what is happening. I love my daughter and grandchildren so much I can't continue to bite my tongue — it's all bruised now." I'm afraid I can't advise this lady specifically, since she didn't give any further details. I don't know if her son-in-law is cruel or irresponsible, or whether he just happens to disagree with her, or whether she doesn't like the way his ears stick out. And it surely makes a difference.

It's extremely difficult in any family relationship to figure out when it may be necessary to interfere and when you have to tell yourself it's none of your business. I knew one grandmother who lived with her daughter, and we all used to get angry at her when she complained bitterly about her son-in-law. She said he was a cruel, horrible man and that he was ruining the lives of her daughter and two grandchildren. After grandma died, those of us who were close to the family realized she'd been quite right and that something should have been done, long since, at least to protect the children, who grew up with serious emotional wounds.

On the other hand, we all know people who have so few genuine satisfactions in their own lives that they meddle compulsively in the lives of others, and in-laws are often the targets. A very common problem occurs when a daughter or son marries someone who has quite a different temperament and lifestyle, and a parent cannot bear to believe that his or her child could be happy. One mother I know hasn't spoken to her daughter or son-in-law for fifteen years because her daughter was in law school when she married a truck driver and became a homemaker. Because her mother's ambitions for her daughter were thwarted, she cannot allow herself the pleasure of seeing that her daughter has found just the right marriage partner for her.

The best way to decide whether or not to interfere in anybody else's life is first to clarify your own motives. Is there real danger and pathology in a situation, or is it simply your own need to participate more fully? Is it a way of expressing disapproval over the fact that your child, in choosing a marriage partner, may have strayed far from your dreams? It's a good idea to talk this over with a family counselor before you stop biting your tongue. After you've had some help assessing the situation, you'll have the advantage of knowing a good resource for your daughter if she's really in serious trouble.

Jealousy

JEALOUSY, THE GREEN-EYED MONSTER, is rarely the reflection of what somebody else is or has; it is usually an indication of how we feel about ourselves.

It isn't so much the fact that the new baby sister is cute that bothers a four-year-old brother; the real issue at the heart of his jealousy is

"Can I compete with that cuteness? Am *I* lovable?" When a young bride is jealous of her husband's preference for his mother's cooking, it isn't really the homemade pies or the baked lasagna that are the problem; the jealousy stems from self-doubt — the panicky feeling that her own gifts and talents in many other, nonculinary, areas such as being a competent lawyer, or an attractive woman, or a devoted companion may not be qualities which make her worthy of love and respect. When a man is constantly preoccupied with jealous feelings about his wife's or girlfriend's men friends, he is having self-doubts about his own attractiveness. When a middle-aged woman can't bear it if her husband's co-workers happen to be younger women, her jealousy stems from her own misgivings about whether or not it is still possible to be lovable at the age of forty-five. Jealousy is nature's way of telling us that we are in short supply of an essential ingredient for successful relationships with others — the healthy capacity to appreciate ourselves.

Like most of my fellow human beings, I have lived through the full variety of jealousies in the course of my life. What I have discovered is that the more I learned to value my own life, the qualities that made me uniquely myself, the less often such episodes seemed to occur. Prolonged and intense periods of jealousy are an indication of *self-hatred*, and the only cure is not to get rid of baby sisters and brothers, mothers-in-law, rivals for a spouse's interest and attention, but rather a careful and thoughtful examination of what makes *us* feel *inferior*.

A friend told me that when she was unable to shake an unrealistic fear that her husband would leave her for a younger woman, she began seeing a psychotherapist. During the course of that experience she began to appreciate her own virtues, and one day, euphoric with a new sense of what a decent and able and lovable woman she was, she suddenly thought to herself, "Hell, if he doesn't appreciate me that's his problem, not mine!" That attitude is the only antidote for jealousy that I have ever discovered.

Failure

TWO MEN I KNOW have been involved in an intensive research project for five years. It has failed. They have lost precious time and a considerable financial investment. One of the men was back at work on a new project immediately, the other went into a serious depression. If we can figure out the difference, we might know something very useful about how to deal with failure.

John, who was back in the research library within a few hours of having faced the failure of five years' work, is a man who expresses his feelings very openly. Every time he experienced some new frustration in his work he would rant and rave, but after a few minutes he'd turn around and apologize to everyone and go on with his work. When he reached a dangerous level of fatigue, he'd quit for a while and go off on some kind of vacation that satisfied some secret need he'd had for a long time. He would come back refreshed and be able to work with a new level of creativity. He's a man who can swear loudly and laugh with enormous gusto, and who drinks in the pleasures of life. He had never worked harder on any project in all his life, and he lost a great deal of money, as well as the time he'd invested in his work; when the research failed, he was beside himself with fury and disappointment, and cursed everyone out very colorfully. Then he sighed and went to the library to start all over again.

Charles has never appeared in public without a tie. He stands straight as a ramrod, and is the kind of polite and proper gentleman we associate with the Victorian age. Very strictly reared, he lives by the strictest of codes of behavior. John has never heard Charles raise his voice or speak ill of anyone, no matter how valid his reason might be. When Charles heard the news about the failure of the project, he told John he was sorry, but they must both make the best of it. Then he hung up the phone, went to his room, lay down on the bed, and stopped talking or doing anything. Now he sits in a chair and stares out the window most of the time, but he never says one word that would indicate he is angry at what happened to him.

The interesting thing is that John and Charles were raised in similar ways as children. There was a time when John probably would have reacted in the same way Charles did, but during the course of John's life he has done everything he possibly could to become a more open person, more in touch with his real feelings.

What we can learn from this comparison of two men is that people respond to failure in the same way they are likely to respond to any traumatic event. The person who has the courage and the psychological health to allow his or her feelings full expression can recover much more quickly and constructively than the person whose feelings of anger and frustration are too deeply repressed, and therefore emerge through depression or psychosomatic illnesses.

Since we all fail some of the time, we ought to get ourselves in emotional shape for the event!

Lying Is a Necessary Art

WERE YOU TAUGHT that it was a sin to ever tell a lie? Whoever told you that was telling a whopper right there.

The telephone rings just as you are about to take a soufflé out of the oven for your six dinner guests. It's Aunt Wilhelmina, who needs to give you the latest news bulletin on the condition of her gastrointestinal tract. Your spouse says it's a shame, but you just left the house to go to a movie. The white lie is a necessary family staple, which makes life endurable for the liar and protects the sensibilities of the person one is lying to.

It seems to me that as long as we and our children are perfectly clear about the fact that such lies have a tender purpose, we have no reason to drown in large buckets of guilt. There is often no other way to protect ourselves from impossible infringements on our own rights.

But we can make good use of such situations if we will take notice of why they occur and of the kind of relationships that seem to invite this kind of minor deceit. When we make up white lies, it is usually because we know the other person involved is too insecure to be able to handle the truth. We also do it when our own feelings about someone else are very ambivalent; we don't really like them enough to tell the truth.

Let's say it isn't Aunt Wilhelmina on the phone but someone you work with at the office. Pamela is a lovely, funny, warm lady, and you have tremendous respect for her talents. In short, she's a happy woman, and you are crazy about her. Under those circumstances, you would probably scream from the kitchen, "Tell her that unless she's dying, I can't talk to her!"

What these two different responses suggest is that the more secure two people are and the more they genuinely care about each other, the less they ever really need to lie to each other. It therefore seems to me that the problem is not to worry about lying less but about loving more.

There is no question that there are people in our lives with whom there will always have to be some evasion of the whole truth. We know the other person is too frightened, too uncertain, too easily threatened by any indication of disinterest on our part, even of a temporary nature. For such people we may have to lie about being busy or about that "wonderful" birthday present — which we plan to return — or we may pretend an enthusiasm we don't exactly feel about some culinary triumph which actually left us feeling definitely queasy.

Life isn't long enough for us to manage to make every relationship a straightforward encounter. But we need to remember the less we demand from others, the more likely they are to be able to tell *us* the truth, and that when we work hard to establish feelings of respect and affection with those we care about the most, lying seldom even comes to mind.

In the best and most profoundly satisfying of human relationships, honesty is not only the best policy, it tends to be the only policy.

Drugs

A WOMAN RECENTLY came up to me in the lobby of a movie theater and said, "I know who you are — you're one of those permissive psychologists who turn all the kids into drug addicts!" I suppose I should be flattered at being awarded such omnipotence, but she made me feel sad and angry all day, because that kind of stupidity is what makes the drug problem get worse and worse.

A friend of mine, a former drug addict now working with a medical team to cure drug addiction, told me that in spite of the fact that all kinds of horrifying and destructive drugs are rampant in high schools all over the country, there are only a few enlightened school systems which seem to take the position that discussing such matters is as important as algebra and physics. The attitude is very often "Sorry, we haven't got time — and it's not our job. We've got to teach skills."

I have never really met a permissive child expert — I don't even know what that means. Dr. Spock was just a scapegoat — there isn't one word in anything he ever wrote to suggest that children could raise themselves. Permissiveness has nothing whatever to do with drugs — but schools where *any* academic subject is more important than helping young people deal with their emotional and social problems have a lot to do with drugs.

Regardless of the particular drug, its use is a form of self-destruction, an indication that life is worthless. It is a way of tripping out of a real world which is too full of pain and hopelessness and confusion. Whether it is some wealthy and famous movie star sniffing cocaine at a Hollywood party or a street kid in Harlem shooting heroin, the two are brothers under the skin. We have a terrible drug problem in this country because drugs make money for the kinds of criminals who never go to jail, and because millions of people live lives of unquiet desperation.

If we wanted to kick the drug habit in America — and I would most assuredly include alcoholism in the drug category — what we would have to do is to look at the people who never become addicts, and who rarely consider the possibility of getting high or drunk no matter how great the temptation.

They are invariably people who are too busy living fulfilling and satisfying lives. They get high on work and high on love and high on the challenge of life. They like themselves so well that, even living in a time of turmoil and anxiety, they feel they have the capacity to live a meaningful, purposeful, creative life.

It's really all perfectly clear: All we have to do is develop a community life in which everyone has the chance to grow up with that kind of strength and maturity. That's all — and that's everything.

Marriage: When Parents Are Critical

A YOUNG WOMAN wrote to me about a very common problem among newly married couples. She wrote, "George and I have been married for six months. Every time I invite his parents to visit us, my father-in-law criticizes everything I do. He complains the food is too salty, or he thinks the drapes are an ugly color, or I see him making faces when he sees the laundry on the floor of the coat closet. I've told Larry that I don't want his parents to visit us anymore — I just get too upset. Am I doing the right thing?" Since she asked, I feel required to say no, she is not, and here's why I feel that way.

During the first few years of marriage, both partners tend to feel very insecure about themselves and each other. Learning to live as a couple, while also holding on tightly to one's personal identity, is no small achievement and takes a whole lot of hard work — and it can be an almost impossible task when there are too many threats from the outside world. Any kind of slight or criticism on the part of parents or in-laws becomes a gigantic issue, out of all proportion to reality, because it appears to be a challenge to the marriage itself, which is still shaky and uncertain.

What I wrote Nancy is that if she'd been married twenty-five years, and if she and George were more confident of themselves as successful and mature adults, her father-in-law's behavior might seem more amusing than serious. Right now, it adds to her feelings of inadequacy and inexperience, and that's why she is overreacting.

There are all sorts of reasons why a father-in-law, or any other relative, for that matter, may be supercritical. Maybe he has doubts and misgivings about whether or not George is really grown up enough to handle being married, and since he can't say that, his anxiety takes the form of being critical. In some cases, a father-in-law may feel some unconscious envy of his son, who is just starting out in life, in a first flush of romantic love with a pretty girl, and since to face his jealousy would be intolerable, he tries to find fault with his daughter-in-law. Sometimes parents try to use the young marriage as a random target for some of the discontents they can't face in their own relationship.

Whatever the cause, Nancy, because she is younger and more flexible, and can probably bring better psychological insights to the situation, needs to grin and bear it — not seeing it as a challenge to herself or her marriage. It's even possible she can joke about it a little, and be just a tiny bit flirtatious, making her father-in-law feel that she sees him as an attractive man, which is maybe what he needs rights now in order to feel less competitive with his son.

A lightness of touch is what's called for, and an inner sense that Nancy and George have a valued and significant life which cannot be destroyed by such acting-out on anyone's part.

The Right to Love

IF ALL GOES WELL, I will become a grandma in the early fall. One day recently, while sitting and talking with my daughter, it suddenly occurred to me that this future baby is going to be loved by so many people that without even giving it a lot of thought, I can immediately think of several hundred people who will adore him or her, unconditionally. No matter what this child looks like, no matter what he or she can or cannot do, no matter how nice or naughty, that lucky baby is going to feel like a national treasure — which of course he or she will be. In the midst of feeling great joy about this fact, I suddenly felt terribly sad; so few of the world's children ever experience such feelings — and yet I know that if anything can save this sick old world, it is only that kind of a beginning.

Theories on child raising come and go: People with excellent training and very good intentions often recommend opposite courses of action. When I was a baby, the behaviorist Dr. John B. Watson was exhorting mothers, mine included, to raise me like Pavlov's dog — all was conditioning. At about the same time Dr. Sigmund Freud was suggesting mysterious recesses of the mind, which might make me a victim of primitive fantasies caused by too much repression and guilt.

By the time I became a mother, Dr. Benjamin Spock was advising me to watch and listen and let my child tell me what she needed. I, who had been toilet-trained at six months, now found myself trying to believe my child was not retarded if she didn't make it to the toilet by two and a half. Where I was fed at exactly the same times, no matter what, I was now being told my child knew better than I did when she was hungry.

Parents, after each child post-psychology generation, have tried their best to adapt, to choose which experts to listen to — and even more important, when to ignore them.

But there has remained, throughout, one underlying theme — and that is that a creative, fulfilling, satisfying life, the raising of decent children who become responsible citizens, is possible only when children are given unconditional love by the adults around them. Not love for being good or smart or beautiful, but love just for being themselves. The mistake we sometimes make is to think that unconditional love means a wishy-washy permissiveness. It means nothing of the kind. Guidance is one of the main ingredients of love.

Criminal violence, neurotic relationships, and psychosomatic illnesses all have their roots in the lack of unconditional love. I am convinced that the right to love is even more important that the right to life — for without *love* life is not worth living.

Education for Citizenship

WHEN I WAS YOUNG, I believed that the right kind of educational system — designed by me, of course — could save the world. It never happened, which makes me sad.

If the goal of education were to create human beings capable of being informed, responsible, idealistic citizens for a democratic society, we'd have it made. Instead, most of our schools focus their attention on teaching children to memorize some facts, to read and write and learn such essentials as geometry, which about seventy-five percent will forget as quickly as possible, the minute they get out of school. I'd like to tell you a story which may explain why so few people seem prepared to live in a democracy, even after twelve or twenty years of going to school.

There is a privately sponsored summer-school program based in New York which is a six-week program designed to help young people understand the problems we face in today's world. The students, from about sixteen to twenty-one, come from every imaginable economic class, and ethnic and political background. They listen to lectures, discuss in workshops, and go out into the world to experience the problems and possibilities in a democratic society. Experts in economics, agriculture, race relations, community planning, international affairs, and other relevant topics come to speak to the students. Part of learning the mechanics of democracy is developed through participation in town meetings and cooperative living.

The program recently took place in Washington, DC. During the first week, the director made outrageous and untrue statements about a great many public figures, both living and dead. The faculty members came late to workshops, although students were penalized for doing the same thing. In general, the faculty were noisy and irresponsible, and appeared to be misinformed on almost every subject.

This was done deliberately to see what the students would do. The assumption was that the students would rise up in fury, that they would challenge incorrect statements, that they would demand that the faculty accept the same responsibilities they had been given. This was supposed to be a lesson in democracy — that we have a right to question authority, and that we have equal rights under the laws of the land.

Nothing happened! The students mumbled and complained to each other, seemed restless, angry, and unhappy, but not until they were *told* what was going on could they respond directly and openly. Their attitude was, A teacher is a teacher and a boss is a boss, and even if you know something is wrong, you keep your mouth shut — or you'll be punished.

These were young people from all parts of the country, and their behavior was, I think, a terrible condemnation of our educational system.

What we teach in our schools is how to compete with everybody else, how to be richer, smarter, more succcessful than others. What we ought to be teaching is that we all live in the same world and what we need more than anything else is cooperation — sharing, mutual understanding. When we get out into the world we discover that the skill we need most, and haven't learned, is how to go about finding answers for ourselves as questions and problems arise in daily life. We discover that the right answers keep changing with each generation of scientific progress. What we needed to learn was how to think, how to plan, how to analyze, how to question, how to search. We need the capacity and the courage to take risks, and that's about the last thing we ever learn in school.

People might stop messing up the planet if they learned to cooperate instead of compete. They need to value the sacred obligations and opportunities of being a citizen in a democracy. It's time for parents and teachers to change the curriculum or give up the dream.

Father's Day

I DON'T DISCRIMINATE: I dislike Father's Day just as much as Mother's Day — but this seems an appropriate moment to reflect on the fatherhood revolution of our times.

One of the family jokes when I was a child was that every time my diaper was wet, my father would silently hand me to my mother. Aside from this tale about his being so fastidious in that area of parenting, there was never any family story about his not feeding me or dressing me, for it was assumed that fathers never did such things. I suspect he must have given me a bath once in a while when I was old enough to wash myself, and I know he told me bedtime stories, but the fact that I never saw him buying food, cooking, or doing laundry was in no way surprising.

My daughter's experiences with her father were more varied. My husband was a much more willing diaper changer than I was, and because I worked and the household help of our childhood had passed from the scene, he did a lot of playground time, a lot of baths, and a lot of evening baby-sitting. But I still shopped and cooked and did the laundry.

My grandchild will have the best of all possible experiences with daddy, for he will be doing breathing exercises with his or her mother before the child is born, and will probably help to officiate at the birth, and there is no part of growing up in which he won't be an equal partner.

We've come a long way from the "Life with Father" authority figure — but I sometimes wonder if the revolution is really as significant as it appears to be. Perhaps a lot of it has to do with *function* rather than attitudes.

Whatever chores my father may or may not have done, I always knew he loved me a lot. He was also a great moral force in my life, responsible for my sense of right and wrong, my deep concern for ethical issues. Most of all, if I had to pick one particularly important characteristic I remember from childhood, it was that he made me feel safe. I saw him as big and strong and powerful, and believed that no harm could come to me as long as he was around. I think my daughter felt the same way about her father and I suspect that this represents something quite primitive and instinctive about fathers; and I would hate to see it washed away by a self-conscious refusal to see that there are psychological as well as physical differences between men and women. If I felt sick, I wanted my mother to feed me chicken soup; when I heard there might be a war, I wanted my father to tell me that couldn't happen.

Fortunately, by the time Prime Minister Chamberlain came along and my father promised me there wouldn't be a war, I was old enough not to be traumatized by the discovery that he was not infallible. But believing he was infallible was wonderful when I was little, and I hope that whatever daddies do or don't do, their children will see them as knights in shining armor — at least for a little while.

If Your Kids Are Off to Camp

THE ONLY THING WRONG with sending the children to sleep-away camp is that parents tend to feel too guilty about how happy they are to have some time alone, and their feelings of guilt ruin the whole thing. My advice as a much older parent is very simple: DON'T SPOIL IT FOR YOURSELF.

When my daughter first went to camp, I felt so guilty that I spent most of the time she was away painting her room. That was a terrible mistake. What I should have been doing was reveling in candlelight dinners with her father.

If you wait until children are really ready and eager for the adventure, and if you have chosen wisely, knowing it to be the kind of place where your child will feel at home and cherished, for heaven's sake relax. There is no better way in which to greet your child on his or her return with genuine pleasure and delight than to have thoroughly enjoyed every minute of being deliciously childless.

No matter how much you may love your offspring, I have never yet met an adult parent who didn't feel that there were certain activities in life which are enormously improved upon when there aren't three kids supposedly sleeping down the hall.

It is extremely good for children to learn that they can adjust to life without their parents — but even more important than that, if you tend to feel guilty, think of it this way: Maybe having some uninterrupted time with your spouse may save you from the misery of divorce, and surely that's nice for the kids!

Married people need time to talk quietly, to relax, to follow their own hobbies and interests — even just to *rest*. One mother saves all the books she's dying to read until the summertime, when she knows she won't be interrupted thirty times and lose track of the story. One father waits until his kids are gone so he can mow the lawn; he loves doing it, but when they're home, he feels they should have that responsibility.

If you feel too guilty, you not only ruin your own special time, but guilt makes you bring the children food they are not allowed to have, and guilt makes you cry when you go to see them. And guilt makes you mad if the counselor doesn't tell them to wear their sweaters. You figure acting sad and upset will make your relief at your child's absence more tolerable. But whatever it does for you, guilt can ruin the child's enjoyment of this adventure. The poor kid gets so worried about how lonesome you are, he figures maybe he should come home. A lot of homesick children are really just trying to be decent to their parents by making them feel they miss them more than they really do.

If you can allow yourself the perfectly normal emotion of relief and happiness, you can refresh your soul by figuring out what you miss doing the most the rest of the year, when parenting takes up so much of your time — and do it. When the bus brings the children back, you'll really be glad to see them.

The Preoccupation with Externals—
The Youth Cult

A WOMAN WROTE ME that she's becoming increasingly concerned about her future, because she is married to a man who is ten years younger than she is. At the moment, he's thirty-five and she's forty-five. They have been together for ten years, and she has two daughters from an earlier marriage who are now in college. She's afraid that in a few more years her husband will begin looking around for a younger woman, and she asked me what I thought about face lifts. I suggested that she have a *mind lift* instead. Unlike a face lift, a mind lift need never sag.

It doesn't surprise me that we have become so preoccupied with externals or such worshipers of youth. We are bombarded constantly, with the clear message that, unless we use the right deodorant and mouth wash and skin freshener, we will be rejected by the rest of the human race. The ads that really knock me out are the ones in which a beautiful young face appears on the screen and in a hushed voice confesses she is *thirty years old!* She sounds as if she were admitting to having a social disease – and I guess, in a way, that's exactly what she's got: the social disease of thinking that what really matters is how she looks on the outside.

We must all try harder to remember that for all the propaganda pounding away at us – encouraging our anxiety, making us feel we can't possibly be lovable without several major surgical operations – the truth is that some of the happiest and most loved people are very frequently a little bald and a little fat and a little pimply, and have noses of odd and assorted shapes, and don't gargle unless they're sick, and are generally too busy living to spend a whole lot of time getting hysterical over the graying of their hair.

The woman who is worried about her husband's straying ought to be spending whatever worry-time she has in becoming a person of such worth – so exciting and interesting to be with – that the aging process will only make her more lovable and attractive. Men – and women – stray from home base most often because of boredom and anxiety. Neither of those conditions can be saved by longer eyelashes or larger breasts or a more streamlined behind. The only people I know who go on loving each other indefinitely are gloriously beautiful on the inside.

When It's Too Late to Be Sorry

THERE ARE TOO MANY men and women in the age group from forty to sixty who now regret having divorced in haste, some ten or fifteen years earlier. Their decision is almost always irrevocable, but their experience can be a lesson to younger couples.

Some people most certainly do need to separate and/or divorce, when staying together is really destructive and life becomes unbearable. But it seems to me that there is now a good body of evidence suggesting that many divorces have been entered into too rapidly, and a whole lot of lonely, anxious, unhappy people have discovered that life alone is no bed of roses.

A contributing factor was the emergence, about thirty years ago, of a new idea — that individuals had a right to personal fulfillment. It's a wonderful and civilized concept, and I'm quite delighted with this turn of events, but as with any new idea, some people misinterpreted it and overdid it. Among those who I think got a little drunk with this concept were some psychotherapists and marriage counselors. In their genuine concern for a patient's quest for self-fulfillment, they assumed, often wrongfully, that fulfillment could be obtained only by divorce. Too many men and women thought, or were encouraged to believe, that the answer to all their disappointments and frustrations was to get unmarried as quickly as possible. Then self-fulfillment would lead to a wonderful, creative, satisfying life.

In some cases, of course, this was true. If a marriage partner wants to keep you chained in a psychological cage, you have to try to break out, but most situations are not that simple or that clear-cut.

Let me give one example. Ginny and John had been married for twenty-two years. The children were grown and gone. There was plenty of money for travel and good times, a beautiful home, and all the accoutrements of success and contentment. But Ginny and John had been so busy getting rich and raising children that along the way they had lost touch with each other. They had also postponed a whole lot of problems that surfaced during these years because they were too busy to deal with them. Ginny grew restless and angry. She felt she'd wasted all her talents just being a homemaker. She now began to feel resentments that went a long way back. John, feeling unappreciated, went in search of younger, more understanding female companionship, and Ginny started therapy, in which she was encouraged to assert herself, become independent, make a life of her own. After a few months, in a moment of irrational and impulsive excitability, she told John to get out — their marriage was over.

Each now lives alone in an apartment. They miss each other. They had plenty of good material to work with, together, but they threw away the chance to grow with each other. They each grow separately, and while there are new insights and satisfactions, the decision that change could occur only when alone was made in too much haste.

People need to be more careful. Sometimes it's better to try to seek self-fulfillment with a marriage partner than alone.

Car Drivers: Dr. Jekyll and Mr. Hyde

I'VE BEEN TOLD by people who certainly ought to know that if anyone happens to be listening to me on the CBS Radio Network, he or she is likely to be driving a car. It therefore seems appropriate to spend a little time thinking about the fact that, psychologically speaking, many drivers fall into the Dr. Jekyll and Mr. Hyde category. There seems to be something about getting behind the wheel of an automobile that can turn the nicest people into monsters. Before you scream at the dumb creep who is going on so slowly ahead of you, hear me out.

My husband is a very learned gentleman, of serious mind and tender heart. He is ordinarily the most polite and thoughtful of men until he gets behind the wheel of a car, when he undergoes a complete change of personality. Suddenly the entire world is his enemy, everyone is out to drive him crazy, and it seems obvious to him that only the feebleminded are out there driving their cars. He doesn't drive fast or recklessly, you understand; he just screams and shouts at other drivers in language I don't care to repeat. He's a peaceful man — he never even watches football or boxing, and ordinarily displays very little heated aggression beyond an occasional academic debate with his colleagues — but when he is driving a car there are times when I almost have to physically restrain him from getting out of the car and beating up another driver.

I used to think this was just a personal eccentricity, but after careful research I have discovered that the world is full of adorable people who go crazy behind the wheel of a car. I began to suspect this when I was driving with a friend whose voice I have never heard raised above a gentle whisper. We got stuck in traffic, and all of a sudden I was riding with a truck driver whose entire vocabulary seemed to consist of four-letter words.

That part of the story is amusing; its probable meaning is not. There is really no harm if someone can release a lot of pent-up aggression, hostility, rage, and frustration by a verbal barrage, as long as it doesn't come to blows — but the problem is that if relatively *mild* people let off steam in their cars, what happens to people who have serious problems in life, and also use their cars as weapons for release of emotions? We all know what happens: Fifty thousand people get killed in car accidents every year.

My husband, the car screamer, is also a learned professor of psychology, and by some strange coincidence he wrote his Ph.D. thesis on accident proneness! So next, I'd like to discuss this more serious side of the driver personality.

Accident Proneness

PEOPLE WHO TEND to keep their feelings all bottled-up inside are the ones who have most of the automobile accidents.

For the past thirty years there have been numerous intensive studies of people who have all kinds of repeated accidents. The term *accident proneness* has resulted from this research. The first observation that some people have most of the accidents occurred, appropriately enough, by accident! A psychiatrist, Dr. Flanders Dunbar, was doing pioneering research on psychosomatic illnesses. She was studying hospitalized patients with heart and stomach disorders, and she needed a normal group of people as a control group. She decided to use the fracture ward, thinking this would be an average, normal group of people, hospitalized by chance accidents. Much to her surprise, she discovered this was a very special group, which had a far higher percentage of accidents than the general population. Since her work, there have been many studies of accident proneness. In one case, a group of people with high accident rates was removed from dangerous jobs and placed in safer, more sedentary jobs. The people continued to have a high rate of accidents.

My husband, a research psychologist, became interested in the early research and began a study of his own in the 1950s, and since then most research on accident proneness has indicated very clearly that people who have repeated accidents tend to be people who resent authority, have great difficulty expressing anger, have difficult relationships with family members, and tend to be impulsive and unable to set long-range goals. Often they are people who want very much to change their social status, but don't have the necessary skills or the personality to move upward.

In the last few years, automobile insurance companies have begun to acknowledge that a small group of people accounts for the high cost of insurance for everyone, by giving deductions to people who almost never have any accidents. For the accident-prone person, there is a clear need for psychological help. For the rest of us, we need to drive very carefully, because accident-prone people often get us safety-prones in trouble, as well as themselves. And if you are one of those Jekyll and Hyde characters who gets all steamed up but drives very carefully, there is no harm at all in some colorful cursing as long as you keep the windows closed. Chances are your capacity to release your feelings verbally keeps you from using your car as a lethal weapon.

In the Swim of Things

WHILE I WAS at the beach the other day, I was reminded of the fact that for years I've been wanting to ask a special favor of all the young parents who have preschool children and who go to beaches and pools. It has to do with being in the swim of things.

The other day at the beach the same thing happened to me that happens every summer and that always ruins what otherwise would be a lovely day. It is the sound of children crying because their parents are forcing them to go into the deeper water, and are forcing them to kick their feet and splash their hands in what I presume is supposed to be a process of inducing swimming readiness.

It drives me crazy for several reasons, the first being that it ruins the day for the children as well as for me; they could be so happy if allowed to build their sand castles and sand pies and collect shells and dabble at the edge of the water. But parents have this uncontrollable tendency to want their children to grow and develop faster than nature seems to have meant them to for quite a few thousand years.

It would make life much more restful and serene for me if I could just convince even a few of you that the second reason such behavior drives me crazy is that children learn to swim best (as with all other skills) if they start when *they* are ready, not when their parents are ready.

Fear of water is a sign of maturation. Any two-year-old will step off the edge of a pool or crawl into a tidal wave if you don't watch carefully. The reason is that a baby doesn't know any better.

A three- or four- or five-year-old is a whole lot smarter. He or she has lived long enough to know that water can be dangerous — you can choke on it, you can even drown in it. Caution is being far smarter and more sophisticated, *not* babyish at all. It takes a while for a kid to regain the confidence needed for getting into deeper water, and that experimentation is best done without adult interference.

If your kid loves being carried into the deep water, by all means enjoy yourself, but please, for my rest and relaxation, let the others find their own way, at least for a few more years.

And while we're talking about my comfort at the beach, how about turning down that eardrum-splitting music on your radio!

Inflation and the Preoccupation with *Things*

NO MATTER HOW EXCELLENT your state of mental health may be, it is more than likely that inflation is driving you toward that padded cell.

For those who live at the edge of poverty, inflation offers nothing but terrible deprivation and growing anguish. For the middle class, inflation can mean such disasters as the disappearance of life savings and a terrifying level of indebtedness. It may also mean the necessity for mothers to get jobs outside their homes even when they would prefer to be at home with their children. There is no doubt that a high rate of inflation can play havoc with our lives, as well as with our society as a whole.

But there is one aspect of inflation that might in the long run, if things don't get any worse, do us some good — and that is the end of a kind of crazy insatiability to buy and to have all kinds of junk that we don't really need, that clutters our lives and enslaves us by making us take care of and worry about *things.*

From what we know about human history, people have always wanted some luxuries in their lives. The mosaics on Egyptian, Greek and Roman walls speak clearly of a desire for aesthetics above and beyond mere necessity.

There is nothing wrong with wanting beauty in our lives, and some creature comforts, as well. But let's face it: Since World War II most families have succumbed almost completely to the blandishments of advertisers selling us products we don't need, never use, and have to keep clean. Until we began to feel the pain of serious inflation, people who could afford it — as well as a great many who couldn't — were inclined to walk through their local shopping center as if in a drunken stupor, buying anything that was the least bit enticing. *Usefulness* and *need* were words no longer heard in the land.

One cause of feeling miserable is not having too little, but having too much. We have drowned ourselves in *things* and lost our freedom in the process. One reason so many people enjoy camping is that there are so few utensils to wash, no beds to make, no rugs *not* to spill things on, and no electrical appliances to break down. It is also a time of escape from the enticements of the hard-sell gang.

As an exercise in improving your lifestyle, I suggest you go from room to room in your home and count the things you don't need, don't use, hate to take care of, and that cause you to have too many fights with your kids because they don't put them away. This is an especially useful exercise if you have a house and can count the junk in the garage as well.

When you finish, I guarantee you will feel less depressed about inflation — even possibly relieved that the shopping spree is over.

On Losing One's Job

WHEN I HEARD a news report about four thousand men being laid off because of poor car sales, due to the very clouded crystal ball of the automobile industry, I found myself flooded by memories of the Great Depression of the 1930s. I remember men standing in line at soup kitchens, selling apples in the street, huddling on benches in the park. I remember my mother talking about how *ashamed* the men were about not working, and how *devastated* they were if their wives were able to find jobs. I remember great *silences* between husbands and wives, and children who shrank into corners silent and wide-eyed.

Losing one's livelihood is a disastrous and terrifying experience at any time, but there seem to me to be aspects of life today which make a difference.

There are, of course, such practical measures as powerful unions, unemployment insurance, and food stamps (so far!), but I think there are other even more significant changes.

In talking with a number of men who have been laid off, I didn't find one who was ashamed. There is far more understanding today of the economic issues which create unemployment, and if a man is deeply distressed by the loss of a job, he can often talk about it. The reactions I heard were: "Sure, I'm scared — I'd be crazy not to be!" or "I cried like a baby the first day off the job!" or "I'm *damn glad* my wife is working!"

What all these reactions mean to me is that the macho man who had to know he was in charge at all times, and who thought it unmanly to show his feelings or be dependent, seems happily to be passing from the scene and hopefully will become as extinct as the dinosaur.

Life seems so complicated today that we sometimes wonder whether or not all the changes in our thinking over the past fifty years have made life better or worse. It seems to me that being able to express one's feelings more freely, to face crises more openly with one's family, and to see marriage as a partnership of equals are enormous assets in such situations as the loss of a job. Such insights don't solve the problem, but they leave less of a residue, less havoc psychologically, after the problem has been solved. In one sense a person is never out of work, because during a period of unemployment there is a lot of work to be done in dealing with one's feelings.

The comment I felt most heartened by was from a man who said, "Me and my wife and our kids are closer than ever before." Even a time of great stress and worry can provide some secondary gains.

Life Has Calories

I WAS TALKING TO A FRIEND about a subject that comes up very frequently in my life — dieting. We were trying to figure out if there was *any* really satisfying food that we could eat as much of as we wanted, without adding calories, and as it became clear we were foolishly dreaming, my friend sighed a big, sad sigh and said, "Life has calories!" Oh, how right she was! I'd like to pursue this profound philosophical observation.

What I think my friend was saying is that nothing in life comes easy, nothing is for free. Anything we do has a price of some kind or other. It's a terribly important point because many of our psychological problems stem from the irrational hope that somehow we will find a way to avoid the calories of life — and we can't.

One of the phrases I remember from childhood, which still echoes dimly inside my head, is "Everything will be all right." It is surely a natural and understandable inclination on the part of a loving parent to want to comfort a child, but too many of us grow up thinking that it's really true. Everything *will* be all right, if we only do what we are supposed to do — if we are smart, or if we make a lot of money, or if we marry the right person, or have the right number of children, or choose the right job in the right town. Life is not like that at all. No matter how clever your plans or brilliant your choices, I have never heard of *anyone* who didn't have problems. Tragedy and frustration and the unexpected are part of the very fabric of the human experience, and the sooner we accept that fact the less disappointed and angry we will be when life has calories.

That doesn't mean that we might as well give up in hopeless despair because we can't arrange the universe. What it does mean is that we live and work and love as fully as possible, but don't expect to avoid pain and unhappiness. The minute we give up the idea that we *should* be rewarded for good behavior, we will have given up one of the heaviest emotional burdens and will feel a whole lot better. The *shoulds* seem to me to have become one of the most serious hurdles we need to overcome in order to be reasonably satisfied with our lives.

I visited the home of a friend shortly after she'd lived through a very painful divorce. On the kitchen wall she had tacked up a piece of paper which said, "*Life is what happens to you when you have other plans.*" I now have a piece of paper over my desk with that sensible saying on it, and I recommend it to you as a way to keep a realistic sense of balance.

The Traveling Man

A FRIEND SAID that she'd like me to talk about husbands and fathers who are traveling men. Very little seems to be said about how difficult it is to keep a family together when the father is on the road all week and is home only on weekends. It puts a terrible strain on everyone, she told me. She's quite right.

It takes a lot of trust and love and plain hard work to be a traveling man or to live with one, and there are no easy solutions to the problem; but here are a few suggestions which may be of some help.

One of the major hazards for such part-time fathers is that they become the heavies. Mother, who gets tired of being the constant disciplinarian, says, "Just wait until your father gets home" — and the family is well on the road to a miserable weekend. Or mundane and unpleasant things get left for the weekends, such as a leaky faucet or the unmowed lawn or the bad report card or the electric bill that seems to have been short-circuited in the computer and says you owe nine hundred dollars for one month!

Whatever needs to be done during the week ought to be done during the week. If a husband is away, it is necessary to include in the family budget money for plumbers and other helpers. It's also necessary to assume that telephone bills will have to be higher than most people's, so that junior can talk quietly with his father about that report card when it arrives, on Tuesday, and does not have to wait until Friday night for the ax to fall.

Letter writing is a lost art, but it's one that could help family members keep in touch. I know of one father who put a map up on the kitchen wall, and as he calls or sends postcards, his kids stick red tacks on the map to show where he is. I know another father who keeps a chess game going with his daughter — one move per nightly telephone call.

The most important thing to keep in mind is that weekends are far more important than they would be if daddy weren't a traveling man and that great efforts must be made to make that precious time together count. That doesn't mean becoming self-conscious or over-organized and planning activities for every minute of the time. It just means not gathering up all the unpleasant, difficult tasks and putting them in a bag labeled "For father"! A whole lot of things can get settled by phone and mail so that weekends can accentuate the positive in family life. One father told me his eleven-year-old daughter keeps a daily diary of the events in her life and reads it to him on Sunday morning, in bed, curled up close to him. That's a dandy way of making up for lost time.

The Immoral Minority

IT SEEMS TO ME that each day I sense more emotional stress over the words *the moral majority,* and I'd like to discuss what I think these psychological reactions are all about.

The term *moral majority* comforts some people, because they have been feeling extremely uneasy about some of the things that have been happening in the United States in recent years. Life seems to have become too free, without moral or ethical purposes, and there is a feeling that the new salaciousness of soap operas or the more sleazy and distasteful movies and magazines ought to disappear. There is also tremendous anxiety about the serious social problems that beset us, and the words *moral* and *majority* give many people a feeling of confidence and security.

For others, the expression produces only greater anxiety, for they have the feeling that those who proclaim to *be* more moral and a majority may not be either. I myself happen to fall into this second group, and I decided that I would feel better if I tried to figure out who those of us are who, by innuendo, are being labeled "The Immoral Minority." Clarification is needed about who we really are.

I think of myself as being a very moral person. I have a profound sense of the sacredness of human life, and, because of that, some of the highest priorities on my list of things that need attention have to do with keeping life on this planet from disappearing. In that connection, I abhor war and feel we must struggle desperately for world understanding and peace before we blow ourselves into atoms. I also worry greatly about runaway science and technology that poison the earth, the air, the water we need for human survival. I would like to live in a world where there was far less rage and violence, so one of my deepest moral concerns is that every child who is born, anywhere in the world, is given the loving care he or she needs to grow up into a responsible citizen.

Next to human life, I value freedom and believe it to be the essence of a democratic society. I want people to be free to believe what they please and to do what they want, so long as their personal actions don't interfere with my personal beliefs and actions. We need rules to protect human life and freedom, but we need to limit those rules for the greatest fulfillment of all our differences.

I think it is very moral to be honest with children about all aspects of being human — talking with them frankly and openly about some of the subjects we have tended to hide and repress. We need to talk about anger and love and sex and all the feelings and emotions that can lead to either a wonderful or a terrible life, depending on our openness.

I think it is immoral for someone to tell me that my values are immoral, and I think it is immoral to frighten public servants into accepting other people's opinions in order to get elected.

I really believe that I don't belong to a minority at all, but simply to a majority that is much too quiet in expressing its ideas about morality. I don't plan to be quiet anymore.

Once the War Is Over

A FEW YEARS AGO I went to London on a theater tour with a much younger woman. I was somewhat apprehensive; usually I travel with my husband, and we are very congenial traveling companions, so I wasn't at all sure this new arrangement would work out. Actually, we had a glorious trip. We were completely compatible, and I realized that my traveling companion was one of the nicest people I'd ever met. Are you getting bored with this commonplace story? Well, if you are the parent of a teenager, I think you'll perk up a bit when I add that my London roommate was my daughter, and the two of us were pretty surprised — and if you are the parent of a teenager I'll bet you know why!

When my daughter was thirteen, I wrote an article for *Parents' Magazine* called "The Year I Became a Monster Mother." That was the time when I wasn't sure whether the look in her eyes couldn't kill. It was also the year she refused to go to a school dance because I was supposed to be one of the chaperones and she was too ashamed of me.

A demolition program was also under way at the time — the slow but steady disintegration of her bedroom. All clothes were hung up on the floor; this was necessary in part because the closet was full of dirty dishes, leftover food, towels covered with makeup, and an expensive and discarded guitar with no strings.

When she was fifteen, I forgot what my child looked like, because she wore her hair parted down the middle of her face. Once in a while, in an unguarded moment, you might see the tip of a nose, but that was it.

Roughly from her thirteenth to her eighteenth year, I accepted the fact that I was the rottenest mother alive and that there was no hope for a reconciliation. And then, quite suddenly, the war was over. My daughter began to feel like an adult, at last, and didn't have to fight every inch of the way to prove it. We suddenly found ourselves talking to each other. She even *asked my advice* about what kind of mop to buy for her first apartment!

Well, to make a long story short, the slob with the food and shoes under the bed now starts washing my coffee cup before I have a chance to finish drinking the coffee. The natural enemy is now my best friend; that silent, angry, rebellious child is now one of the loveliest women I've ever met.

My message should be loud and clear by now: All you have to do is wait.

You Never Can Tell . . .

It seems to be a human tendency to have the feeling that, no matter how well things may be going, everything could change overnight and we could be in terrible trouble. Over the last few months I've seen a number of people whose lives once looked quite hopeless who are now doing beautifully, and it occurred to me that we need to cultivate the fine art of saying, "You never can tell . . ." and to mean by that that things could get *better.*

Ten years ago Fred was in a federal prison for selling heroin, and Betty was a prostitute. Neither their relatives nor society in general were taking any bets on their ever becoming happy, successful, responsible citizens. I visited them a few months ago. They met at a center for rehabilitation of ex-convicts, married five years ago, and have recently built themselves a house in the country. And I mean *built the house themselves:* dug up every tree, cemented each brick in place, nailed each nail, did all the wiring and plumbing — learned it all so well that they passed every inspection with flying colors. At one point during our visit, I was waiting impatiently in a car to go, when my husband came out of the woods where he'd been with Fred. "We won't be leaving soon," he said; "Fred is straightening out the forest!"

Fred and Betty couldn't be happier if they'd built San Simeon or Versailles. Their neighbors are crazy about them, and now they are helping other people build houses. You never can tell. . . .

Marian was widowed at thirty-five, with five children to raise and no insurance. It looked as if she was done for. Nobody was offering any odds on her survival. It's fifteen years later now, and the business that Marian started in sheer desperation — a tiny gourmet restaurant in her own living room — is now a famous restaurant, in larger quarters, where you sometimes have to wait several hours even if you have a reservation.

When I went to visit my daughter and son-in-law a few months ago, there were some charming, delicate sketches on the mantelpiece that I'd never seen before. They had been done by a woman who had been paralyzed from the neck down after a car accident and had been existing like a vegetable in a hospital until she was brought into a rehabilitation program, where, through trial and error, she found that she could paint with a brush in her mouth. Her work is gaining considerable recognition, and she is finding it hard to keep ahead of the orders for her work.

It's natural, I guess, to worry that, when things are going well, something awful might happen. But we need to remember that when everything seems just about as terrible as it can get, something wonderful might happen.

Men's Liberation

IT SEEMS TO ME that there must be some, like myself, who feel they have learned just about as much as they need to know about the awful attitudes people used to have about what little girls could be allowed to do and how much discrimination there has been against women. Is there anyone among us who doesn't know how upset and angry many women feel? What about thinking about men's liberation for a change!

During the same period that little girls were being told it wasn't nice to shout or climb trees, and that they could be nurses and airline stewardesses but not doctors and pilots, little boys were being taught a whole lot of very stupid things, too. At the top of that list was the idea that being a boy meant being tough and getting to be number one — at everything. The best baseball player, the smartest kid in the class, and certainly, most of all, the sexual stud of the century. The macho image which little boys began to sense when they were still in diapers has, in my estimation, done as much if not more damage to human relations, and human society in general, than any of the restrictions which were placed on girls. The goal of purity in womanhood certainly caused some miserable and unnecessary sexual repressions and frustrations — but having to be a macho man has caused most of the murders, rapes, wars, assassinations, terrorist groups, torturers, gas chambers, and other assorted wonderful human artifacts. It has also caused the much higher mortality rate among males of all ages, has deprived men of the human necessity to be able to cry, and finally, has been the source of a whole lot of unnecessary impotence.

While women may have felt enslaved by doing dishes, mopping floors, and going to PTA meetings, men have felt enslaved by trying too hard to be best, by expectations both in and out of bed that can't be met, by the terror in the night thinking they will never pay off the mortgage, and by the certainty that no matter how much they might hate what they do, they are as imprisoned by necessity as women.

During a social revolution ideas get oversimplified. As women successfully climb the barricades to freedom, a lot of men feel that the only way they can keep their identity is by more macho behavior than ever before. Afraid of grown-up women and their apparent demands, they begin to go the Lolita route; afraid they won't be able to prove their manhood, they go to more porno films, and beat each other up with such aggression and violence that games that used to be fun to watch now seem more like the Roman ones of lions eating Christians.

What seems to me to be needed is human liberation.

Human Liberation

I KNOW A MAN in his early seventies who is still in full possession of all his marbles and works as a top executive in an advertising firm he started forty years ago. He sold the company a few years ago with the agreement that he would continue to work there until he was seventy-five, if he wanted to. He needs retirement like a hole in the head, but he is leaving this year — because he now has a woman boss who is thirty-six years old and treats him with so much contempt and hostility that he knows there will not be a moment's peace until she has his job.

I think this is a sad story for both the older man and the younger woman. They are both victims of rapid change — a revolution in the relationships of men and women. She has apparently interpreted freedom and equality as the right to be mean, and he is making the very serious mistake of thinking that women's lib is the cause of his misery. What neither of them is ready for is human liberation, in which we live together and judge each other and care about each other as human beings.

There is an inevitable self-consciousness when rapid social change occurs. If she'd been a man, he would have just said, "I really hit a bummer this time." If he'd been a woman, it's possible she would have seen her co-worker as a sister instead of an adversary. The challenge, now, is that men and women regroup. There have been many absolutely fantastic gains in honesty and increased equality, and the beginning of excellent and constructive communication about real needs and feelings. It's time for both sexes to agree, once and for all, that *both* boys and girls were taught untrue, awful destructive lessons when they were young, and that grief and despair have no gender — and neither do tenderness, compassion, cooperation, and love.

Both sexes can be assertive, and both can be gentle: Both are often miserably exploited, and both can achieve fulfillment — and the sooner they can see each other as members of a common race, the sooner they will be able to enjoy their absolutely terrific differences.

Of course, it's all beginning to happen already. Both in and out of my crystal ball, I am overjoyed by the young couples I see who are discovering how much fun it is to cooperate instead of compete.

Bisexuality

I WAS SORRY when Billie Jean King spoke about the complexities of her life as having been a big mistake. It seemed to me that any love relationship in which one person eventually suffers rejection is tragic for everyone concerned, but that doesn't make it a mistake. Bisexuality is a far more common phenomenon than many people would like to think.

Some years ago I met with a group of men and women who acknowledged being bisexual. Most of them were married, and many of them were parents. Among the group there were three or four corporation executives, several doctors and lawyers, and a few teachers, artists, and writers. Together we discussed some of the issues that concerned them — their strong commitment to their children, their wish not to hurt a spouse who was not bisexual, the ever-present fear of discovery because of the general attitudes of prejudice they felt all around them.

They were intelligent, caring, successful, creative, and sensitive people, and I found myself full of admiration for their struggle *not* to be exploitive or hurtful to others.

I found them the same as any other group of men and women, except for the single factor of their bisexuality. If they were different in any way from a lot of other people, it was their strong desire to be open and honest about themselves and their great concern for all the people they loved.

The only thing that was unusual about the group as far as I was concerned was their willingness to talk to me about their interrelationships with such candor. Otherwise they did *not* represent a tiny minority: It's a rough guess, of course, because secrecy is so much more the usual behavior, but I think most sociologists and others who may be experts in psychology and sexology would probably agree with me that at least thirty percent or more of now married adults have had bisexual experiences of some kind.

As far as I am concerned, the only important distinction is not what adults prefer to do in the privacy of their own homes, but the attitude with which they do it. Some people are mature and loving and responsible, and some people are ugly and dirty and exploitive in their relationships. That has nothing whatever to do with being heterosexual, homosexual, or bisexual. It has to do with personality and behavior.

Insomnia

IF YOU WANT TO BECOME a millionaire overnight, all you have to do is invent some harmless substance which will guarantee eight hours of sleep. There are few normal human experiences about which people lose more sleep than insomnia.

Most chronic insomnia is caused by the fear of not getting enough sleep. If you don't believe me, I suggest this experiment. Make up your mind that breathing is something you must be in charge of every minute; unless you notice exactly how you are breathing, it just won't work right. Count every breath you take, note the depth of the breath, and the time between breaths. If you do this for about five minutes, you will probably hyperventilate and get dizzy, and until you quit this silly game, it will seem as if you are not breathing properly. That's exactly what happens to most people who worry about not getting enough sleep. Insomnia is the hyperventilation of the sleep worrier.

There is nothing dangerous or abnormal about variable sleep patterns. It's perfectly natural to get out of breath after running, and it's perfectly natural to be restless after a party and too much drinking, or five extra cups of coffee on a busy day. It's natural to be restless and uneasy if you're worried about something or just had a fight with someone. There are all kinds of things that can interfere with sleep, but they are all temporary and would go away if we didn't get into the double bind of worrying so much about not sleeping.

This is particularly true of people over the age of fifty or sixty, when the amount of sleep that is needed for good health decreases just as the need for food decreases. We get fat because we go on eating as much as when we were young, and we become insomniacs because we are trying to force too many hours of sleep.

Of course there may, in some cases, be serious problems which need medical attention if insomnia is chronic and severe and is causing genuine fatigue. It's always wise to check first. But if you discover you are in good health, the best cure for insomnia is to stop worrying about it. Read, listen to the radio, let yourself fall asleep in front of the television set; rest with your eyes closed and enjoy the quiet and the dark, and allow yourself brief catnaps once in a while. It's truly amazing how well the human body will take care of things like breathing and sleeping if you just go away and mind your own business!

The Search for Unconditional Love

I'M GETTING REALLY FED UP with a whole bunch of new books which all focus their attention on what they call the "me generation." By that they mean that young adults who were raised in the 1960s or 1970s were all so terribly pampered and overprotected that they are really getting their comeuppance in the tough 1980s — and a good thing too. Absolute, total nonsense!

The children of the sixties and seventies really had it easy: All they had to face was the history of the forties and fifties! The fact, for example, that there was now loose in the world the atom bomb, and all the terrific, wonderful, really imaginative weapons which followed, and which can now destroy us slowly by leaking radiation, or quickly if someone presses the wrong button. They were born into assassinations of decent men, into a violent struggle for equal rights of blacks and women, and they faced an immoral and terrible war in Vietnam. They had lots of bicycles and guitars and big allowances and time — and then they also had the privilege of being the first generation of young people ever, in all of history, to feel that none of them might live to be old, or to father and mother future generations. They were the first generation ever to find themselves poisoned by insecticides or damaged by drugs given their pregnant mothers, and by chemicals seeping into wells.

What a wonderful time they've had, this "me generation"! If they have problems dealing with the realities of life, it may well have to do with the fact that so much of reality is so awful.

But it isn't even true that the majority of the so-called spoiled kids of the so-called permissive generation is copping out. Most of them are struggling very hard to give their lives some shape and meaning. It's true that at least some of them seem less interested in financial success and power than other generations, but that doesn't seem too surprising to me, considering the fact that money and success can't stop the planet from being polluted, and in their lifetime there will probably be standing room only on the planet, polluted or not.

The "me generation" experts claim that these young people spend all their time searching for unconditional love — and on that score, I sure hope they are right.

There is a very good reason why there has been so much preoccupation with the idea of unconditional love. It is not selfish or weak or lily-livered. It is what I consider to be the very wise observation that the human race may very possibly wipe itself out completely in the next half century, and that we haven't got much time to figure out what's wrong with people bent on species suicide. The conclusion a lot of us have come to is that most of the really dumb and destructive things people do happen because too many human beings hate themselves and live in quiet — or not so quiet — despair most of their lives.

Depending on the degree of conditional love, children grow up expressing their self-hatred in a variety of ways, ranging from mild headaches to becoming terrorists or dictators or murderers — and even people who appear quite normal may behave in destructive ways, showing little sense of the sacredness of human life.

That's where conditional love got us — a human species that hates itself. The search for unconditional love is not weak or selfish at all — it is the civilized struggle to save the human species by making people care for their own lives *so much* that they will be able to care for the lives of everyone.

Dreams to Grow On, I

IN THE EARLY DAYS of psychiatry and psychoanalysis, therapists often gave us the feeling that only *they* could understand our dreams and find them useful — we who were *having* the dreams were helpless without their scorecard. Today there are dozens of handbooks for the use of dreams in such endeavors as mate selection or reading the future. Somewhere between these two extremes, it seems to me that dreams can be useful to us as a way to grow and change.

All of us dream every night, whether or not we remember our dreams. Researchers have discovered that when we dream there are specific eye movements that can be measured, called rapid eye movements, or REM. We also know that not being allowed to dream can cause severe physical and mental disturbance — apparently we need our dreams. In a general sense, our dreams are a kind of contact point between our conscious and unconscious minds. We handle some of our problems when we dream; we deal with feelings about which we are uncomfortable, and with ideas that seem irrational to us when we are awake but which nevertheless play an important part in our total makeup. The more we make the effort to get in touch with our dreams, the richer and fuller our lives can become — we are able to explore more dimensions of ourselves, and self-understanding is a major part of growing and changing.

There are of course situations in which we are so frightened, anxious, unhappy, and self-destructive that we need expert help. Dreams are useful in therapy for the same reason they are useful in everyday living — they are simply another country, another language, which can tell us more about what we feel.

I have found it very helpful to keep a daily journal as a way of increasing my self-understanding. It's especially useful to record your dreams in such a journal and then to play with them in a number of different ways. Describe all the different characters in your dreams and how you feel about them. Do you like them or hate them? Are they just the opposite of things you think about yourself? Since you dreamed them, they are all parts of yourself in some way or other and have things to tell you about yourself.

Sometimes it's helpful to continue a dream after you wake up, to make up a story using the dream as a beginning. You may be surprised by where it takes you and learn something new about yourself.

Often we learn about childhood feelings in our dreams — feelings we were ashamed of, unnecessarily mixed-up ideas about ourselves and others. Now we have the opportunity for clearing up childish confusions.

I'll give some examples of dreams and the ways in which you can use your dreams for growing in the next commentary.

Dreams to Grow On, II

I'VE SUGGESTED THAT our dreams can be useful to us in exploring ourselves and using what we learn for personal growth, but it is difficult to explain that without using examples, so I'd like to share some of my own dreams with you.

Each of us has our own special language in our dreams, and we can learn to understand the messages we are bringing to ourselves only by exploring our own dreams. Your images will undoubtedly be different from mine, but I hope that if I describe some of the ways in which I have learned to use my dreams for self-understanding, it will give you some clues for finding your own unique style for doing likewise.

Both in and out of therapy, I've used my dreams so extensively that I seem to have developed a shorthand; my unconscious cooperates — perhaps because it knows I will give it no peace if it doesn't! For many years now, I have had a recurring dream in which I am in the brownstone house where my family and I lived from the time I was four until I was seven. Whatever the content of the dream, I always know that being in that house means that the dream is dealing with very ancient feelings, with things that happened to me when I was very young — primitive feelings of anger, fear, jealousy, and rage are likely to be evoked by the dream and, most of all, feelings of childish guilt for crimes I never committed. When we dream of childhood homes, or if we dream that we are tiny in an enormous room, chances are we are picking up some feelings we had as young children, when we did not yet understand that *all* feelings are normal, and that only actions can be unacceptable. We could not distinguish between wishing a baby sister had never been born and actually pushing her off the bed, so just having the thought made us feel as if we were very, very bad. Now, as adults, we have a chance to straighten out some of those childish misconceptions. For example, for several years I had a recurring dream that someone was lying on the basement floor in that old house and that I had killed him. I stopped having that particular dream when my aunt happened to mention that there was a man who used to come to fix the furnace who had epileptic fits. I then realized that whatever my childish angers may have been against my father or my grandfather, the guilt about such feelings was reinforced by an actual event for which I had no responsibility at all.

If I dream of being on a boat or crossing a bridge or being in an airport, usually I can be pretty sure this means that it is time for me to explore something new — take a trip into my inner world in order to develop some new aspect of myself.

But the most common dream of all has to do with an abandoned little girl, whom I neglect or cannot reach, and I'll tell you more about her next.

Dreams to Grow On, III

I'VE BEEN TALKING about the ways in which we can use our dreams for our own growth. Now I want to talk about the most important theme that can occur in our dreams.

A few weeks ago I dreamed of a little girl, who seemed to be about seven or eight years old and was living all alone in the house where my daughter had lived at that age. In the dream I was very agitated and upset because I couldn't seem to do anything about the situation. It was terrible to think of a young child being all alone. Apparently she went to school each morning, but then came home to an empty house, where there was no one to buy food or cook it, and when she went to sleep, she was alone in the house. I couldn't seem to reach her — something always kept interfering.

I woke up greatly agitated and wrote the dream in my journal. Then I went back and read what I had been writing in the journal for the past few days. I had been trying desperately to spend time alone so that I could get to work on a new book. While the process is lonely and difficult, writing is still the most important part of who I am at this point in my life, and for weeks I had failed utterly in spending the time alone that I needed in order to develop the concentration it takes to write. Every day there were dozens of phone calls from people who wanted my attention. I had accepted too many invitations to do things I didn't really want to do; I had made too many morning appointments with dentists and hairdressers, when I knew perfectly well that my mornings are for writing only. Too many people were making demands on me that were fracturing my attention and energy.

Whenever I dream of a young child in trouble I know that child is me. The dream is a reminder that unless I take care of the child inside myself I will become self-destructive, unable to work, and furious at all the people who, in the name of love, can't learn to leave me alone. When I neglect that inner self, I start to eat compulsively. The dream and my self-destructive behavior tell me I am hungry for attention I need from myself.

Dreams about a child almost always reflect attitudes we have toward ourselves. A crippled child, a naughty child, a rejected and unloved child — these are all attitudes toward ourselves, attitudes accumulated through childhood when we often felt we were not worthy of love because of adult disapproval.

Whatever the child may be whom you dream about, the most important value of your dreams is whether or not you can figuratively take that child in your arms and love it, however misshapen or ugly you may think it is. The only road to genuine growth is in nurturing that inner self, loving that dream child — for he or she is the source of your compassion for others, your creativity, your life force. What could be more worthy of your attention?

The Most Endangered Species

I LOVE TO WATCH such television programs as "Wild Kingdom," where I can get an appreciation of all the beautiful and fascinating animals there are in the world—and I worry terribly about the fact that so many of them are on the way to extinction. But there is one endangered species that I worry about all the time.

The most endangered species on earth are human children. What we need to do is take over one of our National Parks, put fences all around it, and try to raise human children in an environment that would save the species. I would want this park to be at least a thousand miles away from the nearest nuclear plant. The water the children drank would have to come from some spring having its origin somewhere near the North Pole so it couldn't be contaminated. The soil would have to be tested before a vegetable garden could be planted, to make sure there hadn't been any seepage from industrial plants or the use of insect sprays or chemical fertilizers. A canopy would have to be built over the entire park so that acid rain couldn't fall into the ponds and lakes.

There is no place on earth anymore where we could guarantee such environmental safety, but let's pursue this process of saving the species, anyway.

All the mothers in this park would be given medical care and the best possible nutrition. With all the money we are now going to save by *not* providing vitamins and milk to the pregnant poor in our cities, we could certainly provide such things for this small group in the park. We will be saving so much money on everyone else's prenatal and infant nutrition and on medical care that the kids in the park will be able to have all the things that will make them grow up strong and intelligent and healthy. We'll give them the hot lunches we've taken out of the schools, and of course there will be good teachers and small classes and plenty of recreational programs, and special education for their parents, so they can have a happy home life.

Then we can take all the books from the libraries we are closing, and all the ballet companies and orchestras we are no longer funding, and send them all to the park so the children can have a rich cultural experience. And finally, all the professors from all the colleges that will have to close because of cuts in student loans can be sent to the park so that every child can have a college education.

The nice thing about my plan is that these wonderful children would be so smart and so healthy and so responsible that they'd probably run away from the park when they were grown up and would try to save whatever was left of the rest of the other children. I hope it won't be too late.

The Extended Family

I RECENTLY SPENT SOME TIME living with my daughter and her husband, and fortunately we remained friends. But it occurred to me (as it does quite frequently, as a matter of fact) that if the extended family is to be a successful lifestyle it needs all the wisdom and sensitivity relatives can bring to it. If you are already a member of such a household, you hardly need me to tell you it isn't always a cozy haven but can turn into a hornet's nest. I think there are some useful guidelines for keeping these alternatives at least in balance.

Barbara, a thirty-five-year-old lawyer with two preschool-age children, wrote me that she thinks the only way having another woman living in one's home can work is if roles are clearly defined. Barbara's widowed mother is in charge of the household — a task she knows well and loves. Barbara says, "I hate cooking and shopping, and while my husband and I spend a lot of time with our kids, especially on weekends, my mother is there if they get sick and when they come home from school. She's a vigorous woman, with lots of outside interests of her own, and we respect each other. We each feel we have separate jobs and we don't interfere. I don't tell her what to cook for supper, and she doesn't tell me how to write a brief. I don't tell her what kind of grandmother she should be, and she doesn't tell me what kind of a mother to be."

In addition to clearly defined roles, the ability to communicate about feelings seems to me to be essential. Quietly nursing wounded feelings, or trying to deny festering angers, is a sure road to the hornet's nest. A grandmother told me that she had sworn to herself that she would never criticize her son-in-law if she moved into his house. She told me, "Instead of talking about it, I began keeping a secret list in my head of all the things he did that drove me crazy. I just stopped talking to him altogether. There were these terrible silences, but I couldn't seem to do anything to stop it."

Her daughter and son-in-law found her company so upsetting that they decided they would have to ask her to move out. They went to a counseling center for advice about how to unload one old lady, and a family meeting was suggested. The secret collection of annoyances turned out to be matters that could be negotiated, and this episode started the flow of communication.

Respect for privacy is another essential. No matter how small, most adults need their own special turf: a place, a corner, a closet that is absolutely off limits to everyone else. Psychological space is far more important than square inches.

With rentals soaring and mortgages becoming as extinct as the dinosaur, more families will be trying to join forces. In every family there are times when people get stung, but if honey is a by-product, it's worth a try.

Retirement

Dr. Hans Selye, the medical researcher who has done more than anyone else to make us aware of the meaning of stress, said at the age of seventy-two, "I have nothing against retirement as long as it doesn't interfere with my work." You will never hear wiser words on the subject.

Few experiences in the course of human events cause more anxiety and stress than facing retirement. It is often viewed as a kind of dying. Preparing for, or adjusting to, retirement calls for seeing ourselves as persons embarking on new adventures.

The three most common mistakes made by retirees seem to me to be these: first, viewing our work as that which gives us our identity, forgetting we are also men, women, parents, husbands, wives, citizens — in general, people with many talents and interests. The second mistake is thinking that being paid for what we do is the only thing which gives us dignity and status, and the third mistake is assuming that retirement means not doing anything.

One wife was terrified that when her husband, a school principal, retired, he would be moping around the house all day. She was greatly relieved when he offered his services to a day-care center as a foster grandpa to children mostly from single-parent families. Sitting in a rocking chair, holding a sad little kid, he said, ''I feel just as useful as I ever did, and getting paid has nothing to do with it.''

A widower who became seriously ill after his retirement told his doctor, ''I have nothing left to live for.'' The doctor asked him if he'd ever had any secret longings, and he said he had always wanted to take a trip around the world. Since he expected to die, anyway, he took all his life's savings and went on a world cruise. He came back thoroughly refreshed and quite healthy and decided to try a new career as a travel agent. That was six years ago, and he's about to retire again. ''I think I'll try something just a little less taxing this time,'' he says.

A woman moved from New York to Florida. ''I worked hard all my life,'' she said at first, ''and now I'm going to rest.'' After two years of resting and becoming increasingly bored and irritable, she went to work in a department store modeling clothes for senior citizens. Then she became a very successful fund raiser for a charitable organization. ''These last five years have been the best years of my life,'' she said.

If we plan it that way, we can use retirement as a beginning, not an ending.

Sex in Old Age

THERE IS A SCENE in a masterpiece of a film called *Tell Me a Riddle* in which two very elderly people kiss each other quite passionately and hold each other with great tenderness. During this scene we see flashbacks to when they were young and newly married. At another point, toward the end of the film, when the wife is dying, the couple lies in bed holding each other. I understand that there was some shock and criticism over these scenes, and since I found them beautiful and real, I'd like to talk about sex and old age.

This generation of elderly people is lucky in two ways. They are living longer, but what's even better, they're having more fun! The sexual revolution has had as much influence on the lives of older people as on the young, and it seems to me that in many ways the oldest generation has benefited more than the youngest.

The greater freedom of exploration among teenagers, the constant titillation they experience through all kinds of media, the lack of adult supervision means that kids with no experience and less maturity are experimenting sexually but, if the truth be known, not really having that much fun. They feel pushed into behavior for which they are very often not ready; and for all the big macho talk, there are a lot of scared and confused young people who are having a hard time dealing with so much sexual freedom.

Young adults also seem to be having a rough time of it. Being single and free can lead to loneliness in the midst of a crowd. They are not so sure what was wrong with getting married and having babies. As people reach their mid-thirties and find careers not quite enough, many middle-aged marriages founder on the shoals of open marriage. In this sexual revolution the only folks who really have it made are the Social Security crowd!

Having been told that it is normal and healthy to be a sexual person indefinitely, they have been discovering that this is true. In addition, years of experience and maturation have taught them that the best sex worth having goes with love and commitment, and because their sexual drives may be somewhat less overwhelming than that of eighteen-year-olds, it's worth having only where it matters a lot. They have also learned through a long life that sex does not mean only having intercourse. They know that sex is the way in which two people who care about each other touch and caress and speak so as to give a special kind of pleasure to each other. They see sex in its infinite variety and richness, garnered from a lifetime of experimentation.

There are, of course, those who were so deeply repressed in their sexual drives by Victorian parents that they cannot recover even in old age — but I get the impression this is a smaller number than we think. I for one look forward to those twilight years.

Betrayed by the Working Woman

I'M FEELING EXTREMELY SAD, and it's going to take a while for me to recover. I feel betrayed by the new working woman.

I guess I've suspected all along that it would happen. While I want every group to have its freedom of opportunity, I know from more than half a century of personal history that whatever good cause I may espouse, sooner or later those who have been victimized are likely to become too much like their persecutors.

My current sad disillusion was crystallized recently on the front cover of a magazine for working women. The headline in large print was "MAKING IT!" and under that were listed, in this order, the apparent ingredients of making it: money, success, power, and love. Just look at what's at the bottom of that list.

Instead of forging a new and better value system as they gain in prestige and opportunity, women — at least an important number among them — are going to opt for all the wrong values, which an important number of men have set as their goals in life. I suppose I wouldn't be quite so sad if I hadn't gotten caught up myself in some of the starry-eyed idealism that went along with the beginnings of the women's movement. I should have known better.

What I now must accept is the simple and inevitable reality that, as in all social revolutions, you win some things, but not everything.

The rank order of money, success, power, and love has been operating in human relations under male influence for all of human history, and as far as I'm concerned it's been a big bust. It has led to major and minor wars, stealing, lying, cheating, organized and unorganized crime — it's even hit the world of sports, where love of a game is now buried under reports on contract negotiations. In my time it has led to plenty of political scandals, and — far, far worse — to men who value money, success, and power so much more than love that they continue to pollute our planet with poisons, even after they know the horrendous consequences to future human life on earth. With love at the bottom of the list in "MAKING IT!" guns before butter becomes the way of the world, and we are all stuck with an international stockpile of weaponry that is already totally out of control.

I guess I hoped that maybe the new working woman would change the order and put love at the top of the list. There was just that small chance it might have made all the difference.

I'll recover, because I know there are men and women who *do* put love at the top of their lists – and I can't help myself; I go on hoping for a miracle.

Talking Can Be Highly Overrated

DURING A RECENT WEEK'S VACATION, my husband and I hardly talked to each other at all. We rode silently in the car; we took long walks through fields and along country roads, often not saying a word for half an hour or longer. We walked on the beach for hours, fully aware of each other's presence and glad to be together, but silent. It was a very refreshing week, and it reminded me that talking can be highly overrated.

The reason we were able to tolerate, even enjoy, all that silence is that we have already communicated with each other at great length on the issues that matter to us; but that's only part of the story. What is more important is that we each have cultivated a rich inner life and have learned to respect each other's right to plenty of time for fantasy and reflection and free association. When we can allow our minds to wander freely there is a special kind of refreshment. It's like a mountain stream being filtered into a lake, cooling and cleansing.

There has been so much emphasis in recent years on the art of successful communication through expressing feelings and thoughts that I'm afraid we may have forgotten that silence is another way of communicating. Sometimes silence says, "I love you enough to leave you alone with your own thoughts!"

There are people who drive me mad with their chatter; they cannot stop talking for a minute, wherever they are, whatever they are doing. The push of speech is a way of handling anxiety, the fear of one's own thoughts. People who talk incessantly are not really communicating with anyone else, except to the degree that they are letting others know how anxious they are.

Sometimes it seems to me that we need to allow the flow of speech to cease for a while even when we are communicating effectively about important issues. Endless confrontation wears us down — we need time to regroup! After a big, unsettling argument with someone, the most refreshing thing you might do is to have a silent meal together or a silent walk. It's amazing how the issues at hand can get clarified when people talk to themselves as well as to each other!

Talking is great if you really have something worth saying, and the best way to figure out if it *is* worth saying is to allow yourself some silent thought.

Divorce and Mourning

I RECEIVED A LETTER from a young woman who cannot understand why she feels so depressed. She wrote, "I'm newly divorced from a man who made my life a living hell. Shouldn't I be overjoyed?" My answer to her is that if she were overjoyed, it would mean she didn't understand the situation.

It is perfectly true that many people feel a sense of relief when they divorce after a long period of pain and suffering. But many of those who feel wildly elated for a time experience a good deal of depression later on. Men and women who tend to be in touch with their feelings often start to go through a period of mourning even before the divorce is final.

What we are learning is that human beings need to mourn about any traumatic loss. Somewhere, way back in the beginning of a marriage, there was some awakening of love, some exulting in being alive and together. When two people fail at keeping the initial hope and promise, it is sad. Chances are they tried hard for some time, and the sense of failure can be very acute. Recovery from the anguish of misunderstandings, of falling out of love, of discovering a partner cannot measure up to your expectations, of facing your own human frailties — all of these mean that divorce is a kind of death and that homage ought to be paid to the struggle and the loss.

If your spouse dies, at least you are permitted to weep, to be inconsolable, to fall apart for a while. In a divorce it is a rare friend or relation who fully understands the necessary interlude of grief.

A young man, newly divorced, with custody of his two children, told me that his mother called him on the day of the final divorce decree. She asked him how he was celebrating, "having gotten rid of that rotten woman who made your life so miserable!" This mother was stunned when her son began to weep on the phone. She couldn't understand at all — isn't this what he wanted? Hadn't she been a disloyal wife and an irresponsible mother? Wouldn't the children calm down and have a happier life now that they wouldn't be beaten anymore? Wasn't he well rid of her lying? Quietly her son explained as best he could. He said, "It's not what *was* that hurts; it's what it *could* have been!"

Some time ago I heard about a church which was now offering divorce services to families. The couple and their children stand before the minister, who talks openly and honestly before the gathering of friends and relatives about the sad but inevitable failure of the marriage, how each person will go on caring what happens to the others, and how worthy their struggle has been to make the best arrangements possible for the children, who are assured that everyone present is concerned about their future.

Whether one agrees or not with this procedure, it is an indication that we are learning to respect the need for a period of mourning before we can celebrate a new beginning.

When People Leave Therapy Too Soon

WE HEAR A GOOD DEAL about people who remain in therapy too long, developing an unhealthy dependence on it; but there is an opposite side to this: the equally complicated problem that occurs when a person leaves therapy too abruptly – often when the "good stuff" is just getting started!

Alice had trouble keeping a good job. Therapy helped her to have a better attitude toward herself, and she got an excellent job and quit therapy. Now she suffers from chronic headaches. Ben is a widower, and therapy helped him a great deal to cope with the early months of crisis and trauma. He learned to deal very effectively with his children and is doing well at his job. He quit therapy when these two areas of his life seemed back under control, but he finds his relationships with women unsatisfying and is extremely lonely. Carl went into therapy because his parents were critical and overprotective. He stayed in it just long enough to find out how angry he felt, and then he quit. He and his parents aren't speaking to each other at all now.

Often, what happens in therapy is that people who are really very fearful of self-examination try therapy for a while when they are suffering so intensely that it seems the only way out. They reach a point where to go on means to examine some really painful wounds of childhood, and they get the mistaken idea that continuing will be so unpleasant and so frightening that they would rather do it alone.

Finding out that there are reasons you may be very angry at your parents, and being able to express that anger, is the first half of therapy. The other half is learning to care so much about yourself that your anger can turn to compassion for and understanding of your parents.

Finding out why you can't keep a good job and eventually getting one is the first half of therapy; the second half is exploring the sources of tension and anxiety that have to do with needing to be a perfect person. Getting help in living through grief and mourning is the first half of therapy; the other half is finding out what some of the sources of your strain may have been in the relationship with the person who has died, which now interfere with making new and satisfying heterosexual relationships.

Nobody can tell you how long to continue in therapy or when it is time to take charge of your own life. All I can do is to point out that when major sources of discomfort and lack of personal fulfillment are left untouched, the process was probably cut in half.

Young Adults and Their Parents

IF YOU ARE IN YOUR THIRTIES and feel you are doing very well as a grown-up, but your parents still seem to treat you like a two-year-old, you are not alone. It is a common condition — which can be alleviated if not entirely cured.

The first step in changing parental attitudes is to understand how they feel. A friend told me, "I'm sure that my thirty-year-old daughter feels like a kid when I'm around, but I wonder if she knows that *I* feel about one hundred and two when I'm around her. She happens to be a lovely young woman, but in order to try to overcome the impossible, that I will forget she was ever my child, she sometimes overwhelms me with opinions about life and the world today. She's right about the fact that I can't see the world of today through her eyes, but I find myself feeling so dumb and so left out that I begin to pontificate and make speeches, reporting on *my* life and times. Whenever I begin to do this, I see a glazed look come into her eyes, and I know she is feeling that I'm treating her like a child. What I need to explain to her is that *I* feel as if I am being treated as a has-been."

A woman wrote me that she had just come back from visiting her new grandchild. She said, "I love being a grandmother but I don't love being treated as if that's all I am from now on. I'm still a wife and a student and a musician and fairly intelligent!"

Parents and their young adult children need to share some of these feelings with each other. You stop shouting at each other as soon as you can begin saying quietly what you are feeling. Thirty-year-old grown-ups are less likely to need to make their parents feel like worn-out retreads if they can say something like "You know it's crazy, but whenever you start giving me your opinions about anything, I feel about five years old again." Chances are that any reasonably honest and open parent is likely to reply, "I know how you feel, because every time you start explaining life to me, I feel I'm being patronized and belong in a home for the elderly infirm in body and mind!"

The fact of life remains that to some extent a child is a child forever from a parent's view. But retaliating against that awful fact by treating *parents* like children doesn't help.

What is needed is some honest discussion about the hidden agenda of past history and a mutual agreement to have conversations for *adults only.*

Pure Fun

DO YOU EVER HAVE any fun anymore? Do you even *remember* what fun is? Could you give a definition of pure fun? I think I can.

Several years ago a mental health clinic ran a one-day conference which included workshops on dealing with death and divorce and unemployment and marital conflict and teenage drug addiction, and other delightful and enjoyable subjects. One of the staff social workers, looking over the program, announced that she would like to lead a workshop on the subject of pure fun. Her colleagues viewed her as the possible victim of professional burnout, but decided to humor her.

As it turned out, a lot of people shared her exhaustion with dealing with the tragic realities of life, and her workshop was mobbed. To help the participants get into the mood for trying to define pure fun, she asked each person to find someone with the same color of eyes as his or her own. This meant that a whole lot of strangers had to really look at each other, and since eyes come in only a few colors, a good deal of merry rivalry ensued. There was a lot of laughter before the group settled down to figure out the meaning of pure fun.

By the end of the day they agreed that the first task that had been set for them had been pure fun because it was so totally unexpected, just a little silly, and not in the least a serious competition.

Pure fun, they agreed, was something that just *happened,* without planning. It was something that could happen just as often when you were alone as when you were with other people. In fact, it seemed more frequent in solitary form because such events are the least planned. Pure fun happens when there is no competition about anything, no stress, and lots of spontaneity. It isn't something that you *should* be doing or that looks like an accomplishment. It's such things as watching a dog run on a beach, and starting to run too. It's feeding a duck or a pigeon what's left of a picnic lunch. It's watching a bird take a bath, or deciding to join a bunch of kids playing hopscotch, or suddenly taking off your shoes and running through a park fountain on a hot summer day, or just getting the giggles over something silly.

Moments of pure fun are a necessary refreshment for the soul and the only possible way to deal with all those other problems. So while you can't go looking for it, for heaven's sake make the most of it when it happens.

Imagination

SOMEONE ASKED ME RECENTLY what were the two or three most important attributes I would want for a grandchild. A feeling of self-worth would be at the top of the list, which would automatically lead to compassion and empathy for others. Beyond that, I think imagination would be the next on my list of priorities.

Imagination is the capacity to live a full and rich and varied and adventurous life inside one's own head. Imagination is at the root of all creativity. It is the source of all inventions and progress. Imagination helps us to understand other people and makes it possible for us to be alone without being lonely. It is a gift which needs cultivation.

The most imaginative people I know are people who were allowed to have a rich life of free play when they were children; their parents encouraged them to spend time alone and to make up stories. They were children who could turn almost any object into something else, without the slightest difficulty. A pail of sand was a chocolate cake, a shoe box was a train, a pillow was a rabbit.

Imaginative people like themselves a whole lot and place a high value on their thoughts and dreams. They tend to be gentle and caring because their souls are well nourished—they do not feel deprived, because their inner life is so rich.

Of all the imaginative people I've known, Burr Tillstrom, the creator of *Kukla, Fran, and Ollie,* seems to me to represent all the magic that imagination can bring into one's own life as well as the lives of others.

About ten years ago, when I was on tour plugging my book *The Wonderful Crisis of Middle Age,* a beloved friend in Chicago, the host of a program called *Kennedy and Company,* arranged with Burr Tillstrom to surprise me. I was answering questions on the telephone from viewers, when suddenly I heard a rasping, outrageous voice ask, "Tell me, Mrs. LeShan, do you have any advice for a middle-aged dragon?"

I knew at once it was Ollie, the love of my life, and despite getting tangled in wires and cables, I raced across the studio to where the Kuklapolitan Theater had been put up so I couldn't see it. I shouted to the audience, "You see, you see, I *told* you! I'm fifty years old, and this is the best day of my life!" When I reached the little stage, I threw my arms around Kukla and Ollie, and we hugged and kissed, and even while I knew they were realer than real, I was also aware of two arms in a white sweater at the other ends of my dear friends. In a flash I realized it didn't make one bit of difference that the illusion had been interrupted; Kukla and Ollie and Fletcher Rabbit and Beulah Witch were real because they were in Burr Tillstrom's imagination, the best of all possible worlds.

Beulah offered to fly me back to New York on her broom, but I declined. I was quite high enough on a trip into the world of fantasy, created by the gift of imagination. If we encouraged more of that, nobody would need to trip out on anything else.

"Is There Life After Children?"

A FRIEND OF MINE called me recently and said, "Eda, what did I do wrong? David wants to come home and live with us!" David is twenty-seven years old and was recently divorced, and the resulting depression has interfered with his keeping a job. He wants to come home. There are thousands of such young adults returning to the parental hearth. We need to understand why, and what's to be done about it.

I recently saw a wonderful play called *To Grandmother's House We Go,* by Joanna Glass. In it a middle-aged mother turns to her own mother, in her eighties, and asks, "Mother, is there life after children?" The audience howled in instant understanding, but it's a question no past generation of adults would have understood.

There are many reasons why young adults seem to be returning to the fold. Life is more complicated, frightening, and confusing than ever before, for one thing, but a deeper reason is that never before have parents allowed their children to remain dependent on them for as long as we have been doing for the past half century. The reasons for this are many and complex. The psychological revolution made us more self-conscious, more anxious, and more guilty about whether or not we were doing a good job as parents, so we have tended to overprotect our children. In addition, information in all fields of endeavor has expanded at such a rapid rate that it takes much longer to educate a child to the point of becoming expert enough to get a job. The educational process has forced our children to be dependent on us into their early twenties, and the rapid rise of inflation in the past decade has made it extremely difficult for our young adult children to be able to do such things as buy a home without our financial help. In addition, society in general is far less structured than it once was, and young people often feel lost and adrift in having to make choices and decisions about their own lives.

Many young people become depressed and paralyzed, unable to cope with adulthood, but we can't really help them by offering them an unrealistic dependency, a return to parental protection. What we *can* do is to help them find the help they need. Some may need psychotherapy and vocational counseling; some may need a clear message from us that it is time for them to take charge of their own lives. Allowing an adult child to regress to childhood dependency is no favor to the child. We can offer compassion and understanding, but should not allow a total retreat from life. That isn't good for anybody.

What we need to make clear is that we are available for directing a child to sources of needed help, but that it is entirely inappropriate for him or her to give up the struggle for independence and autonomy. That's a burden middle-aged and older parents cannot carry.

There comes a time when a wise bird knows that if its fledgling doesn't leave the nest, it will not survive. We need to have the same courage and wisdom in seeing to it that our grown children learn to use their wings.

Meditation

ARE YOU ONE OF THE MANY people who are curious about the value of meditation? You may be pretty confused by all the conflicting theories and puzzled by the hordes of gurus, each of whom assures you that following his particular techniques will lead to enlightenment. Here is one opinion which I hope will at least be illuminating.

The current interest in meditation seems to me to have developed quite naturally, at a time when the pressures and confusions of our daily lives leave us feeling fractured, vaguely depressed, and dehumanized. The art of meditation is centuries old and often has been thought to be the province of mystics and mysterious sects in remote parts of the world. I think that the current interest in meditation comes from a growing awareness that the human race is in a lot of trouble, and that this is partly due to our having become overwhelmed by the outside world and its demands on us, to the exclusion of the inner life of the mind.

At its best, meditation is the mental equivalent of getting your body in better shape through jogging or weight lifting or playing tennis. It's a kind of mental gymnastics that requires a lot of practice over a long period of time. When practiced on a regular basis, it can lead to deep inner repose and relieve physical illnesses caused by tension and stress.

There are good books on the subject and excellent teachers. There are also misleading books, poor teachers, and charlatans who would like you to follow their teachings while leaving a hefty part of your income at their doorstep.

If you are interested in adding this experience to your fuller growth as a human being, the most important criterion for selecting a program is to find someone who does *not* offer one magic road to Nirvana, but makes it clear there are many roads to inner growth and each person must experiment in finding his or her natural path.

If you sense anything of a Madison Avenue sell — lots of gimmicks, lots of pressure, and lots of money changing hands, run, do not walk, to the nearest exit, in exactly the same way I hope you would with any con man.

There are perfectly good programs which teach relaxation. Free associating and breathing exercises can be quieting and refreshing, if that's your goal. Genuine meditation is much harder work. It is doing only one thing at a time, focusing one's mind completely. It is just about the toughest discipline one can work at, but before you begin to contemplate your navel, contemplate the ethics of your teacher.

We are all more than we think we are, and a bona fide program of meditating is a way to discover new strengths.

Searching for an Adopted Child

THERE HAS BEEN A GOOD deal of discussion in recent years about whether or not adopted adults ought to have the right to try to find their biological parents. One of the main questions has been whether those biological parents *want* to be found. More and more frequently, one hears of the reverse situation, where it is the biological mother who wants to find her adopted child. Then the question becomes "Does the *child* want to be found?"

The more flexible a society becomes, the more problems it encounters. That's not necessarily a bad thing — it just means we have to make more difficult personal decisions.

A young woman of thirty-two, who had a baby when she was sixteen and gave it up for adoption, told me, "Ever since I've known it was *possible* to try to find my daughter, it's been on my mind all the time. I realize now, more than ever, that it was agony to give her up and that I want desperately to see her and know she's all right. In the first few years, when it was impossible to get any information, I never allowed myself to feel my feelings."

A woman who was a drug addict, and is now completely rehabilitated, is eager to reassure herself that her daughter did not suffer any physical damage. Another woman who had seven children by the time she was thirty now wonders how the eighth child is doing; her other children are now all grown up, she's a grandmother — and now she regrets what she did.

The fact that there are now so few children available for adoption is due to many factors, including better birth control and legal abortions. But I think that probably the major reason is that women now, in many cases, are given better counseling at the time they have a child; and because raising an out-of-wedlock child is now much more acceptable, many women are keeping their babies. They are more aware of feelings of grief and mourning at losing a child through adoption.

Many women say they don't even care if they never actually meet the child they gave away for adoption — they just want to know some facts, they want to hear that everything is all right. Others feel that the adoption was an immature and ill-advised mistake and must be undone. There are some important issues they need to think about before taking any action. They need to accept their painful feelings and curiosity and regret, and then they have to decide whether taking *action* is the only or the best way of dealing with their normal feelings. In many cases such actions can be disastrous.

There is no way to assess in advance whether or not interfering with old history and total estrangement is going to be reassuring or perhaps permanently damaging to one or both parties. There are many biological parents who want to let sleeping dogs lie, and adopted children and their parents who feel the same way. Adoption implies total separation and an entirely new family history. We need to think very carefully about tampering with this arrangement.

Adopting Older Children

THERE ARE A LOT OF PEOPLE remaining childless these days because the reservoir of adoptable newborn babies has dried up — apparently for good — because of birth control and legalized abortion and the end of any serious social stigma about raising a child out of wedlock. There are, however, hundreds of thousands of youngsters desperate for a loving family, and if you are in the market for parenthood, I'd like to suggest that you consider adopting an older child.

Most of the people who become criminals were unwanted, rejected children, so that the adoption of some of these unhappy kids may very well be a way of making a contribution to the safety and well-being of this country. But most people who adopt children do it primarily for perfectly normal personal reasons: They want a child to love and to be loved by — one of the nicer experiences available to human beings. So quite aside from the issue of "doing good," I'd like to stress the point that ultimately a kid who's been in five foster homes at the age of ten, or has spent the first few years of his life being battered and neglected, can probably give you more satisfying feelings of being loved than even a newborn baby.

It doesn't come quite as easily, however; you have to really work for it with an older child. A newborn baby doesn't know anything about rejection, so it loves without hesitation. The child who hasn't been adopted because he or she is too old may have suffered too much, may be crippled physically or psychologically, or may feel he would be a fool to trust anyone — and doesn't. Love has to be proved to the wounded and the scarred — but it's a wonderful challenge, and the rewards are quite spectacular.

Fortunately, more and more social agencies are making it possible for older children to be adopted by working closely with the adoptive parents. The most common questions in such situations are: How do you show a child love through setting realistic limits? How do you show flexibility and patience in the face of behavior that cannot be tolerated? Giving the right kind of unconditional love that still sets standards is one of the most challenging and creative jobs any adult can undertake. You can't be a phony or a weak-kneed sentimentalist, but if you work at it, you'll end up with a son or daughter who really understands the meaning of being loved and giving love, having known the lack of both.

Give it some thought. Married or single, rich or poor, old or young, you are likely to be eligible, and a lost child might be found.

How to Prepare for a Trip to the Hospital

I SINCERELY HOPE that at this moment you are in perfect health, but even if you are, I think it would make very good sense for you to prepare yourself for a trip to the hospital.

I have a friend whom I admire greatly. While she was hospitalized after a heart attack, her heart was being monitored by a machine, which suddenly stopped clicking away. A nurse came galloping into the room and was about to do various dramatic things to get my friend's heart pumping again, when my friend pointed out sharply that she was sitting up in bed, drinking some juice, very much alive. The nurse shouted, "But you *can't* be! Your heart has stopped beating!" My friend suggested that maybe the *machine* was the problem, an idea that seemed to strike the nurse as ridiculous, but shortly thereafter an electrician arrived on the scene.

I think that story is a realistic metaphor for what life is like in many hospitals these days. There are exceptions, but the age of technology has turned some hospitals into machine shops in which very advanced life-saving equipment is looked upon with awe, and people are an incidental inconvenience. Machine shop is exactly what I mean. We need to remember that a car has to be fixed by a mechanic because it can't do anything to heal itself. You can; in fact, you need to be part of the act in order to get well. There is something about the hospital atmosphere that encourages us to think we know nothing about ourselves and must submit without question to anything anyone wants to do to us.

While you are healthy, check out the hospital your doctor is connected with. Is there anyone on the staff who deals with patients' rights and needs? Are there ongoing training programs for the staff about the psychological needs of patients?

There is no question that doctors and hospitals save lives. But it is also true that hospitals encourage us to become too passive. You have a right to know exactly what is being done to you and why. You have a right to see your own chart. If someone is thoughtless, you ought to say so; if you aren't getting the care you need, someone should call your doctor for you. If you know your own special reactions to certain medications, be sure your doctor puts these on your chart.

Tell yourself that you do not stop being yourself, even when caught in a helpless state. The medical care you get can do only part of the job of helping you recover. The other half is staying in charge of your life.

Parent Kidnappers

I'VE SPENT A GOOD part of my professional life trying to encourage parents to dump their load of guilt about their failures and their imperfections in the raising of children. Guilt immobilizes a person and makes it very difficult to change and improve; and struggling for perfection is a denial of being human. But there is one kind of parental behavior that makes me so angry and is so horrifying to me that I find myself wanting to encourage a good bit of guilt — and that has to do with parent kidnappers.

When my daughter was a little girl, she often asked me how she would know when she would meet the man that she would want to marry — how she would recognize that special kind of love. We would go through such questions as would she be able to take care of such a person if he were very ill, and could she imagine loving him if he were old. The other day, while watching a television program about divorced or separated parents who kidnap their children, it occurred to me that the question I would like to ask every couple getting married, is this: "Can you imagine a time when you would hate this man or woman so much that you could destroy a child's entire life?"

I am not speaking here of those situations in which a child's life is truly threatened by a totally inappropriate custody decision, but rather of the more common circumstances in which hatred between husband and wife is the main ingredient.

Parent kidnappers are men or women who do not have legal custody of their child or children and who manage to waylay these children at school or on the street, hustle them into a waiting car, and disappear with them, often for good. It is a form of aggressive hostility which can kill the other parent without committing murder. It is a method for so traumatizing a child that he or she may never recover.

In those cases where a custody decision may have been unjust and even dangerous, and the child's welfare is the main consideration, a mature and reasonable parent would and should fight through every possible legal and psychiatric channel in order to reverse such a decision. But child kidnapping usually has little to do with the needs of the child. It is, rather, the way in which one adult uses the most vicious weapon possible, short of a gun, on another adult, to express an unspeakable fury.

The innocent victim in this struggle is always the child, torn in two by mixed loyalties, fear, separation, confusion, and panic.

We need new and better universal laws about child custody, as well as the facilities for seeing to it that divorcing couples are helped to deal with their anger and emotional wounds.

Any parent now contemplating an act of kidnapping needs to understand that the psychological scars imposed on the child may be the only legacy of all the sound and fury. The only place for expressing this depth of feeling is in the courts and mental health clinics, for the child is being used as a tool for vengeance — and in a civilized community that ought to be unthinkable.

How to Comfort People in Distress

IN RECENT MONTHS I've heard a number of young adults complain that when they were teenagers and were feeling miserable, what they hated most to hear was an adult saying, "You'll be fine, you're just going through a phase of growing up." Here they were, feeling absolutely rotten, and all they got were platitudes about how someday it would be over. I find myself in something of a dilemma when I hear this, because the truth of the matter is that what they were being told was the truth of the matter.

How can we comfort people who are unhappy, especially if we are older and the unhappy person is younger? The nephew of a friend recently lost his job, becoming a victim of the general cutbacks in state and federal programs. His salary had been low, with little likelihood of much advancement. He would have unemployment insurance while he looked into other possibilities, and there would be time for training in other specialties which might prove more enjoyable as well as more profitable. His aunt commented that this might turn out to be the best thing that ever happened to him, and her nephew flew into a rage. He said his aunt was cruel and unfeeling not to see how frightened and depressed he was, and he couldn't stand her cheerful, Pollyanna approach.

I understand how this young man felt. I also understand that a gangly, pimply, self-conscious, anxious teenager who feels certain he or she will *never* be popular might well feel a sense of isolation, betrayal, and fury when an adult calls all this misery "just a stage." But it's still the truth, so what can we do? If you have lived a long time, you know beyond a shadow of a doubt that no matter how terrible any experience may seem at the moment, it does fade with time, and often the deepest anguish is something you can laugh at twenty years later. We know that adolescent misery does pass; we know that a frightening event like losing a job can be a blessing in disguise — in the perspective of ten years later. It would be dumb to lie and say otherwise.

I guess the only answer is to share the misery first — acknowledge the suffering, sympathize with the feelings — and then tell the truth as we have discovered it, that all things pass into history. It may make a younger person angry — but only until he or she is old enough to say the same thing to the next generation!

Feelings of Ambivalence

MY MOTHER WAS AHEAD of her time. Way back in the dark ages of the 1930s my mother knew about adolescence and did her best to explain some of my more peculiar behavior to me. One day, in a high-school class on child development, the teacher asked us if any of us knew the meaning of the word *ambivalent*. I raised my hand and said, "It's something my mother and I have about each other!" The teacher was very impressed. I guess the reason I've remembered the story for more than forty years is that, from that time to this, I don't think I've lived through a single day without some ambivalence, and I have come to the conclusion that it's a special and valuable human attribute.

There are three talents, at least, which I like to think of as forever separating us from computers — one is humor, one is being able to love, and the third is feelings of ambivalence. If anyone knows about machinery which now has these human qualities, I don't want to hear about it!

It's my belief that ambivalence is a feeling that encourages us to hold on to our most human qualities. It forces us to see life in at least three dimensions. It makes us more sensitive to our own natures and therefore has the capacity to help us understand others. You really have the most tender and loving feelings for your elderly parents, and you know how much it means to them to have you travel three thousand miles to see them for Christmas, but if you take off all that time and spend all that money, you won't be able to have that real vacation that you need so desperately, a winter trip to the Caribbean. Or, you understand why your spouse is despondent and cranky after getting laid off at work, and you feel a lot of loving compassion — but oh, how you'd love to leave home for a while. Or, you feel frightened and anxious about your child, who fractured an arm playing football, and while you're tenderly feeding him chicken soup and making nice-nice, you'd also like to scream at him for insisting on playing football in the first place.

We love and hate simultaneously; we want to stay and we want to run; we want somebody to take care of us and we want to be free and independent. We want to work at the same time we want to play.

This human capacity to feel at least two feelings simultaneously is one of the most important things we ever need to learn about being human. It may be the source of confusion and discomfort, but it also forces us to make choices, to explore our feelings, and to weigh our values. Those are exercises we all need to stay in condition — to keep on trying to figure out who we are and what's most important to us. Ambivalence keeps us human. I'm glad my mother told me I have it.

Tips for Divorced Daddies

DURING THE SPRING and summer I find it a little painful to walk or to ride a bicycle in Central Park. I see too many fathers and children trying too hard to act as if they are happy when they are really miserable. Their problem is that daddy and mommy are divorced, and Saturday is daddy's visitation time.

Contrary to what I observe in the park, a divorce need not shatter a natural love between father and child. What frequently happens is that a parent and a child lose their natural sense of connection to each other because the situation has become unnatural. It was easier to enjoy each other's company in the context of family life — sitting around the kitchen table, or watching a baseball game on television, or having the whole family go on a skiing trip. Now, suddenly, there you are, alone, no longer sharing daily events, tongue-tied and self-conscious.

This is more likely to occur when there is only one child, but it can happen with several as well. My tips for daddies caught in such discomfort are as follows.

Talking is a nice way to communicate, but it's not the only way. Don't get anxious about silences — they can be very companionable, especially with a quiet kiss on the cheek or an arm around the shoulder. After reassuring a child that he or she doesn't have to talk or be entertaining, you can also make it clear that when you *do* talk, it isn't going to be about the weather but about real feelings. Not "So how did you do in school this week?" if a child seems sad and withdrawn, but the more crucial and honest question, "Do you want to talk about how sad and angry you feel because mommy and I got a divorce?" Once you begin to ask the truthful and meaningful questions, then you have to cultivate the fine art of really listening — not jumping in every second to explain or justify. You can help a child feel safe about expressing real feelings if you let him or her know some of the normal reactions a child may have to divorce. You might say, "I guess it's hard for you to trust me when you feel I made your mom unhappy." Good listening allows time for silence — don't rush on if a child needs time to talk about feelings. You gave a clue that you want to be real and honest. Let the child have time to think about that.

Tips for Divorced Parents, I ·

THE MAJORITY OF THE CHILDREN of divorce *do* continue to live with their mothers, but that picture is slowly changing, and now more fathers are gaining custody of the children. Therefore my comments about the role of the nonresident parent really apply to both mothers and fathers.

Johnny's mother has called his father and reported that Johnny cheated on a math test at school and was suspended for two days. Mrs. Brown says to her former husband on the phone, "You're still his father, and it's up to you to teach him right from wrong. I expect you to really raise hell with him this weekend!" If Mr. Brown accepts this challenge, he will be making a big mistake. It is true that his role in Johnny's life is still of monumental importance, but he has more choices than his ex-wife seems to know about.

He could start right off in grim anger and say, "I'm shocked to hear about your cheating in school. You will ruin your entire future with that kind of behavior. I was going to take you to the football game, but I gave the tickets away because you need to be punished."

Another alternative would be a bigger hug than usual and the quiet comment, "I hear you've had a pretty rough week: Let's talk about it." Children feel far worse about their impulsive transgressions than their parents do and what they need is help in understanding what happened, not anger and punishment. Something like "I realize now how scared you are about passing math. Maybe we ought to talk about a tutor." Or ``Listen — why don't we spend an hour working on math — maybe I could help you." Or ``I know that when you're really scared it's hard not to cheat, but it would be better in the long run to let your teacher know how confused you are."

Children and their divorced nonresident parent may actually find that they are beginning to communicate more effectively than ever before. When they are together now, it isn't over and through the hustle and bustle of domestic life. It may be the first real chance for getting to know each other in new and deeper ways. It is the wise and brave parent who can have the guts to say, ``I know your mother and I tried hard, but lots of times I feel like a failure, anyway. I feel sad and lonely sometimes, and I'm sure you do too. That's probably affecting your schoolwork."

That will not scare your child or make him irresponsible. Instead it will open the doors to a deeper sharing of real feelings.

Tips for Divorced Parents, II

TALKING IS AN IMPORTANT kind of sharing, but there are many other ways in which a divorced part-time parent can relate to a part-time child. One common mistake is for the parent to think that every en- counter with a child has to be entertaining: before you know it, you've gotten yourself entangled in circuses, movies, baseball games, puppet shows, and a general assortment of spectator activities. That's okay some of the time, but shared activity, doing something your- selves, is more enriching and satisfying for any kid and is of special importance in a divorce: learning how to play chess, going fishing, sharing a hobby such as stamp collecting, going to museums and read- ing up on space science or American Indians. One divorced father has built a workbench in his apartment and he and his daughter have made some shelves and a toy sailboat for the lake in the park, and a footstool for grandma's birthday. Another father is a gourmet cook and he and his son make one really terrific meal each time they get together. Swimming, snorkeling, tennis, bird watching are all a good deal more companionable than sitting in front of a television set in silence, all day long.

But no entertainment has to be on the agenda at all. There is nothing wrong with a quiet, boring afternoon, when maybe daddy has to take a nap because he's exhausted from a business trip, and junior calls a friend to come over to do some homework together. Being natural is the key — not trying to set up some artificial social scenario, which isn't the way parents and children relate to each other under ordinary circumstances.

Further, both parent and child need to talk about the times they *don't* want to see each other! There is so much unnecessary guilt and tension when Maryanne can't tell her dad she'd rather go to a pajama party at her best friend's house, or when daddy grins and tries to be cheerful while his mind is far away with the girlfriend who would have liked him to spend a weekend in the country with her and her best friends.

What divorced parents and their children need to strive for is the same thing as any family: quality time together, not quantity.

Having now ingeniously placed a girlfriend in the background, I have set the stage for discussing the new people who enter the lives of divorced parents.

Tips for Divorced Parents, III

I'D LIKE TO TALK now about the ways in which new loves can be introduced into the picture. Since seventy-five percent of all divorced parents remarry, this is a matter of some importance.

Bill's two kids, aged eight and ten, arrive at his apartment at noon on a Saturday, Their father moved into the apartment only a month ago; the divorce is just barely final. When the children get to the apartment, a lady they have never seen before greets them at the door in a bathrobe and says, "I'm Barbie," in a tone of voice which suggests the children certainly must know who she is. She's right — they should know. Their father has been seeing her for a year and plans to marry her, but hasn't been able to share this news until this moment. As a matter of fact, his lawyer told him not to, because of the divorce negotiations.

This is not an uncommon experience for children of divorce, and having already been shaken by the divorce, this is sometimes the last straw; they react with fury, hate, and rejection, even though the intruder may be a combination of Florence Nightingale, Mr. Rogers, and Bo Derek. Parents and their new partners need to be sensitive to raw wounds. It is far better for the children to meet Barbie in a somewhat less challenging situation than dressed in a bathrobe in the apartment! It will take time and patience and understanding for a new relationship to be established, and it will help greatly if it is clear from the outset that the new love is not a replacement for a parent. He or she can be a new adult friend — even a comfort and a guide — but should not compete with the special love a child has for a parent. Otherwise, children feel disloyal to their own absent parent. The only exception would of course be where a child is very young and where a parent has really left the scene completely; in such instances the stepparent becomes the real parent, to all intents and purposes.

Most children suffer greatly from mixed loyalties; they want desperately to love both parents, and one of the most serious pitfalls for divorced parents is to use the children to go on hitting out at each other. If parents keep their serious conflicts to themselves, making it clear to their children that, while there are problems, the children will not be asked to become pawns in the war game, it becomes possible for the youngsters to begin to imagine the advent of a stepparent. If Judy's mother doesn't spend her days listing all Judy's father's faults, and if Judy's father doesn't give sarcastic messages to Judy to deliver to her mother, Judy will be able to go on enjoying the love of both parents and will not feel obliged to take sides. Under these circumstances the new person isn't seen as a threat to an already wobbly, uncertain, and volatile triangle. When a child feels secure and loved by his or her own parents, a stepparent is much less upsetting.

When divorced parents take the lead in making adjustments with creativity and flexibility, children can too. A part-time parent and a full-time parent can guarantee for themselves an easier road to a new love relationship if they have helped their children to understand that life may change, but love goes on being soul food.

Tips for Stepparents

CINDERELLA'S STEPMOTHER is fortunately moving rapidly into the world of fantasy only. These days the converse is likelier to be true; stepparents often worry *too much* about being popular.

My more recent experiences with stepparents have been that they are so eager to do a good job that they tend to rush things that cannot be rushed; they want to be loved and respected and trusted the day they move in.

What they must remember is that the story never begins with the new marriage; there is a lot of old business, some of which will continue forever — and should. New families don't *replace* old families; they add a new and different dimension.

Taking it slow and easy is the name of the game. Trying to move in too quickly makes children defensive; they feel they must remain loyal to their own absent parent, and so they may try to sabotage even the nicest kinds of discipline. One woman who married a man with three rambunctious young sons, who had been doing pretty much what they wanted to do for several turbulent and insecure years, told me, "I didn't say one word about their table manners, or the garbage in their rooms, or their not doing reasonable chores for the first six months. First we got acquainted; I let them know I would never try to replace their mother but that I knew I could be a really good friend and help them to grow up. Once we were pals, I could lower the boom. The oldest boy said he had wondered when I'd get around to acting like a human being instead of a polite stranger! I realized that a little patience had made them more than eager for some limits."

A father told me that he was stunned by how quickly his four-year-old daughter responded to his new wife. "But," he added, "it was a short honeymoon. She was so frightened and unhappy that she became a helpless baby for a while. Once she saw that my wife was going to be a real mother, she began testing the limits. Fortunately, we weren't surprised and could handle it."

Stepparents need to recognize all the memories, the wounds, the love that are part of the child's past. If one tries to compete, one is bound to fail; comparisons are poisonous, and when they inevitably occur, it's a good idea to clear the air by saying, "When you're with your dad, you and he decide what's okay. When you live with me, you and I have to decide in a different way. I'm not your father, but I'm a man and you are a boy, and when we are together, I have to lead the way."

Most children are greatly relieved to discover that instead of being lost and alone as they expected to be, they are more surrounded by mature and loving adults than ever before.

Labor Day

SOME YEARS AGO, while my husband was driving the car, it began to make some very peculiar noises and to lose power. Luckily, he was able to coast into a small rural gas station, where a mechanic worked on the car for an hour and a half without success. Suddenly he touched one particular part of the motor, and the engine began to hum happily. The mechanic cursed like crazy and seemed absolutely furious. My husband couldn't understand why the mechanic was so angry and assured him he was delighted with the outcome. He asked the mechanic what he owed him, and, still muttering angrily, the mechanic said, "You don't owe me nothing!" My husband said, "But you've been working on this car for an hour and a half — of course I want to pay you!" The mechanic replied, "I should have seen what was wrong the first five minutes, and I'm not going to charge you for my stupidity." My husband knew he had met a lucky man who was proud of the work he did and did what had to be done without being enslaved by a time clock. That's the work ethic.

When my father's family emigrated to America, every member of the family worked six days a week, and about fourteen hours a day. That was cruel and inhuman treatment, and since that time life has improved under the influences of unions and automation. It has also *not* improved in certain ways. Somewhere along the line a whole lot of people have lost a sense of deep personal pride in doing a job well, and a whole lot of young people seem to get more tired more easily than those of us, now approaching our dotage, who can still work twelve hours a day without collapsing. We grew up assuming that life's deepest satisfactions came from doing a job well, and we were trained at an early age to being energized by the work itself.

Unions and automation both brought many comforts and safety factors and better working conditions, but pride in one's work is sometimes sacrificed for these necessary benefits. If a teacher can't make a home visit because the hours are not included in a union contract, or if a healthy, active man sits in a theater every night doing nothing because his union contract says that if an actor moves some scenery the stagehand must also be paid, pride in one's work suffers. If work that once took real craftsmanship can now be done in one hundredth the time by a machine, pride goeth before automation. Boredom and a sense of meaninglessness in life also occur.

When society is unwilling to see to it that anyone who wants to work can have a job with a decent living wage, we are encouraging a cynical and despairing attitude toward work. Thank God there are no more shirtwaist factory fires, and that workers are protected against industrial accidents, and that they have such human services as health insurance and money to live on after retirement. Those are great gains — but it seems to me we lose too much if we don't also make it clear that work itself is a necessary ingredient to a feeling of fulfillment and a sense of personal worth. Making an extra effort to do a job well sure makes a person feel good!

Great Teachers

ONE OF THE SPECIAL benefits of talking on radio is that you begin to hear from people you haven't seen in years. The other day I got a letter from a most beloved teacher who taught me a good deal about education and young children back in the 1940s. Her letter delighted me and set me to wondering about what the qualities of a great teacher are, because if we can figure that out, we'd have an important clue to how to have a meaningful life.

Thinking back to my childhood and young adulthood, I remembered there were about ten teachers who influenced my life enormously, who inspired me, and who I think can take some credit for my successes in life and are in no way culpable for my failures!

The first was the teacher in second grade who loved me even after I told a whopper of a lie. The second was a teacher of short-story writing who I'm sure knew that I sometimes came to her after-school club with nothing written in my notebook, although I acted as if it was all written down while I made the story up as I went along. She told me I had a wonderful imagination, and what I remember about her is how she loved reading.

There were several teachers in high school who taught me subjects in which I was absolutely awful, and while they insisted I get passable grades, I knew they loved me even if I didn't fully appreciate their subjects. And then there were a couple of teachers who told me some day I'd be a writer, and I didn't believe them until I was forty-three, but they were right. There was a teacher who raised serious moral and ethical questions, and finally the teacher who just wrote to me — a very great lady, who helped me learn about little children by understanding myself. She taught me how to be a good teacher simply by her example.

The teacher I grew up hating the most was the one who saw two of us cheating on a grammar test, called us up to her desk, and lectured us for twenty minutes, predicting a future life of crime for both of us. At fifty-nine, I still shudder at the memory and hate that woman for making a childish impulse into a federal offense. It may well be that the reason I've written fifteen books, without understanding a single rule of grammar, is my way of paying her back!

Think about the teachers who influenced your life. I'm sure they had certain common characteristics. They loved children and loved you, while being fully aware of your imperfections. They loved the subjects they were teaching, and you were infected by their enthusiasm. They were eager to hear your ideas, and they taught with flexibility, not by following a workbook. They raised a lot of questions without giving you the idea that there are answers to every question, but showing you that the *pursuit* of answers is the excitement of learning.

Most of all, they gave you the feeling that you were a special person with the necessary qualities for growing up into a terrific adult.

As our nation's children go back to school this week, let us all pray they will be lucky enough to bump into a few such teachers.

Ages and Stages for Grownups

WE'VE BEEN AWARE for some time of the developmental ages and stages of children; we ought also to be turning our attention to the developmental ages and stages of adults.

Our society decides that one becomes an adult somewhere between eighteen and twenty-one. While learning and growing may be very dramatic during childhood, that drama doesn't hold a candle to the learning explosions of adulthood. The following are some of the major life tasks that lie ahead when childhood ends.

The first adult task is finding one's work niche in life: developing the skills and the knowledge to become self-supporting and to be able to make the final break with dependency on parents.

The second major task in young adulthood is finding one's role in relation to other people. If we have learned anything about human psychology, it is that we wither and die in total isolation; and in today's society of freedom of choice, with so many options, each person must come to some decision about how to find and work at intimacy — the capacity to be a whole person in relation to another whole person. What roles do we play best? Can we love and be loved? Are we strong enough to become emotionally involved and committed to another adult, and on what terms? I have found nothing in my lifetime to suggest that any of the new options leads to a fuller and richer and more meaningful life than the intimacy of a special partnership; but this stage of growth often takes many years, during which each young adult has a chance to experiment with a variety of roles.

The third developmental stage in adulthood is a kind of settling in; for the majority of young people it is usually marked by a specific job or career, marriage, and parenthood. It is the period of focus on activity, of being very busy — preoccupied with "real life" in the form of getting along with the boss, making payments on the car, buying a house — or, for many these days, the terror of unemployment. Learning to survive is the theme of daily living.

The fourth stage of growth has to do with middle age: the emptying of the nest, the challenge of boredom in marriage, the responsibility for aging parents.

Finally, there is the fact of one's own old age and the challenge to develop the capacity to face mortality with courage and dignity. That's a lot of learning for one lifetime!

The Central Theme of All Growing

TWO KINDS OF GROWING are at the heart of all learning and growing from birth to death: discovering our personal identity and making some contribution for good in the world. These are the two essential kinds of maturation that give us a sense that life is worth living and that our own lives have value and meaning.

Self-discovery starts at birth and should never end. It ought to range from the first discovery of one's toes and the excitement of recognizing an image in the mirror as one's own, all the way to figuring out what a whole lifetime has been all about. The people who are still alive at the time of their death are the ones who wake up each morning wondering what new thing they will learn about themselves.

Some years ago a friend of ours came very close to dying from a serious heart attack. During his recovery in the hospital his cardiologist insisted on his starting to see a psychiatrist, since it seemed quite clear the heart attack was due at least in part to serious psychological stress caused by this man's working himself to death at a job he disliked intensely. Even before leaving the hospital he had already faced the fact that he was going to have to make some major changes in his life.

His twenty-year-old daughter came to see him in the hospital shortly before he was to go home. When he walked into the lounge looking well and strong, his daughter burst into tears and said, "Oh, Daddy, I was so afraid you were going to die!" Her father hugged her and said, "Darling, everybody has to die, sooner or later; what's important is *how* you live whatever life you have. That's what I'm trying to learn right now — how to live with *style.*"

Living with style seems to me to sum it all up. We need to search constantly for what makes us unique and special and then to use our gifts. The degree to which we have the courage to make this search will also be the degree to which we serve others and see life as meaningful, for whether we end up painting a Sistine Chapel or inspecting meat, writing *Hamlet* or driving a bus, if we do our thing with zest and commitment, we make the most of being alive.

The Importance of Saying No

TWO OF THE MOST important words in the English language are *yes* and *no.* I've talked many times about the importance of saying yes to life — of taking risks, seeking new adventures, opting for flexibility and spontaneity in decision making. I think it's time for me to give equal time to the importance of saying no.

Parents usually go bananas when a nice, sweet, cute little kid suddenly begins to say no at about two years of age. Too many parents get angry and see these first nos as a test of parental power. They find themselves at war with a twenty-pounder. They don't know how

lucky they are. Saying no is a sign of integrity; it is the wonderful announcement, "I am a person, and I have to make choices." There are
few signs of growth that should give us more pleasure and comfort.

In order to say no at serious and important moments, we have to
practice. A child who resolutely turns down scrambled eggs and insists
on oatmeal probably likes the scrambled eggs better, but he or she is
practicing the fine art of being a person and making decisions. The
same parent who would like to bop the kid on the head will be very
relieved when that same child can come home and say, "The kids
were going to climb in a window of that new house and bust it up,
but I said no, I wouldn't do that." Or maybe you'll be lucky enough to
end up with a teenager who has the guts and the courage to say no to
driving with someone who's drunk, or no to someone who says he or
she is chicken for not smoking marijuana.

Learning to say no is nature's way of turning us into responsible,
sensible, mature human beings, who not only learn right from wrong,
but can live up to those values and standards that are essential to a
useful and satisfying life. Learning to say no to demagogues and fools,
liars and cheats, and anyone who tries to offer us quick and easy
solutions to serious and complicated problems is an art that must be
cultivated all the days of our lives.

So when a little kid looks up at us with innocent eyes but a determined manner and says no, we ought to take the family out for dinner
and celebrate. Here is the lovely beginning of a *person* with *opinions*.
What we have to do is applaud the courage and tenacity, and give it a
sense of direction by setting a good example.

Caught in the Middle

IF YOU ARE BETWEEN the ages of forty-five and sixty, and if one or both
of your parents is now alive, and if you have teenage or young adult
children — welcome to the club. You are a member of the caught-in-
the-middle generation, and it's not one of your more contented clubs.

When we were young parents, the experts informed us that whether or not our children grew up to be terrific or terrible lay entirely in our environmental hands. Heredity was out during our turn at bat. If a kid was happy, that was just dumb luck. If a kid was miserable, that was because we were rotten parents.

Wonderful people that we are, we survived all of that; most of us did such a nifty job that our grown-up children are crazy about us. When they get sick or when they are unemployed, they love and trust us so much that we are always the first to know their troubles. We are the first generation of parents whose children love to come home.

We are also the first generation of children whose parents often live well into their nineties. When we were children, we were taught that children are supposed to please their parents while they are young and take care of their parents when they are old.

We are caught in the middle for a very simple reason: Most of us *love* our children *and* our parents. Recently finding myself far behind schedule, I needed desperately to finish some writing assignments. Instead, I took my father and his second wife to the country, because they needed some fresh air and a change of scenery. I figured I'd work the following week. But that didn't work out because my daughter fell and broke her leg in four places, and I rushed to her bed of pain and tried to comfort her.

The truth is that while I worry about what could happen if *I* got sick, that almost never happens — and when it does, I want to be left strictly alone; I don't want the ministrations of either the younger or the older generation. My training is that I have to *give* to both, but never to take!

The only way out of this trap is to get over the brainwashing of our younger years. Yes, we love our children and our parents, but there must come a time when we can also be for ourselves. I don't think the solution of my friend need be the only answer: She says, "I pray every night that Dad will stay in Florida and the kids will stay in Oregon and I'll stay in Ohio!"

As for me, as soon as my daughter could get around on crutches, I ran away from home for a week!

Middle-Aged Men

I WROTE A BOOK some years ago entitled *The Wonderful Crisis of Middle Age.* I found out that this was an accurate assessment of how most women felt about middle age, but not at all the way it was for most men.

Middle-aged women had lots of complaints, but they were doing something about them. If they felt they had missed out on something they'd wanted, they were doing it — going back to school, changing jobs, taking a trip, joining some civic organization. Whatever may have once cramped their style, they seemed to have a sense that there was a lot of hope for their future. They could cry about the past and the present, but most of them were fighting for change if they felt it was necessary.

When I began to interview men, I really got scared. I found them a depressed lot. The first man I tried to interview said, "Thanks *a lot,* Eda!" And didn't speak to me again for several weeks, because I had suggested that he was middle-aged at forty-five. The next man said, "It's all downhill to the cemetery." He was forty-eight. A third interviewee sighed and said, "I'm not the man I hoped I'd be and I guess I never will."

Contrary to what we used to believe, it seems to me that men worry more than women about getting older. They are more fearful of losing their sexual appeal and performance; they are less able to change what they are doing with their lives, and if they are unhappy with their work, they have less flexibility about midstream experimentation. This seems to be true even if the wife and kiddies are willing to help in every way to make it possible to try something new.

A lot of the problem has to do with what these middle-aged men were taught when they were little boys. Most of them believe that a macho image is a matter of life and death. A real man never cries, and a real man is a conqueror of women; real men aren't supposed to get too close to other men, so they grow up having very few of the intense, intimate friendships that sustain women.

It's very hard to get through middle age if you can't cry, and if you can't tell your troubles to a friend, and if you worry about your sexual prowess all the time. If we could only convince men that real masculinity doesn't require *any* of these silly postures, but that sensitivity, flexibility, and the sharing of feelings would be as helpful to them as they are to women, middle age might have half a chance of being a wonderful crisis for men, too.

Autumn—and Aging

I COULD NEVER LIVE in a climate where autumn did not happen. There is something wildly exhilarating about seeing the countryside afire in magnificent Technicolor. But even while I glory in this natural wonder, I feel like weeping. Autumn reminds me of my mortality — but it also says, "What a way to go!"

Kazantzakis, the author of *Zorba the Greek* and many other books, wrote that when he died he wanted there to be nothing left of him except a bag of bones. What he meant by that was that he wanted to live so fully that he would use up everything he was or could be. That's what autumn does for me — it reminds me that while only the stark cold of winter lies ahead, there can be an explosion of living before it comes.

A woman I know became the chairperson of an educational institution when she was seventy-five. In her nineties, I could find her on street corners, stumping for her favorite presidential candidate. Another friend of mine, widowed, working at a job that no longer excited her, took all her savings and entered law school at the age of fifty-seven. Now in her late sixties, she's doing what she seems to have been born to do — protecting the legal rights of helpless people.

There are those who say, "Sure, it's great to go on like that *if* you have your health." The seventy-five-year-old was blind and arthritic when she got to her nineties, but, with a little help, still managed to climb that soap box. The lawyer has had a mastectomy and suffers from a slipped disk. Another friend of mine just changed jobs at the age of sixty-nine because she felt she needed a new challenge. She had a hip operation five years ago and walks with great difficulty even with a cane.

I cannot speak with any authority about the political or economic aspects of the current question about what the age is when people ought to be able to retire on Social Security — but I can speak knowledgeably about the psychological aspects of early retirement. Unless a person has prepared for this for a long time and is going *toward* something he or she has been dying to do for years, early retirement is the pits. For those who retire without exciting plans, with the thought of just taking it easy, the mortality rate is much higher than for those who go on working and enjoy what they are doing.

Wherever you live, try to find some place where you can look at some maple trees turning red and yellow and pink, where you can be witness to how spectacular the autumn can be — and then, if this is your autumn in life, go out and create your own fiery glory.

The Lost and the Found

THE OTHER DAY I saw a nursery-school class crossing a street in front of me. Each child had a great big card pinned to his or her back. I hurried along to see what it said, and read, ''If I get lost, I belong to . . .'' and this was followed by the name and address and telephone number of the school. I felt a wave of pleasure, for these children might get lost but they'd always be found. I was especially happy for them because I live with a permanent ache for the millions of lost children who are never found. What was so wonderful about that little class of little kids walking ahead of me was that, if they got lost, somebody would want them back. There is nothing, absolutely nothing, that matters more in the life of a child. This sounds so simple, but it is not.

How do you feel about kids? If you're in your twenties, you may wonder from time to time if you will ever want to have any. It costs such a terrible lot to raise a child, and there seems to be so little room in the modern world for children: city or suburb, life feels dangerous, tense, frenetic, crowded. If you're in your thirties, the issue becomes sharper. Career and kids? One or the other? Will you be missing something if you opt for childlessness? People in their forties and early fifties mostly have some children, and chances are that the nature of life in today's world has made them pretty nervous parents. Will their adolescents get involved in the drug scene? Will a child be ripped off in the locker room or mugged riding a bike in the park? How in the world to find money for college, when a year's tuition may be half a family's income? Older people seem to run to extremes, from doting grandparents to people who move as far away from children as they can possibly get, and savor every moment of the peace and quiet.

But whatever our age, how many of us ever think about children as being an endangered species? How many of us think about kids as being the only future the human race can have? Until the twentieth century, the greatest treasure a family could have, rich or poor, was living children. So many died early; so many were needed in the fields and in the factories to help a family to survive. Children were an economic asset. Now they are, without question, an economic liability of monumental proportions. But do we care enough about children to avoid extinction? It's a very serious and pertinent question. About fifteen years ago, U Thant, then Secretary General of the United Nations, said we had ten years in which to stop the arms race, deal with pollution of the planet, and find some way to control the exploding population. If he was right, we are already behind schedule. Our children may be lost and never found. There is really no getting along at all unless we all think about lost-and-found labels to pin on all the world's children.

Taking Risks: Columbus Day

WHETHER OR NOT Christopher Columbus was actually the first person to discover our hemisphere, most of us grew up admiring the symbolism of what it means to take risks. It takes a whole lot of courage to set sail when most of the people around you assure you you'll fall off the earth when you get to its flat end!

Sometimes it seems to me too few of us hold strong enough beliefs to take important risks. So many people feel so overwhelmed by feelings of doubt and uncertainty that they seem unable to act, even to assert an opinion, much less fight for it. Political scientists report that there have been few periods in our national history when there has been so passive and immobilized an electorate. Parents are full of doubts about raising children. Many religious leaders sound far less sure of the light of truth. So much has changed so rapidly that the majority of people, whatever their roles in life, seem fearful of taking a stand about anything lest they turn out to be wrong.

What seems to me to be happening — and to a dangerous degree — is that the least thoughtful and responsible people, those with the most rigid and inflexible ideas, begin to influence our lives the most because so many of us are paralyzed by self-doubts.

It is understandable that we feel confused, afraid, uncertain. Understandable, but not to be endured. What we desperately need is the taking of new risks, the willingness to adventure into the unknowable future on the grounds that we surely can't solve problems by backing away from them, and there is a reasonable chance that being an active participant in the present and the future may just work out better than we expect. There was the chance that maybe the world was round and surely that was a fact worth proving.

Whether or not we are successful in our adventure, we will certainly *feel* a whole lot better. Since I can't assess this matter personally, I can only conjecture — but I bet Columbus was too busy to feel afraid or depressed. As things turned out, the world was round after all — and it might also be worth saving.

Bigger Is *Not* Better

I FINALLY GOT AROUND to visiting the World Trade Center in New York a few weeks ago, and I had a perfectly miserable time. The view from the top is spectacular, the restaurants at the bottom are sensational, the shops and services fascinating, the design and the architecture remarkable — and I hated the whole thing. Standing in the plaza, looking up at the two monumental, overwhelming towers, I felt like a flea, and inside, the mobs of people made me feel crushed and helpless against a tidal wave of humanity. The noise level in the restaurant made me cringe in pain, and my companions and I had no conversation whatever until we were safely in the car and on our way home. This episode reminded me that there is one principle in this age of technology that is absolutely, totally wrong, and that is that bigger is better.

I think my first awareness of the terrible dangers of bigness came when I went back to visit a college I'd attended for a while about forty years ago. It was a big university then, and I left after a year and a half because I felt lost and alone. It is now about fifty percent bigger than it was then — tall and massive buildings have been added — and the young people who attend this institution of higher learning spend more time relating to administrators and computers than to teachers.

Bigger airports and airplanes make me more tired; bigger stores exhaust me. Bigger offices make me want to go home and crawl into bed. Bigness separates people, makes them feel like ants lost in a maze. We become anonymous in the mass.

For many years there has been a good deal of disappointment and a whole lot of anger about the fact that when a slum neighborhood has been razed and enormous new apartment complexes have been built for the people who were taken out of the tenements, they often tend to destroy the wonderful, new, clean housing project. In one city, the new housing was so badly vandalized and the area became so dangerous that the buildings were finally razed. In more recent years, city planners have become aware of the fact that tearing down private homes and small apartment buildings destroys a neighborhood — that people who can relate to each other intimately, personally, get along far better than those who are put in a rabbit warren of hundreds of apartments one on top of another.

A group of students with one talented teacher sitting in the market place can have such a terrific learning experience that people have been reading Plato for twenty-five hundred years. I don't believe anyone gets educated in a school of thirty thousand young people. Tremendous factories and offices take away pride, individuality, a sense of community. Co-workers become cogs in a machine. Highways and high rises turn neighbors into strangers. "Smaller is better" would be a great slogan for saving the world.

How to Choose a Day-Care Center or a Nursery School

BECAUSE SO MANY MORE mothers are now working, the issue of choosing the right day-care center or nursery school has become increasingly important. Infancy and the preschool years are crucial in the psychological development of children, and the selection of child caretakers is about as important a decision as parents make about child raising. I happen to have some fairly unorthodox views on this subject, and since my major professional work has been in the field of child development, I'd like to share my theories with you.

First of all, I am unalterably opposed to day care by franchise. Maybe you can make good hamburgers or fried chicken that way, but it's a rotten way to care for children. I would run, not walk, from any child-care center that was a national institution: too big, too hard to monitor properly.

Second, having qualified teachers with state certification would *not* be my top priority in choosing a day-care center. In too many states certification means that the teacher is equipped to teach kindergarten through grade six, and that is not the right kind of training for infant and preschool care. What I would look for is a place where at least some of the teachers have had specialized training in early child development. A teacher who has been to a junior college and majored in nursery education may be more qualified to work with little kids than a teacher with a master's degree and public-school certification who has never had a course in nursery education.

If I walk into a nursery school or day-care center and see letter charts on the wall, with three-year-olds uniformly and laboriously writing their names, and if the teachers proudly tell me they are doing a lot of reading, writing, and arithmetic readiness, I race for the door and get the heck out of there. If two-and-three-year-olds were ready for first grade, that's where they would be. It is *not* the appropriate or healthy or sensible time for such skills. There are plenty of far more important things to learn first.

The school or center ought to be a physically safe place, quiet and small and unhurried, with good equipment and space — but only one qualification stands out all by itself as essential. Visit long enough to find out if the teachers understand that their most important task is to help a child learn to love himself or herself. Nothing matters more than that — and nothing is a tougher challenge to parents and teachers. It is the special drama of life during the preschool years.

The Drama of the Nursery Years

WHAT HAPPENS TO A CHILD from the age of about two to five is more important than anything that ever happens later. I make that statement because I believe it to be true — but with great trepidation, because I'm so afraid of being misunderstood. At the same time that I think the greatest drama of life occurs in the first five years of life, I am also absolutely convinced that there is never a time when it is too late to change, and that we have the whole of our lives to either reinforce or discard the influences our early experiences may have had on us.

Having said that, the way in which a human being comes to feel about himself or herself begins in infancy and depends on whether or not parents and other adults encourage and endorse individuality, and make it clear that there is no feeling or thought that any human being can have that is not normal. Respect for individuality means loving a child for not being anybody else but just being the self that he or she was born to be. Not smarter, not cuter, not prettier, not bolder, not sweeter, not better at climbing a jungle gym or faster at getting toilet-trained, not quieter or more noisy. It means making a child feel that the world is a richer and better place because of the unfolding miracle of a new and special self, not to be compared to anyone else. Children make up their minds about all this by the time they are five. Unfortunately, all too many of them arrive in kindergarten feeling exactly the opposite: No matter how much they try, they are failing to measure up to adult expectations — they believe they are really no damn good and never will be. If we could turn that around, we might save civilization!

The second part of the drama of the preschool child is learning the difference between thinking a thought and doing an action. What children need to be told is that all thoughts are normal — even hating the baby, or wanting to kick Aunt Betty, or sock the kid next door who keeps taking your wagon. No one is ever a bad person for having bad thoughts.

The big problem is not letting thoughts turn into action, and no young child is ever a bad person when he or she can't stop an impulsive action. The reason there are grown-ups is to keep you from *doing* what you are *thinking*. Later on you will get old enough to stop yourself, but little kids who bite or hit or take things that don't belong to them are not bad, only little. When *bad* and *naughty* get out of the language altogether, that will also go a long way to saving the world. Anybody who grows up thinking he or she is a bad person can get us all into serious trouble. But how can we avoid chaos if children are never to be called bad? By good discipline, and that's my next subject.

The Real Meaning of Discipline

THERE ARE FEW THINGS more confusing to young parents than what they should or should not do about disciplining their children. They are right to be concerned. Those of us who were disciplined wisely and with love when we were children get along pretty well in the world; those who were poorly and ignorantly and angrily disciplined as children are often the self-haters who end up trying to destroy the rest of us.

By the time children can talk, most of them have been burdened with some formidable lies. These include the lie that they could behave much better than they do, the lie that some children are good and some bad, and the lie that they should be able to control childish impulses even though they are children.

One psychologist got a report from a nursery school that his son was immature. He sent the report back, having written on it, "If you can't be immature when you are four, when *can* you be?"

Children have impulses that need to be controlled. You can't go around hitting and biting and screaming to get your own way all your life, and you need to learn ways of behaving that, it is hoped, will allow you and others to live in a civilized way with each other. But good discipline has nothing whatever to do with punishment, and even less with spanking. It is the way in which an adult helps a child understand human nature, accept human frailty, and become wise and strong enough to seek personal fulfillment while getting along with other people.

That's a mouthful, all right. Let me give an example of what I mean. When Johnny hits David for taking his truck, you *don't* hit Johnny and say, "That should teach you not to hit people!" When you think about it, that's pretty stupid, if learning by example has any merit. You *do* take the truck away from David and give it back to Johnny, explaining to both of them that, when you are little, it is very hard to learn to share and not to hit, and grown-ups are for helping you learn; maybe we'd better all sit down and talk about it for a minute.

Discipline that shows understanding, compassion, patience, kindness, and good sense helps to create human beings who are understanding, kind, and sensible. Children learn to discipline themselves best when they see themselves as good human beings, able to learn and grow. Inner discipline can never grow in a climate of self-hatred.

When our daughter used to kick the leg of the table and eat with her fingers, her father would shout, "Civilize up!" At least he was on the right track: The goal of discipline is nothing less than civilization.

Parapsychology

SOMEONE WHO HAPPENED to know that my husband has been exploring the subject of parapsychology wrote and asked if I could try to explain why certain things we believe are impossible keep happening to us.

The woman who wrote to me described an event in which she had known the exact moment when her son had been killed in a car crash thousands of miles away. There is nothing at all abnormal or unusual about such an event. People frequently have information we cannot explain, if we think that the only way we know anything is through our senses. The only reason ESP, clairvoyance, and other kinds of paranormal events strike us as abnormal or strange is because we don't yet fully understand why such events occur. If you had told anyone in the fourteenth century that someday there would be a box which would sit in the middle of the living room and show you a picture of men landing on the moon, chances are you would have been stoned to death or burned at the stake for having such ridiculous fantasies. The day is not very far away when paranormal events will seem as ordinary as television.

What we are discovering is that there are many different kinds of reality, and that different things can happen depending on what reality you are using. Paranormal events occur when, perhaps for a split second, we enter a reality which is quite different from our everyday, ordinary reality. It is a moment of deep meditation, in which the most important element is that we are all connected to each other in a larger universe. There is overwhelming evidence that, without being conscious of making a switch, people who get information without the use of their senses have entered an altered state of consciousness.

The reason this field of research is of enormous importance is that it is making us aware of aspects of being human that Western civilization has tended to bypass and ignore. We do so at great peril. This attitude has crippled our natures, for we, like the amphibians, only live fully if we live on both land and sea. We need the everyday reality of our senses in order to survive in the physical world, where we must watch traffic lights, clean our teeth, eat, and sleep in order to live. We need the world of oneness with the universe for spiritual survival, in which we feel connected to each other beyond the separation of our own skins.

The difference between the smartest computer and any human being is the capacity to shift from one kind of reality to another without direct orders. We smell and see and dream and pretend. We eat and we imagine. We are separate identities as well as ripples in the universe. The current research in parapsychology reminds us of all we can be, and how much we need each other.

Psychic Healing

THE MORE TECHNOLOGICAL medical practice becomes, the more interest there seems to be in psychic healing. That can be a very good thing — and also very dangerous.

Psychic healing, through all human history, has been a way of helping an individual bring all his or her own self-healing powers to bear on illness. Before the modern era of great specialization — a kind of fragmenting of the human body into separate categories of treatment — the family doctor or general practitioner often provided some psychic healing along with whatever scientific treatments were available. Tender loving care is a kind of psychic healing, because the patient is seen as a whole, living, feeling person who needs love as well as medicine.

Psychic healers are usually people who happen to have more paranormal abilities than other people. They are able to go into an altered state of consciousness in which they make a kind of spiritual connection with the patient, and that extrasensory message of love and care helps the patient use his or her own healing resources. The scientist Alexis Carrel has described watching, under a microscope, a cancer on the hand of a woman while a famous healer meditated nearby. He said that what he saw happening was the development of healthy cells at a more rapid rate than could ordinarily be expected. The healing was taking place within the patient and was not something imposed medically from the outside.

Modern scientific technology is keeping us alive and healthy far longer than ever before, but we have paid a price in feelings of fragmentation, anonymity, depersonalization. Psychic healing and all the other approaches to holistic health are a helpful adjunct to medical procedures. They fill in that missing link of individual care and an awareness of how interconnected all the parts of our selves really are.

Where psychic healing is used to reinforce medical care, or where it is used when the problem goes beyond what medicine can accomplish, it can be an aid to the physician. When it is seen as an alternative to modern medical care, it can kill you.

Because we still know so little about the mind-body-soul mystery, there are certain important criteria you ought to follow if you want to see a psychic healer. The first is that this person insists you remain under medical supervision. The second is that there is no charge for this service. Responsible healers recognize this is an area for research rather than practice and do not use their talents as a way of earning a living. And, finally, it is crucial that the healer does not make any promises about the outcome.

When these rules are followed, psychic healing does seem to help a great many people to feel lovingly cradled in a safe universe; and this feeling enables them to use all their own resources for self-healing.

Working Mothers, I

MANY YEARS AGO, when I was a consultant in a nursery school, a mother came in to see us — ashamed, apologetic, flooded with guilt — eager to tell us she'd give up her job if we felt she should, because four-year-old Andy had started to have nightmares. We suggested that before she turn in her attaché case, she might like to know that most four-year-olds have nightmares and that Andy was a charming, bright little boy who could survive having a working mother.

Much has changed in the intervening years — but not everything. What was different about the time when I met Andy's mother was that fewer mothers were working from choice, there were fewer divorces, and a daddy was less likely to be helping with child raising. But one factor remains unchanged — the heavy burden of guilt many working mothers feel about not being at home while their children are young.

Whether one is a single parent raising children alone, and whether or not mom and dad have achieved a comfortable balance of sharing child-raising duties, many mothers still seem to be feeling some concern and some guilt about whether they might be shortchanging their children's emotional health by having jobs outside the home. Well, I'm here to tell you that there is no reliable information indicating that a career woman can't also be a terrific mother.

There was a time when working mothers were being brainwashed into believing that they were responsible for juvenile delinquency, among other serious emotional traumas. Working mothers who love their kids, and who feel a sense of joy in also being fulfilled as persons using their full talents, tend to bring something quite wonderful into their children's lives; it is the clear message that people are happier and more loving when they are allowed to discover their fullest potential. And that children have a right to beat out their own music, too.

Working mothers often spend more quality time with their children than mothers who are home all the time and don't feel guilty! Women who stay home to be full-time mothers, and are *glad* to be where they are, are likely to do a fine job, but if they are *not* happy, their discontent and restlessness is perfectly clear to their kids.

Children can be neglected and mistreated by any mother, with or without an outside job. Emotional problems don't occur because of one factor, but in the total climate of life. If anything, my experience has been that because a woman has a life of her own, she tends to be more concerned, not less, about the welfare of her children. But it's not easy when women try to lead a double life, and I'll have more to say about some of the realistic problems, and what can be done to alleviate them, next.

Working Mothers, II

I HOPE I HAVE MADE it clear that self-fulfillment for a mother is not a cause for alarm — quite the reverse. However, motherhood and a full-time career outside the home call for some pretty clever juggling, and I'd like to offer some suggestions from a card-carrying member of the working-mothers club — me!

It's long past now, but I remember only too vividly getting up in the morning and discovering my daughter had a high fever when I was due to conduct an important meeting at 9 A.M. I also remember the day my daughter had an accident at school and the nurse couldn't get in touch with me, which made me feel pretty rotten.

In the first case, I had planned ahead for such an emergency. I always saw to it that I had a list of at least five baby-sitters who were mature women and had raised a family themselves. That way I knew they could handle a virus without getting rattled. When I interviewed baby-sitters, I chose people who were very relaxed and loving, and who didn't feel that it was their job to be disciplinarians. I wanted my child to enjoy their company; my husband and I would take care of setting limits when we were home. I was not interested in having sitters who could cook and clean; I wanted them to care about my child and nothing else.

A single parent *must* rely on relatives and baby-sitters, but even though my husband was present, I didn't count on him for emergencies because there were times he was no more able to stay home than I was.

When the school nurse couldn't reach me, I almost drowned in guilt, until a friend pointed out to me that the same kind of thing had happened to her when she'd gone shopping and then had lunch with friends. No parent can always be available, but what we all need to do is to see that teachers and school nurses and baby-sitters have a list of other relatives or close friends to contact — and, of course, the name of the doctor who is caring for our child.

During the period when children are young, we need some clear priorities. Those are *not* the years to worry about a neat and clean house or to feel obliged to cook gourmet meals or have a wild social life. Children grow up so much faster than we ever expect, and there is plenty of time for all that later on.

Quality time together is far more important than quantity. Playing a game with a sick child when you get home from work or feeding soup to a sick eight-year-old who needs to regress a little can be more satisfying than a whole day of scattered attention.

One mother came home and said she needed to rest a while before she could play, and her little girl said, "Mommy, why don't you lie down and suck your thumb, and then you'll feel better." The best thing a working mother can have going for her is such compassion from her child!

The Creative Art of Homemaking

FOR THE PAST FEW YEARS career mothers have been getting a good deal of approval, encouragement and respect. It seems to me to be time to say a good word for mothers who choose to stay home.

Many years ago a friend of mine who wanted to be, and was, a full-time homemaker told me that she saw herself as a set designer. She said, "I see my job as setting the scene in which life can happen, for Jerry and me and the two boys. By creating an atmosphere, a climate, the background scenery of a comfortable, attractive home, I elicit from all of us the best we can be." I thought her attitude was lovely and valid. She saw herself as a creative, intelligent, loving force in the life of her family, and she was right.

Women who choose not to take outside jobs while their children are growing up in fact develop a great many careers through daily life experiences. They learn to be nurses, psychologists, teachers, nutritionists, judges, cooks, plumbers, electricians, chauffeurs, doctors, economists, interior decorators, and other assorted roles. If they become sensitive, wise, patient, and loving parents, they are doing more than most of us to raise a decent, responsible next generation.

When I was a young woman, homemakers were greatly admired if they took their roles as wives and mothers seriously and performed them well. At that time we still understood that our children were our most precious asset, so we wanted them to get the best possible care.

It takes a whole lot of courage to stay home these days. We don't value children much at all anymore, and we value money and success-ful women with outside careers far more. In the early days of wom-en's lib the emphasis quite naturally was on encouraging women to fulfill themselves, and many chose careers alone or careers combined with homemaking. The woman who could become the head of a big corporation or a bank, the woman who could become an airline pilot, the woman who could break down the taboo against women con-struction workers all caught our fancy because they represented prog-ress — something new and different.

It takes not only courage but remarkable fortitude to be a full-time homemaker today, when inflation has played such havoc with family economy. It's obvious that it is all but impossible from the fact that so many women who want to stay home can't anymore.

Homemaking can be a creative art, and any society that penalizes women, or men, for that matter, who choose that career is taking a big chance with the stability of its society and the well-being of its children. We ought to applaud instead of smirk at that profession.

Prescription for Recovery from Traumas

A FRIEND OF MINE works as a volunteer paramedic in a rural area. On a recent night of horror, her ambulance was called to an accident in-volving two cars on a highway. Two people were dead in one car, and in the other, two parents were seriously injured, while their two children, fortunately encased in proper child car seats, were uninjured in the back of the car.

As soon as people began to gather, there was much shouting about the necessity of getting the two children away as quickly as possible. My friend told me, "I raised bloody hell! I pushed my way through, got both kids out of the car, and walked around the whole accident with them, showing them exactly what had happened to both cars. Then I took them into the ambulance with their parents, let them see they were going to be all right, let them touch them and talk to them, and then off we went to the hospital, including the children. Well, you would think I was a murderer the way everyone reacted. How could I let two little kids see such terrible things?"

My friend was absolutely right to involve the children in this awful trauma to whatever degree the children seemed to want — and even to encourage them to see it all. If we have learned anything at all in the field of psychology, it is surely that human beings of all ages can come to terms with fear and tragedy far, far better when events are confronted directly. Nothing in life is ever as bad as what we can imagine.

During and after World War II, there were occasions in many countries when children were evacuated — separated from their parents and sent away from such dangers as bombings and floods. Over and over, the same thing happened. Those few children who stayed with their parents, even though living through terrifying experiences, showed far less emotional damage than those who were sent away. We have the capacity to endure the unendurable if we are permitted to experience our anguish. If we deny it or cover it up or run away from it, we become crippled, unable to cope.

The parents in the car accident lived in the same town as my friend, the paramedic. After they recovered, they told my friend that their children had been remarkable about the whole experience. Occasional nightmares and some normal apprehension, but other than that, they were doing just fine. They talked about the accident, and it was clear that their familiarity with the event had given them the strength to deal with it. We need love and support and care when something terrible happens. What we *don't* need is running away.

What *Psychosomatic* Really Means

THERE IS A GREAT DEAL of confusion about what the word *psychosomatic* really means. The most common confusion seems to be the idea that when an illness is called psychosomatic, it means the individual has deliberately given himself or herself the disease and should therefore feel guilty and ashamed for having done such a foolish thing. That is just about as far from the true meaning as you can possibly get.

Psychosomatic means that everything that ever happens to us occurs to a whole human being who has a body *and* a brain, and that they are part of each other, without any separation. From that point of view there is no illness which can be relieved or cured without consideration of that wholeness.

We have known for many years that certain kinds of psychological stress can cause changes in body chemistry, resulting in such real illnesses as ulcers, migraines, or colitis. In more recent years there has been a growing body of evidence suggesting that we need to view heart disease and cancer from the viewpoint of wholeness. Rapid and fascinating advances in biochemistry are making it clear beyond a shadow of a doubt that physical distress can cause chemical changes which affect personality, and that emotional distress can cause bodily changes leading to physical illness. We are just on the threshold of understanding the ways in which the hormonal system can trigger all kinds of reactions, and probably the greatest mystery, which may well be unraveled in the next few years, is how the human body sets up its immune system and what factors tend to break down that immune system.

For example, a fascinating study at a New York hospital indicates clearly that men who are grieving after the death of their wives show dramatic changes in their body chemistry. In another study of grief reactions, it was shown that changes in body chemistry move in the direction of such imbalance that the craving for chocolate which many people describe during life crises is the result of these chemical imbalances, not just some psychological need.

Some of the things that happen to us are best treated by medicine, others by psychotherapy. Neither should be used entirely by itself. Grief, for example, may be treated partly by medical means and partly by psychotherapy to help the body rebalance its own normal chemistry.

If you think holistic medicine is some crazy new fad, it isn't. It may be fumbling and uncertain at the moment, but its goal is most definitely to bind us to our whole selves inextricably, so mind and body are one. That's what psychosomatic means.

The Healthy Aspects of Anxiety

ANXIETY HAS GOTTEN a bad name, but I think that there are some healthy aspects to anxiety.

There are, for sure, some kinds of anxiety that don't do us one bit of good, and can in fact do a good deal of harm. For example, irrational anxiety about getting killed in an air crash, or about falling out of a window, or about someone else being hurt are all a screen for unconscious feelings that have nothing to do with the things we *think* we are anxious about. Anxiety as a substitute for anger or feelings of inadequacy has nothing whatever to recommend it.

But there is a productive kind of anxiety that revs up the motor and gives us the opportunity to do something so well that the end result is exhilarating and reassures us about our talents.

Whenever I have undertaken a new challenge, I always experience a great deal of anxiety. I drive my poor family and friends crazy as I moan and groan and threaten to kill myself, assuring anyone who will listen that I'll never measure up to the task at hand. My anxiety usually leads me to a period of very tough and intensive work, with weeks of rising at dawn and working a twelve-hour day. When I finally get to the new assignment, everything goes off so smoothly that I am stunned. This is a difficult period to live through, but it is a kind of healthy anxiety that pays off very well.

Healthy anxiety can occur only in a situation where two things are operating. In the first place the individual must have background experience and training for whatever the job is. Helen Hayes claims to have had nervous butterflies in her stomach before every perform-ance, but she acted from the time she was about eight years old and probably had more experience behind her than almost any other ac-tress. Experience and expertise form a basic partnership for healthy anxiety to work like an outboard motor for bringing about a high level of achievement.

But I think the second factor is even more important. Much as I may drive my poor relatives and friends crazy by my frenzied cries and moans, much as I may shake and tremble, much as I may have some sleepless nights, I have to admit that somewhere way down deep I really know I'm pretty good at what I do, most of the time, and that when I fail, it has never been the end of the world.

Healthy anxiety is a kind of driving force which can work only when it is the expression of *self-confidence*. That ought to teach us a thing or two about our children as well as ourselves. A little less criticism and a whole lot more enthusiastic support would help our kids become able to tolerate healthy anxiety.

Getting Along Black

A FRIEND OF MINE walked into a large department store in downtown New York. A beautiful model was handing out perfume samples, and my friend put out her hand to take one. Beth is middle-aged and col-lege-educated, and she has two daughters with graduate degrees. Her husband is a famous artist. She was wearing a fur coat, and she always looks elegant. The model asked her if she did "day cleaning" and whether she had any free time. If you are confused by this story, there is a simple explanation: Beth is black.

When I heard the story I was shocked. My immediate reaction was that this department-store model must have been some kind of rare weirdo, but Beth laughed at my disbelief and said, "That's exactly the reaction I get from my white friends. You just can't believe our lives are still like that. Well, I'm here to tell you that we middle-aged, middle-class black women are *still* being asked by doormen in apartment buildings to please use the service entrance."

Beth proceeded to tell me that, while she likes the things I talk about on "Getting Along," I really didn't know anything about "Getting Along Black." Of course she's right — and there is no way in which I can fully share her experience. All I can do is try to listen as sensitively as I can and to empathize with what she tells me about how she feels.

Beth lives in a beautiful home; she has traveled extensively; her husband has received many honors and awards for his work; and he and Beth are loved and admired by many people, both black and white — and yet Beth feels a deep sense of sadness and anger, and she tells me that she doesn't have any hope that things will improve in race relations.

I, on the other hand, think I've seen remarkable changes in my lifetime. If anyone had told me thirty or forty years ago that I would live to see a black Supreme Court justice, black mayors, black sheriffs in the South, and a television comedy series in which interracial marriage is a secondary theme, I would have said this was much too optimistic. When I was a child I knew only one black family who weren't servants. The only blacks I saw in the movies were either servants or musicians or comedians — and even in these roles they were portrayed as obsequious and childlike. I never saw a black salesperson in a store or black diners in any restaurants. I never met a black lawyer or banker. When I was a college student I worked on a committee which was trying to get Nedick's and Macy's to employ black people, and it was a tremendous uphill fight. As a teenager, traveling in the South, I was horrified by the "white" and "colored" signs on park benches, at drinking fountains, and in public bathrooms. When my parents had to explain to my younger brother why we had to sit in front of the bus, he asked, wide-eyed, "Who thought *that* up?" When I see young men and women, black and white, working together wherever I go, I marvel at how easily we take that for granted now, when such relationships could not have existed fifty years ago.

Beth and I see the world through different eyes. I need to understand her pain and anger, and she needs to examine my perspective. Together we need to work for change, since those who suffer the most in "Getting Along Black" are not middle-class women like us.

They are the children who are being rejected in white schools and neighborhoods. They are the young blacks, fifty percent of the unemployed in some places, who can't get jobs. They are the poor who are too malnourished to have the energy to change their lives. Whether or not Beth and I understand each other's perspectives, we have plenty of work to do — together.

The Tragic Nature of Life

IF MY MOTHER had not died nine years ago, she would have been eighty-seven years old today. I remember that at the time of her death a friend told me that I would never recover from this death. Her mother had died five years before, and she still found herself running to the telephone to call her mother about some good news. My friend was both right and wrong. I'll never get over it, but I have recovered.

When my mother died, we planted a tiny red maple tree outside our house and held a memorial service there — a circle of friends and family, all holding hands around the tree.

Today the tree is a glorious miracle, the wonder of the neighborhood. It has grown so fast and so abundantly that its branches are already strong enough to hold climbing great-grandchildren — an idea my mother would have loved.

Immediately after my mother's death, I cried every time I looked at the tree, but as the years have passed, I have come, instead, to glory in its beauty. I think this is a useful metaphor for how people can deal with the tragic nature of their lives.

I don't know a single human being or a family that hasn't had to deal with tragedy and anguish. What separates the cowards from the brave is how we deal with that inevitable part of our lives.

I have a friend who has gradually been going blind for about twenty years. Now she is almost totally blind. I am in anguish for her — and at the same time, I am inspired by her courage. In the course of this developing tragedy she has become ten times the person she was before it all began. The depth of her understanding, her honesty, even her humor seem to me to have reached heights that would never have been likely to occur if life had not honed her to a fine edge by terrible pain.

I have a friend whose mother died about three months ago. She was in her nineties and had been sick for a very long time, and my friend hadn't seen her very often in recent years. My friend's mourning seems endless. She's taken to her bed, is unable to do anything, and has enslaved her family by her endless tears.

No one asks for pain or loves it. But since it is inevitable, it matters a lot what we do with it — whether it does us in or helps us become more than we have been before.

Martin Gray wrote a book called *For Those I Loved.* It was the story of his lonely survival from a concentration camp, the rebuilding of his life, and then the loss of his wife and children in a fire. Since that time he has remarried and has another family. A new book by photographer David Douglas Duncan, *The Fragile Miracle of Martin Gray,* is a magnificent testament to the human spirit. In it, Martin Gray wrote:

> And when tragedy comes,
> as it will, we must take this
> suffering into our hands
> and, through willpower,
> transform it into a fruit
> that will nourish us
> as we begin life again.

I still miss my mother terribly, but that pain has helped me to grow and bloom, along with my mother's tree.

I Love You

IT'S A SAD FACT of life that many of us find it much harder to say "I love you" than to express our anger at each other. If you love somebody, *say* it. The telling will be good for *both* of you.

At first glance it may seem amazing that so many people who love each other hardly ever say so out loud. But maybe it's not so surprising, since the words "I love you" are probably the most complicated words we can ever say to each other.

Yesterday I had two telephone calls from friends. I was very busy, and I guess I sounded annoyed by both interruptions. The first time I asked if there was anything special on my friend's mind, and she said, "No, I just wanted to tell you that I love you," and she hung up. I felt a pleasant glow and went back to my work, making a note to call her back later in the day. When the telephone rang the second time, I explained immediately that I was in the middle of a tough writing assignment, and my friend interrupted and said, "I know, I know, you always have something more important to do than talk to me! I really love you and miss you and wish you had time for me." When I hung up I felt guilty and angry.

Whether or not we like to hear somebody else tell us that they love us depends on the message behind the words. Does "I love you" mean "I want to own you" or "I need something from you," or is it really an unconditional message of caring, without any strings attached? I certainly felt very differently about my two telephone calls, and that difference tells me something *I* need to know about saying "I love you."

When Betty said "I love you," I knew she wasn't asking for anything from me at that moment. She was just letting me know she'd been thinking of me. We both know how much we care for each other, and that sweet reminder nourished my spirits. Sarah, on the other hand, doesn't really love me, or she wouldn't resent my work. She wants my attention, and when she speaks of love I perceive it as entrapment.

One of the reasons some of us are scared of saying "I love you" is that we are afraid of becoming too vulnerable. Suppose the other person rejects us? We will feel horribly foolish and embarrassed.

If you can say "I love you," meaning only that and asking for nothing in return, it need not be the end of the world if the other person can't respond. Quite the contrary: It means that you are capable of the highest form of courage — the capacity to care more about someone else's need than your own. It means that despite the dangers of being rejected or misunderstood, you are willing to take a risk, to say the most brave and civilized thing we ever dare to say to each other. It's nice if the other person can enjoy it. It's even nicer to be the person who can say it.

Do It Now

HAVING TALKED ABOUT the courage it takes to say "I love you," I want to add a note of urgency. If you want to say it, do it *now.*

A woman wrote me the following story: She and her widowed father had had an argument some months ago. It was really over something quite trivial, but both their feelings had been badly hurt, and they hadn't spoken to each other since that time. Then she got a phone call that her father had had a stroke and was in the hospital. Driving there from her home three hundred miles away, she had a lot of time to think. She wrote me that she realized she and her father had always been able to hurt each other too easily because they cared so much about each other, and she was shocked to realize she had never told her father how much she loved him. When she got to the hospital, her father had died, and she began to weep uncontrollably, not only for his death but perhaps even more for the unspoken words. Then a nurse gave her a note, dictated by her father just before his death. The note said, "It's all right—I *know."*

I was deeply touched by the story. Even at the moment of dying, it is so hard for us to say what we really feel; yet, this letter was the best effort her father could make, and his words were a gift of comfort and love. But that's only part of the story. The deeper message is that none of us can ever afford to leave for tomorrow a message of loving and caring that we really want to send today. Sometimes we need a reminder of our mortality to help us reach across the complicated barriers of past memories and current misunderstandings in order to communicate what we really feel.

We ought never to wait for a Mother's Day, designated by Congress for the benefit of the flower and candy industries, to call up and say, "Hey, listen, Ma — I just felt like saying thank you for getting me through my nightmares and the measles and acne. I love you a lot!" If we feel like sending a friend a present on a Tuesday five months before a birthday, that's the moment to do it. It is *always* the right day to say "I'm sorry" if we lost our temper over something dumb.

It makes me terribly sad to think how many times I *didn't* tell my mother I loved her while she was alive. Since her death, I think about wanting to tell her that almost every day. The good thing about it is I have learned never to wait again.

Election Day

WHILE I CAN'T REMEMBER where I've left my glasses, or why I've walked from one room to another, I remember with absolute clarity the first time I voted. The voting place was in the basement of an apartment building around the corner, and I was terribly excited. The year was 1943, and we were living in constant grim anxiety, in the middle of World War II. But I had been raised to believe that the act of voting was a sacred right and trust, and that my coming of age was one of the most important days of my life. I wish more young people felt that way now.

It distresses me terribly to hear so many of them insisting that voting is purposeless because, after all, there is no difference between the Democratic and Republican parties, and all politicians are corrupt. It distresses me on two counts — first, because I think such cynicism is a great danger to a democracy, and second, because I can't help but understand how they feel. When I was young, there was a kind of idealistic innocence because we were shielded from knowing a great many things. The first time I voted, I had no idea what a terrible beating we'd been taking in the South Pacific, nor did I have any idea that Franklin Roosevelt had had a love affair. The wheeling and dealing, the political corruption during my young years was Rebecca-of-Sunnybrook-Farm time compared to what today's young people discover every day about the chicanery and greed behind the facade of so many politicians, to say nothing of the constant reports of such problems among our leaders as sexual deviation, marital infidelity, and kids with drug problems.

It's not easy to be an idealist in today's world. The more information one has, the harder it gets. I look back nostalgically to a time when ignorance made life easier, and the less I knew, the more fervent I could be in fulfilling my patriotic duty to vote.

But the truth of the matter is that I wouldn't want to go back to the past. It's better to know when we are in trouble, because then we can do something about it. Watergate surely proved that. And despite all the headlines about the frailties of our political leaders, the majority works hard and does good as it sees it. The temptations that come with power are so overwhelming that it's a miracle so many legislators stay reasonably honest and ethical.

And I have never found one single year when a vote didn't matter. There are always some fundamental differences between candidates. For example, no two presidents have ever been similar to each other in their choices for the Supreme Court, and that august body can change the whole climate of life within any given decade.

As for me, I'd never miss a chance to vote. It's one of my greatest privileges and just about the easiest thing I can do for my country.

Senility Is Remembering

I AM CONVINCED that most of what we too easily call senility is really *remembering*.

Many of us may have had the experience of talking to an elderly person and realizing he or she seems to be out of touch with what we are talking about. We ask a question, and the person mumbles about some childhood event that we cannot comprehend. I suspect that a great many people in nursing homes and homes for the aged are being tranquilized and drugged, and treated like infants, when the problem is simply that the closer each of us comes to our own dying, the more vivid become the memories of childhood. It is a process of reconnecting with one's past in order to set things straight — to figure out who we really are and what our life history has meant to us.

I am well aware of the fact that there are real physical changes with age, such as hardening of the arteries, which can cause a state of confusion. But I suspect we arrive at that medical diagnosis too often because we don't understand the normal, natural work of preparing for death.

Some years ago there was a very old lady who lived down the road from us when we had a summer cottage. She sat outdoors quite often, holding her pocketbook tightly on her lap, and next to her chair was a suitcase which she insisted on having close by, although it was actually empty. Each time we passed and said hello, she would tell us with great pleasure that she was waiting for her son to take her home. It became clear after a while that she was talking about a time and a place where she and her husband had lived while they were raising a family. She spoke as if her husband were still alive and her children still very young. If we took the time to listen, she was talking about what I imagine she felt to be the most important years of her life, when she felt most loved and most useful. It may have *seemed* crazy to hear her speak of her daughter's skinned knee and her husband's first Studebaker, but I think she was learning to accept the fact of her mortality by remembering those times and places that had given meaning to her life.

What we ought to be doing with people who we think have become senile is to encourage them to talk into a tape recorder, to tell us their stories. We might discover that we too can share a rich past we knew nothing about.

One of the best and most humane movements in this country is the growing number of hospices — places where people can live in peace when they are dying. The men and women who work in such places are learning how to be better listeners, and in many cases they are discovering some beautiful and touching life stories. It is a crime to keep old people from this natural process, and it deprives all of us of the richness of these voices that sing of the past.

Friendship

DRIVING ALONG A ROAD one day recently, I saw a sign which I'm sure was supposed to be helpful to drivers' safety, but which appealed to me on psychological grounds. The sign said, "Shoulder for emergency only." What it made me think about was friendship.

A friend is someone who always has a shoulder available for emergencies, and that is surely one of the great treasures of friendship — but of course there's more to it than that. The cultivation of genuine lifelong friendships is a high art, and it's surprising how little attention we focus on this human need.

There are three women who have been my friends for over fifty years. When I try to analyze how that has happened, it seems to me that a deep friendship has the same characteristics as a good marriage. We have interests in common, we share the same basic values — and then, beyond the points of similarity, we have learned to accept, even enjoy, each other's eccentricities. As in a successful marriage, we have a deep sense of each other's hopes and dreams and talents, and no matter how angry we may sometimes get at each other, always in the background, for each of us, is that feeling, "They see me as I really am and they love me anyway!"

The most profound friendships are a kind of unconditional love. You know that no matter how stupid or insensitive or mean you may sometimes be, you will not be deserted. Reprimanded — even yelled at, yes — but not abandoned.

Such friendships are possible even among relatives, and even some brothers and sisters manage to achieve this high level of human relationship, despite the normal rivalries of childhood. The main ingredients of these relationships seem to be mutual feelings of self-confidence, a high level of tolerance, and the sustaining belief in one's own and the other person's capacity to become more than we are at any given moment in time. It's a mutual dream for each other's fulfillment.

The ending of a friendship can be as painful as a death or divorce. There are times when one person grows and changes and the other doesn't; there are times when rivalry or envy or deep personal hurts destroy a relationship that was very important. At such a time we need to experience our grief and allow a period of mourning. We tend to take friendships so for granted that we underestimate the depth of our feelings for each other.

Learning how to be a friend and to allow someone else to be your friend is a very high art indeed, and it deserves our intelligence and creativity. A shoulder for emergencies is a special treasure and needs nurturing.

The Limits of Friendship

WHEN I MET A FRIEND for lunch recently, she apologized for yawning and not being quite as peppy as she usually was. She told me that a friend had called her up at three o'clock in the morning to tell her her problems, and had kept her on the phone for two hours. I assumed immediately that there had been some terrible emergency — the death of a child, an impending divorce, a fatal illness — some truly heartbreaking event that required immediate comfort. "Oh, no," said my friend, "Judy does this to me all the time. She has something on her mind, and she can't sleep, and she needs someone to talk to." My response was, "With a friend like that, you'll never need any enemies." I think there is an important distinction between genuine friendship and unacceptable exploitation.

There will always be people who take advantage of other people. If they can get away with it, I guess that's nice for them, and in any event, I don't think for a minute I could influence their behavior; but what I *am* concerned about are the *victims* of exploitation, because I think they can change *their* behavior.

The lady who doesn't complain about losing several hours of sleep one or two nights a week because her friend has insomnia has a big problem. She goes to work every day, is raising a daughter alone, and spends a good deal of time with an ailing and aged mother. Her big problem is that she can never say no to anyone's needs but her own. She's always available for the burdens of others — and, of course, word has gotten around. All the neighbors and relatives know that when anything goes wrong, Janet is always available — and with a smile and a hug and whatever else may be needed. Now, it's wonderful to be a sensitive, giving, loving human being, but as in every other aspect of life, balance is an essential. When we allow others to take advantage of our good natures, we are telling ourselves that we don't count, we don't matter — and that the only way we can get the love we need in our lives is by being a doormat saying "welcome" to anyone who wants to wipe his or her feet on us.

Janet happens to weigh over three hundred pounds. She has diabetes and high blood pressure. She's feeding herself food to make up for the lack of loving care she's not giving herself. She needs to call herself up in the middle of the night and scream, "Help!" — and see that she gets it. Real friendships are reciprocal. The day Janet can say, "I'm sorry, you can't call me at night unless there is a real emergency because I need my sleep," she'll be ready for genuine friendships.

When a Friendship Wears Out

I'VE SPOKEN OF the special joys of friendship and the art of cultivating lifelong friendships. But there is another side to the coin, and most of us have had to face the sad fact that a deep friendship has worn out. We need to experience our mourning and grief, and then let go.

Jennie and I were professional colleagues for about ten years. It was an enormously satisfying friendship. We were both raising young children at the time, and we helped each other through many crises. We respected each other's opinions, we loved going to the theater together, we shared some very private secrets with each other. And then I began to succeed at some things we didn't share. I wrote my first book; I was more often in demand for speaking engagements; I began appearing on television. Other people told me Jennie was jealous of me, but I didn't believe it. I had been so sure we would be friends for life. But in the course of the next year or so I had to begin to face the fact that something had gone wrong and that neither of us could set it right again, although we both tried, time after time. The events of life, as well as the differences in our patterns of growth and change, were wearing out our friendship, and finally, with terrible pain, we relinquished each other. It left a hole in both our lives, but I think it would have been worse to try to hang on.

Claire and I met while taking a summer course away from home. We had a marvelous time — we hiked together and laughed a lot, and told each other our life stories. We seemed to have so much in common, to agree about so many things, to share the same dreams — and we looked forward to meeting each other's families. Claire was at a low point in her life, and I wanted to help. But I allowed her to become too dependent on me, and, with my encouragement, our relationship gradually became that of mother and daughter. That wasn't a problem while we were away from home, but when the course was over, I began to see that Claire expected me to go on taking care of her and that she was furious when I indicated I had to go on with my own life. Two or three months after we were back home, I realized I had permitted Claire to have unrealistic expectations and that her dependency was a burden I wouldn't and couldn't assume. The relationship ended abruptly, and there are many pieces of it that I miss — but it wasn't wearing well and it would have been worse to hang on.

Each of us sooner or later comes to such a decision. We have to allow the grief, but then move on. It's sad, but it makes the lifetime friendships more precious.

When Children Take Over from Elderly Parents

"YOU'VE WRITTEN a book about the death of a parent," someone wrote me, "but what about when a parent just gets old and can't take care of herself? My ninety-two-year-old mother was still completely independent until she fell and broke her hip a year ago. She can't do anything for herself, but she refuses to stay in a nursing home. I've had to take over completely — she can't even pay her bills — but she won't tell me anything about her bank accounts. I'm the mother, and she's the child, and it's unbearable." I think that letter sums up very well the dilemma so many middle-aged people face. It's painful and frightening and frustrating when the roles shift and we find ourselves becoming our parents' parents. It's also unavoidable.

The first task we face is understanding our feelings as well as those of the elderly parent. Neither one wants to change roles. No matter how old we are, we still want to be children to our parents. When our own lives are the most difficult we often remember the years of our dependency with longing. We also need to understand that an elderly and increasingly dependent parent hates the role reversal as much or more than we do. When you have had a full and independent life as an adult, when you have been in charge for as much as half a century or more, it is unbearable to feel helpless, to lose one's autonomy. There is no way of eliminating this human drama, but it can be endured, even made into a special time of love and understanding, if we insist on *talking* about these feelings. It isn't easy to do it, but it is possible and necessary. Middle-aged children need to say, "Sometimes I wish I were still a little girl, and you were taking care of me again," and middle-aged children need to give their parents the encouragement and freedom to say, "I wish it were still that way, too." Sharing the agony of change is the only way we get through it with love and respect intact.

There are different styles of taking over, and that can make all the difference. John tells his father, "Listen, Dad, you have to tell me about your safe-deposit boxes because I'm in charge now." Jane says, "Daddy, I know it's hard, but we need to help each other. I want to help you to still make your own choices, but I can't do that unless I know what's possible." The same problem, but a difference in sensitivity. However dependent and helpless a parent may appear to be, the need for pride and respect is more important than food or medical attention. And no matter how old a child may be, he or she still longs to be comforted by a parent — and can be, if parent and child will only reach out to each other in these years of parting and share the agony of good-bye.

Selecting a Nursing Home

IF YOU ARE IN the very painful and stressful situation of having to select a nursing home for a sick or elderly relative, I have an important tip for you.

This is part of a letter I received recently. A man wrote, "One of the most striking things that happened had to do with the use of Mom's name and her mental health. When people at the hospital called her by her first name, it was a devastating assault on her dignity. At the first nursing home they called her 'Honey' and treated her like the village idiot. Questions were routinely addressed to me while Mom was right there in the room. We could see our mother slipping into a very withdrawn state. I moved her to another nursing home, where she was called by her last name and treated as someone with the ability to make her own decisions. She responded immediately and since then has made a wonderful recovery."

I think this son was a wise and sensitive observer. Our full name is an important symbol of our identity. When total strangers call us by our first names, especially if we happen to be sick or old, we feel infantilized. All of a sudden we have been demoted to childhood. Our life experiences, all that we have learned, our very identity is suddenly negated, wiped out.

Of course if someone stays in a nursing home for a long time and friendships develop with some of the staff, they may well arrive at a first-name relationship, but if I had to find such an institution for someone else — or for myself, as a matter of fact — one of the first criteria I would use for judging whether this was a good and decent and human place would be the respect and dignity with which patients were treated. Nothing ages us faster or makes us sicker than losing a sense of who we are.

It is true that a much greater social informality has made it possible for people to call each other by their first names far more quickly and comfortably than in the past, but there are some situations in which we need to be reassured that we are clearly seen as special, worthy of respect and dignified attention.

Given the choice between a not-so-perfectly-clean and somewhat rundown place where people are treated with great dignity, and a very clean and well-organized place where new arrivals are greeted as "Betty" or "Jim" or "Honey," I'd take the first place. What's in a name? At certain crucial moments, everything.

What Is a Woman?

A FRIEND OF MINE who was trying to explain how she felt about some feminist issue said, "But of course you're not a feminist, so I don't think you can understand what I'm talking about." A few minutes later I did a double take. I've been a working woman all of my adult life; I've been married to the same man for thirty-seven years, and he still seems pleased to find me on the other side of the bed; and I have a grown daughter who is my best friend. If that's not feminist, somebody better tell me what is!

The woman who started this whole train of thought worked for a few years before she had children. Then she was a marvelous and devoted wife and mother, but now that her children are grown she appears to be quite paralyzed. The only thing she seems to do with any enthusiasm is to *talk* about the feminist movement.

There needed to be a revolution for women's rights, but to tell you the truth, I'm getting pretty sick and tired of all the clichés about women. As human beings all women ought to have human rights and equality of opportunity. That's hard to get, and I respect the struggle. I'm certainly for equal rights — but while too many women are talking about getting what men have and about the joys of sisterhood, pre-adolescent models are what's supposed to be alluring and feminine. At the same time that women report on sexism, the whole country is obsessed with the rear view of tight bluejeans. *Real* women seem to me to have become an endangered species, lost somewhere between thirteen-year-old Lolita types and aggressive, self-consciously purposeful women who never relax and just enjoy themselves.

I have a friend who is sixty years old. Her hair is gray, she wears no makeup, she is about forty pounds overweight, she wears sloppy old clothes — and a perfectly darling young man of thirty-seven is absolutely crazy about her. She's a rip-roaring character, so full of life and love and talent that she just knocks you out, for being around her is so exciting. She's a talented sculptor, a terrific cook, and an adored grandma, and she just lives, without wondering or worrying about being a woman. That's why I think she *is* one.

The problem of equality is surely not to be taken lightly, and there are necessary readjustments — often very painful and difficult — to be made between men and women; but I sure look forward to the time when women can become less self-conscious about their rights and can enjoy just being as fully human and as womanly as they can be. Then we might stop treating adolescent infants like women and be able to recognize the real thing.

Thanksgiving: Preparations

I HAVE AN ABSOLUTELY FOOLPROOF METHOD by which you can enjoy your family Thanksgiving dinner more than ever before.

The secret of a really sensational family gathering on Thanksgiving is to go through some mental exercises the day before the event. You have just the time you need to get ready.

The first mental exercise is to accept the fact that there is nothing you can do to make Uncle Charlie stop slurping his soup; it's just one of those family traditions you might as well sit back and enjoy.

The second exercise is to tell yourself that while you absolutely adore your children and/or your grandchildren, you are not a depraved person if, by seven o'clock in the evening, you wish they'd all go home. You need to assure yourself that if you can avoid raising your voice more than ten times in the face of spilled gravy, rock-and-roll on a transistor radio in the pantry, four people who insist on helping when they increase the confusion and double your workload, burned sweet-potato pie, and several children competing over who can do the best cartwheel in the doorway between the kitchen and the dining room, you surely ought to be up for sainthood.

A third exercise is recognizing those things you cannot change on Thanksgiving day or any other day. Those two adult sisters who have been jealously competing with each other for thirty-five years probably won't stop on Thanksgiving Day. And that old wound, that fight over somebody's will that still festers between two branches of the family—well, you'd best settle for civilized politeness. They're just never, ever going to be crazy about each other, and that's that.

The fourth mental exercise is to prepare yourself in advance for the questions you're not going to want to answer—for example, when your rich cousin wants to know how much you paid for your new car, making it quite clear he disapproves of your extravagance. And then there's that four-year-old who has just begun exploring all the wonders of life and, while you have a mouthful of stuffing, says, "Grandma, are you and Grandpa going to make any more babies?" You see, if you anticipate the questions, you won't choke on what you're eating; you'll have some suave and sophisticated answers ready.

And finally, the most important mental preparation for a joyous Thanksgiving with all your loved ones is to remember that you will be just as glad to see them all leave as you were to see them arrive.

Thanksgiving: The Macy Parade

THERE ARE DAYS when the levels of noise and carbon monoxide in New York City have me dreaming about a permanent escape from my hometown, but I could never leave altogether for one simple reason: the Thanskgiving Day Macy Parade. It nourishes my soul.

I've been watching the Macy Parade since it started. When I was a child we lived in an apartment house overlooking an empty field, where the first balloons were blown up. That's so far back that there was so little air traffic, the balloons would be let loose after a parade, and one could see them floating off, flapping their ears or wings or tails or whatever they had.

I've missed a year here or there, but never without considerable suffering. There was a day a few years ago when I was just about ready to kill myself: The puppeteer, Bil Baird, had a float in the parade and was going to let me ride on it, but I had the flu and a temperature of 103 that morning, and it was pouring outside. My friends still reminisce from time to time about the depths of despair to which I descended on that ignominious day.

The reason I'm so utterly happy at the parade is that, first of all, it's one of the few parades where there are no guns and soldiers, and second, that it is a parade totally devoted to childhood. We grown-ups have the perfect excuse for allowing ourselves to become children again; and watching the faces of mothers and fathers and kids screaming with delight at the clowns, waving to familiar fairytale characters, and laughing with delight when the ropes holding Mighty Mouse or the Dragon get stuck in the lamp posts remind me once again that we come about as close to being civilized as we ever are when we can allow ourselves to be childlike.

Standing among the crowds watching the parade, for one hour out of the year nobody in New York is mad at anyone. Nobody is afraid. Strangers talk to each other, help each other out. An older man who wishes he were a grandfather offers to take a turn carrying a child on his shoulders when the father standing next to him gets tired. A young woman offers the mother standing next to her some tissues for the runny nose of her four-year-old. Old-timers tell the first-timers that you know it's over when Santa Claus appears. The police on duty all act like daddies, and if it's cold, people bring them coffee.

And then I watch thousands of parents and children pouring down the subway steps, with all the paraphernalia of parade watching — scattered smears of mustard, a few tears over busted balloons, a little struggle about who gets to carry the peanuts — and as I watch, I know that, for this magical moment, nobody is mugging anyone, and the city is safe. Such are the wonders of childhood and love, and of the best parade in town.

Windowless Offices

DO YOU WORK in an office without windows? Do you often feel jumpy, irritable, depressed? There may be a connection! I don't think that the architects of all the office buildings which have been built in the past twenty-five years were aware of the dangers involved in putting people into boxes. They were so overcome with excitement over the new wonders of fluorescent lighting and air conditioning, they were so ecstatic about the money that could be saved by the use of internal space, that I think they forgot we were *not* like white rats, who seem to live quite comfortably without knowing whether it's day or night or whether beach sandals or boots are the order of the day.

One of the stresses of modern life is the way in which technology has encouraged technicians to stop looking at us as members of the human species. I think we have a basic human need to be in touch with the outside world of nature, but it is too late to cry over spilled concrete.

What we have to do is humanize our surroundings as best as we can. Plastic plants won't help, but I have a friend whose office looks like a jungle; she's got whole trees growing there. Another friend has a diagram of his *family* tree on the wall, going back about four generations, with pictures of as many of his ancestors and current relatives as he can find. Two different approaches to setting roots!

You need to think very carefully about what it might be that will make you feel you are not merely in a *working* room but in a *living* room. How about bringing in your favorite painting or sculpture? Or souvenirs of your travels? Another friend has a wallboard for recipes he wants to remember to try. A sampler with a favorite saying embroidered on it is another possibility. One that appealed to me on an office wall said, "Don't worry. Nothing will be all right!"

What I'd really like to do is get those architects back to the old drawing board. If their technology is so great, they could at least give us fake windows — a section of glass covering an inset area about four inches in depth, with a background screen on which could be projected whatever scene and weather there was outside or whatever weather you happen to like best. It could all be done with computers and buttons to make the technicians happy, and as we looked at our artificial outdoors, we could at least be reminded that a weekend in the *real* country is available when the stress gets too heavy. The best antidote to the windowless world is to remember to do *a lot of looking around* whenever you can.

Laying a Trip on a Trip

WE HAVE ALL BECOME familiar with the expression "Don't lay your trip on me." Sometimes it may be an evasion of responsibility, an avoidance of helping another person. Sometimes it is an accurate and justified announcement. I just heard a story about how one couple got away with laying their trip on another couple while they were all on a trip.

Millie is a friend of mine who was recently widowed. While reminiscing about her life with her husband, Martin, she happened to mention a time when the two of them had taken a trip to New England with another couple. She told me, "It was the strangest thing that ever happened to us! From the moment we got in the car with Phyl and Dave, we began fighting with each other. Of course Martin and I had our arguments and misunderstandings — but this time it was different. Neither of us could have told you what in the world we were so mad about — it was really crazy! We ended up not speaking to each other, had a perfectly miserable time, and Phyl and Dave kept trying to reason with us; but I wouldn't even sleep in the same motel room with Martin, and he wouldn't go with us to the beach.

"When we got home and were dropped off in front of our house, suddenly everything was fine! We began laughing hysterically, and we *never* were able to figure out what in the world we were fighting about!"

I asked Millie how soon after that trip Phyl and Dave were divorced. She looked at me as if I had suddenly become a gypsy fortune teller. "Now, how did you know *that?*" she asked me. No tea leaves, no crystal ball — what Millie had just described to me is one of those fascinating and mysterious events which we don't fully understand but which occur frequently enough to be identified. Phyl and Dave were putting on a wonderful front of being the happy, loving couple, but under that surface a terrible storm was brewing. There had been awful battles, and they had already talked about separation. Millie and Martin were unconsciously picking up the denied tension and anger, and, also quite unconsciously, they picked up the load, the "trip," of their companions and were acting out for them.

Next time you get unusually angry or feel a great deal of stress — especially when you are in very close proximity to others — and these feelings come up very suddenly and feel inappropriate, you'd better look around and see if persons who can't deal with their feelings are laying a trip on you, and whether you have unconsciously played the nice guy and picked it up. If that's what's happening, you're doing somebody else's work for them, and that won't help *anybody*. "Don't lay your trip on me!" is a necessary response in such situations.

Envy

WE USUALLY THINK of envy as a sin, something bad we ought not to feel. I think that depends on the sorts of things you find yourself envying in other people.

When I was a child there was a very rich little girl in my class. At her birthday party she sat on a throne covered with flowers, and she had a dollhouse with running water and electricity. The furnishings included a tiny vacuum cleaner that *worked*, which was pretty good, considering that this was in the middle of the Depression and few people had *real* vacuum cleaners. I thought I'd die if I never had a dollhouse like that.

Well, of course I didn't die, and when I grew up I found out that she was a rich little girl because her father was a bootlegger during Prohibition, with very shady connections in the underworld, and I concluded with remarkable maturity — at least by the age of thirty-five — that I had been much better off being the daughter of a poor but honest lawyer!

The most common, garden-variety type of envy usually has to do with things other people have which we think we want desperately. We assume that if we had a house with a two-car garage, had lots of money in the bank, belonged to the best golf club, and had three fur coats, life would be perfect. Every once in a while, we get a sudden jolt of reality when we see that the people who *have things* seem to be just about as unhappy as anyone else, but we soon talk ourselves out of the facts and go back to envious dreaming.

A more significant kind of envy comes from deep inside, where we hurt the most. We envy certain characteristics in other people because of what we hate in ourselves. The tall, thin, gorgeous, young redheads are few and far between whom I haven't envied with a passion at one time or another because of my painful assessment of my physical self. We envy people who have the qualities we wish we had, and in that sense envy can tell us a good deal about ourselves, our hang-ups, and our dreams.

I find that the older I get, the less I envy things, or other people's beauty, or even their talents. What I envy are the qualities I wish I had that would make me a better person. I envy a friend who had the courage to protest against racial discrimination during the 1950s and spent several months in jail; I was never that brave. I envy another friend who never allows any social obligations to interfere with his work; I wish I had this self-directed willpower. I envy people who are more patient than I am, who tolerate frustration with more grace, and who don't blow off steam quite as loudly as I sometimes do. I envy people who have the courage of their convictions, have a sense of history, and who maintain their integrity even if that makes them un-popular.

If you are going to be envious, then let it be for qualities you wish you had—and use your envy to get there.

Holiday Dieting: Forget It!

THE PROPER DIET for the holiday season is no diet at all. I never heard of anyone who succeeded in losing weight between December fifteenth and January first. I'll eat my calorie counter if anyone can produce such a paragon of virtue. There is a good reason *not* to go on a diet between Christmas and New Year's, and you may now go get a fattening snack from the kitchen before I continue.

The main reason for not going on a diet during the holiday season is that it won't work, you won't enjoy yourself, and you'll be drowning in guilt, which is very high in calories. But even more important, the best way *to get ready* to go on a diet is to give yourself a little loving kindness first, a little compassion — the permission to enjoy life fully and intensely for a short period of time. The secret of later success with a post-holiday diet is to really savor this festive season — don't stint on being a greedy glutton. If you later regret the things you didn't eat, you will never be able to stick to your diet. Happy memories are much more helpful.

You have to not diet with a full and open heart. If, every time you take a drink of eggnog or eat a piece of Christmas fruitcake, you think to yourself, "I'm a rotten, weak, miserable excuse for a human being, and I deserve to be ugly and fat," you will feel too guilty about your inevitable transgressions and will never have a genuine feeling of well-being, no matter how good the stuffing or plum pudding may be. If you say to yourself, "I'm really a wonderful person, and it's a shame I gain weight so easily, and it's unfair I have to live with that painful truth — I deserve a really good time before I come back to reality and get down to business," chances are that you will have had enough fun to endure the later discomforts and deprivations of dieting. Two weeks of pleasure with no strings attached — no anger at yourself, no guilt, no self-condemnation — are the best route to a happy stomach and a satisfied soul, and the perfect Christmas present.

On January second there will be all those lovely memories to keep you company during the lean days. For a week or two you'll just have to wear your baggiest clothes to cover your holiday sinning. I'm convinced, from a long life of facing that moment of truth on the bathroom scale, that if we give ourselves permission to "pig out" once in a while for a limited amount of time, we will gain less than if we try to be good when the Christmas cookies come around. If we are enjoying ourselves, we don't eat as much as we would if we were miserable while we were eating.

Self-denial works best when it is carefully planned at the most appropriate times — and between January and the chocolate Easter bunny is plenty of time to do the job!

Lending Money

SOMEONE WROTE TO ME recently that she had lent a friend some money and was having a very hard time getting it back. She wrote, "It's only fifty dollars, but I have a hard time budgeting my salary, and I resent it. I know it's going to spoil our relationship. I've tried joking, and being serious, but no matter what I do there's always another excuse. What can I do?" Not an awful lot, I'm afraid, but here are some suggestions for people who might be asked for a loan at some future time.

Mixing money and friendship is a very difficult thing to do and rarely works out very well. Some years ago, when a friend asked to borrow some money from me, I decided to give her only the amount that I would be willing to give her as a gift if she were in trouble. She was always in financial hot water, and I was sure the money would never be returned — but it never affected our relationship, and I never felt resentful, because I had considered it a gift from the beginning.

If someone you really care about a great deal wants to borrow more than you could spare as a gift, it seems to me it's a wise idea to make the arrangements through a third party — someone objective, who isn't directly involved. A lawyer can set up a legal agreement and then be the intermediary if the friend or relative defaults on the loan. Even in as close a relationship as parent and child, the objective outsider can be a great help. One father told me that he wanted to lend his son the money to go to a school for auto mechanics, and he was even willing to help him buy his own garage, but he knew that if things didn't work out smoothly, it would ruin what was thus far a good relationship. Instead of giving him the money directly, he set up a loan to be administered by his bank. "This way," he told me, "my son is fully aware of how serious his responsibility is, and I know that the bank will not tolerate any of the kinds of things a son might expect a father to put up with, nor, on the other hand, will they be as demanding as I might be."

An occasional small loan to someone who is thoroughly reliable may turn out all right, but we need to be wary of the compulsive borrower who sees money as a symbol of love. The unconscious bargain you are making with such a person is that you love him when you lend it, and you are rejecting him when you want it back. We need to try to avoid getting caught in that unfair game. If it happens, and if repeated requests for the return of the loan go unanswered, we have the choice of silently turning it into a gift or going through legal channels. At that point we have to weigh our financial loss against the loss of the relationship. But the best solution is to lend only in dire need and whenever possible to consider it a gift.

Oh, My Aching Back!

THERE ARE FEW MISERIES that occupy more of our thoughts than backaches. The more stressful life becomes, the more I wish I'd bought stock in a heating-pad company! There are, of course, serious medical problems in some back troubles, and people with chronic back pain certainly ought to seek medical advice and counsel. But what I'd like to discuss now are the backaches that start in the head bone.

It took me quite a long time to notice that my chronic episodes of severe back pain always began *before* I moved from one home to another. Not a single box lifted, no couch pushed from wall to wall, no bending into barrels; before all that even started, I would begin to feel twinges that turned into spasms that turned into days and nights of agony. My early explanations were that we were about to move, until a friendly psychologist had the audacity to point out to me that the pain started *before* the packing. I was furious at her, naturally.

The difficulty with back troubles is that very often there *is* some physical problem at the coccyx of the trouble. Some old injury from a fall, a slightly slipped disk, muscle strain from poor exercising can start the ball rolling, but stress, fatigue, anger, and a whole assortment of mental and emotional problems then make excellent use of whatever the weak spot may be. After a careful medical checkup, what we need to do is check out the relationship between the spinal column and the events in our lives.

Let me give an example. About twenty-five years ago, a woman I know was walking down a snowy hill. There was ice under the snow, and she fell very hard on her tailbone, or coccyx. There was enough real injury to cause a number of weeks of genuine discomfort, which ended eventually after heat treatments and painkillers and many consultations. For the next fifteen years, she had occasional episodes of severe back pain, some lasting for six to eight weeks, during which the pain was simply terrible and living came to a standstill. The muscle spasms were so severe that she could not imagine anything but a physical cause for such agony.

But for the past ten years this woman has had no backaches of any consequence, beyond an occasional reminder of past misery after sleeping on a lousy mattress or overdoing some exercise. The reason for this remarkable change was that she finally dealt with the fact that her backaches were mostly a way of saying, "Get off my back!" when too many people were making too many demands on her. The old injury served as the weak spot for release of tension — anger at the world, exhaustion, a feeling of being exploited by others. When these reactions were finally faced through psychotherapy, the backaches diminished. The spasms of emotion returned to the head, where they had started, leaving the muscles relaxed and happy.

I know this case very well and recommend psychological X rays as a possible means of relief, because this lady was me!

Men Who Are Allergic to Commitment

ALL OF MY WIDOWED and divorced women friends, from thirty to sixty, tell me a good man is just about impossible to find. They aren't looking for Prince Charming — just somebody nice, with a capacity for caring. I gather the woods are full of men interested in a one- or two-night stand, but the word that terrifies, even disgusts, them is *commitment*. I suspect that a whole lot of men think freedom is an end in itself. In the end, that's all they will have, and I think they will find it very cold comfort.

Relationships between men and women have been shaken up so dramatically over the past few decades that it's hard to figure out what is really happening. But my impression is that, with some exceptions, women have come to the conclusion that it is possible to be a free and self-fulfilling person within a love relationship; and men, with some exceptions, have come to the conclusion that self-fulfillment is possible only if you carefully avoid caring about anyone too much. It may be that we will have to face the painful conclusion that there *are* some basic differences, biological in origin, between men and women, and that perhaps the earlier social structures and strictures — such as early and permanent marriages — that have been dominant in human history represented this inner wisdom. Or — which seems more likely to me — women may have adapted more quickly and easily to a more open society, in which commitment is self-chosen, because biology demands a certain amount of commitment from them in relation to childbearing. Or perhaps women are still more encased in the attitudes of the past.

Whatever the contributing factors, I am saddened by the singleness of so many of the women I know, who seem to be making one of two choices. Either they have settled for loneliness and celibacy, or they have settled for whatever brief encounters they can find. I have been especially saddened when these choices have been made by close personal friends.

But I am far more sorry for the men they meet: the men who live in single splendor, never dating anyone long enough to get emotionally involved, reporting gleefully that they are gloriously free of the encumbrances of women who want to be loved.

I tell my single women friends to be patient. These men who are so allergic to commitment are apparently slower learners than they are. But sooner or later I think they will figure out that the freedom to remain unloved is a hollow and lonely freedom, happily rejected by children and other living things.

Battered Wives, Husbands, and Children

DESPITE ALL THE SOCIAL PROBLEMS that beset us, *some* things *have* been getting better! There are quite a few problems that we are now facing more openly and offering more help for, and one of these areas is what happens to battered and abused wives.

Nobody gets beaten up repeatedly without cooperating, and abusive husbands and battered wives are more alike than they sometimes realize. What they share in full measure is self-hate.

A friend of mine, a nursery-school teacher, is involved in a special research project in a western state. Whenever physical abuse is reported to the police and the courts, the judge sends the husband, the wife, and the children to a Family Learning Center. Here skilled therapists and teachers and social workers try to find the cause of the violence. What my friend reported to me was that she was finding that the husbands who were beating up wives and children were often compulsively repeating treatment they had received when they were children, and that in many cases their feelings of unworthiness, of being horrible, unlovable, terrible people were even greater than those of their wives.

Women who allow themselves to be physically abused also often have a history of such treatment as children and unconsciously feel that in some way they deserve exactly what they get.

If husbands and wives want to know why they feel it is their fault if they got beaten as children, all they have to do is look at their own battered children. When they begin to get help, they are almost always shocked to discover that *their* children also assume they must deserve to be abused. One father, part of the research project, said, "I heard what made me a beater by listening to my seven-year-old son talking to the shrink in family therapy. I'm sitting right there, and the doc asked Joel why he thinks I hit him so hard, and Joel says, 'I guess because I'm so bad.' I started yelling, 'No you're not — it's me, it's me —' and suddenly I realized my kid and I are the same."

All children tend to blame themselves for anything that goes wrong; it's just the way a child's mind works. Adults who are emotionally ill — and beaters and their victims are in that category — are people who hate themselves because they think they must have deserved the bad treatment they got.

The solution to the problem for any member of such a family is to run to the nearest telephone and call the agencies in your community which offer help. In the mutual search for feelings of self-worth every member of the family will learn that no human being *ever* deserves being abused.

Old-Age Homes

MY AUNT ADA really had a rough time of it. She had lived in the same apartment in the Bronx for over forty years, until it became obvious she would have to move because it had become a slum area. Long-since widowed, she couldn't afford an apartment, and so she went to an old-people's home, at the age of seventy-nine. There she met a lovely man of eighty-three with a heart condition, and they fell madly in love. But the only place they could kiss each other was in the elevator if they stopped it between floors. Aunt Ada had a roommate, so there was no privacy there. The boyfriend had a room of his own, but this didn't work out because it was a rule of the institution that no unmarried people could ever be in the same room without the door being open! Please don't get the idea this was a really lousy home: It was one of the best in the area, and this kind of thinking is rampant all over the country.

Grown children also seem inclined to make it very difficult for the elderly to go on being full human beings. The reversal of roles is astonishing. Now it is the grown children who worry about their parents' involvements, and are embarrassed and ashamed of any indication that their parents are still sexual beings. Many elderly people say with considerable bitterness that, in addition to the fact that their children cannot accept them as sexual beings, another major factor in their disapproval is that the children are afraid a new involvement will disrupt the passing on of wealth to those who are waiting around for it. One old man told me, ''Not only is my son worried I might leave something to my girlfriend – he's also unhappy because he sees that being in love is making me young again, and, who knows, I might live a long time!''

Very bitter indeed, but where there is smoke, we had best look for the people who are stamping out our fires, the ardor of our later years.

When I get too old to manage to live on my own, I may have to start my own old-age home if I can't find the right one. Men and women would be treated like the adults they are, with all the rights and dignities that go with that. I hope a time will come when younger people and institutions will encourage older people to enjoy life to the fullest, so I won't have to start my own old-age home.

There are a few such places, I'm happy to report. I'm especially fond of a hospital for the aged and terminally ill that has a coffee house and a singles bar right on the premises. I may make a reservation for myself any day now.

Taking Pictures on Trips

I RECENTLY CAME BACK from a trip to Europe and my impression is that very few people believe in *real* life anymore. I think an obsessive pre-occupation with camera angles may be distorting the human picture.

We were standing on a mountain top, looking down at a lovely green valley, a charming medieval town, and a beautiful lake. About seventy-five percent of the people on our bus tour never actually saw what my husband and I were looking at — except through the lens of a camera. One man was nearly hysterical because he couldn't find the right angle to get a picture of his wife and also include all the back-ground scenery. He finally talked her into climbing over the wall and hanging on to a tree, so he could get the full picture. If she'd lost her grip she would have been out of the picture forever. The tour guide needed a tranquilizer after the lady had been successfully dragged back over the wall. She could have fallen down a sixty-foot drop, but her husband was furious that his camera work had been interfered with. ''Now we'll never see that view!'' he shouted indignantly at the guide.

I was entranced. What he meant was that he'd never have a slide at home on which he could look at the scenery. And I could understand how badly he felt, because he most certainly would never have any *memory* of that view.

Of course it's nice to come home with some souvenir pictures of one's adventures, to look at later if one can avoid boring all one's friends and relations. But the single-minded intensity with which people travel *in order to take pictures* instead of experiencing life directly seems to me to be a painfully accurate metaphor for the way life is today. We have become so intrigued with technology, with machinery, that we often substitute the machine for real life. Playing a computerized baseball game seems to me to fall into the same category.

There are quite enough stresses and strains in life today without deliberately adding unnecessary ones.

Human beings cannot survive on substitutes for living without paying a heavy price. If all we have at the end of a vacation trip is two hundred pictures, we are not likely to feel very relaxed, refreshed, or rested. In order to experience those nice human feelings, we need to *look* at the world around us, with a hidden camera in our own heads. That camera records not only the landscape but how we *felt* about it—a very different kind of picture, and one that is essential to a living memory book.

Holiday Depression

I RECENTLY READ an article in a medical journal by a psychiatrist who announced that, through various research experiments, he had concluded that there is no such thing as holiday depression. ''The popular conception of holiday depression can be readily dismissed as a derivation of the soap opera,'' he wrote.

Can you *believe* that? It seems clear to me that the man must have been smoking mistletoe instead of hanging it! Post-holiday depression seems to me to be not only very prevalent but entirely normal. It is a syndrome brought on by the spoiling turkey bones in the refrigerator, the six-inch pile of bills on the desk, the five-pound gain indicated on the bathroom scale, and the feeling of letdown that I think hits most of us when the parties are over.

Whether you celebrate Christmas or Chanukah or any other mid-winter festival, it seems to me that in order to survive the holiday season with as few scars as possible it's a good idea to acknowledge the fact, in advance, that a certain amount of manic depression is built into the festivities. How could it be otherwise? There is all that racing around, fighting the mobs in the stores, wondering how long it will take to pay for the kids' toys, and then discovering that despite all your clever maneuvers to settle the matter differently, *yours* is the house chosen by eighteen of your favorite relatives and friends for the big, annual dinner reunion.

There is all that hysterical thumbing through the women's magazines for something new to cook instead of the same old standbys, and then there are the heavy bags of food to shift from the car trunk to the kitchen counter, in order to cook all the same old traditional things, after all. And there's the housecleaning, and the decorating, and the overexcited and sleepless kids who want to wait for Santa Claus — and then, finally, there's the day itself. It turns out that one brother and one sister-in-law aren't speaking to each other, and grandma is terribly hurt and disappointed because junior isn't as thrilled as she expected him to be about the new green bathrobe, and three expensive toys are busted by noon, and if anyone else comes into the kitchen, you know you are going to lose control and come at them with a rolling pin, and by the time dinner is served and indigestion has set in, you wonder what's so great about holidays, and it takes at least a week to recover.

Well, it *is* worth it; you just have to accept that joy and disappointment are inevitable partners. The happier we are, preparing for something, the farther we fall when it cannot possibly live up to our expectations. We human beings can never live up to the fairytales we weave — but there are some funny, sweet memories, too, and after a while what we remember is being close and warm with people we love, at the darkest time of the year.

Will You Leave a Hole in the World?

I HAVE TALKED several times about the ways in which we need to deal with grief and mourning when somebody we love dies. It is one of the great miracles of the human experience that each of us is so unique, so special, that we leave a hole in the world when we die. Or do we? In facing the inevitability of our own mortality, it seems to me that we need to focus our attention on leaving the biggest hole in the world we possibly can when we are gone, for when we do this, we will stop being afraid. Our attention will be on living, and dying will take care of itself.

Some years ago, I mentioned to my psychotherapist that a friend who had recently died had left a gaping hole in my universe. She suggested that I was adding to my grief by feeling such a sense of deprivation. What I should have been doing was celebrating how much this friend had added to my life — how much richer I was for having known and loved him. It seems to me both are true feelings and go together. What they have in common is the profound sense of the uniqueness of each person — that nobody can ever replace anybody. Life goes on, and it may be full of new joys and satisfactions; but the loss of any one person is unique. People are not interchangeable.

I have tried to learn to live with the holes in my life by constantly reminding myself that this sense of loss is accompanied by deep gratitude that I knew someone who mattered so much and meant so much to me. But in the course of grieving it has occurred to me that not all deaths are equal. Some people leave a bigger hole in my life than others; some people have given me far more to miss than others.

The more I have thought about this, the more it has seemed to me that I could come to terms with my own fears of death and dying. The thing to do was to spend my life trying to leave the biggest hole in the world that I could possibly leave. That meant focusing my full attention on doing the very best work I could possibly do; it meant loving and caring a whole lot about the important people in my life; it meant doing as little damage to others as I could possibly do; it meant using my talents, my energy, my self for living as fully as possible, so that when I die, others will feel the loss of me — and at the same time will feel grateful for whatever special something I may have brought into their lives.

This quest leaves us far too busy to worry about the inevitable conclusion — and in the process will hopefully enrich some other people's lives.

Christmas Letters

JUST ON THE OFF CHANCE that you might have me on your list for one of those mimeographed family news letters which come enclosed in a Christmas card, do me a favor — don't send it. I hate to sound like Scrooge, but few things make me feel less merry or full of Christmas cheer.

Here is a brief summary of a dozen such letters I've gotten over the past few years: "We're all just fine and hope you are too. George just got a terrific promotion, and, after raising our wonderful family of four, Judy is now hard at work getting her master's in music education. Donald was Phi Beta Kappa from Harvard last June and is now attending the Yale Law School. Howard is in his last year of high school and has already had early acceptance at three colleges. Suzie is married to a wonderful young man who will probably call you one of these days because he's an up-and-coming insurance salesman, and of course the best thing about this Christmas is Jenny's two-year-old, who has turned us into such doting grandparents."

If the truth were known, George's promotion means he'll be traveling almost all the time, and Judy is boiling mad. She's also not quite sure why she's working for a degree in music when what she thinks she'd really enjoy now is going into politics. Everybody is sighing with relief about Donald, because he had a nervous breakdown during his second year of college. Howard was once arrested for selling marijuana in junior high school, Suzie's husband is very hard-working but something of a bore, and Jenny's two-year-old was an unexpected accident, resulting from a brief and exotic, but definitely unrealistic, love affair.

In case you hadn't noticed, I'm exaggerating, of course, but what really bugs me about those chatty letters is that they are much too cheerful — there is so much denial of the real ups and downs of human life. It wears me out to just think of all the energy it must take to work so hard at denying human frailty. *Nobody,* but *nobody,* has a life of permanent bliss. All of us have our moments of joy and exultation as well as despair and misery. If you have to send me a Christmas letter, I'm willing to share your joys, but only if you will acknowledge that your life is just like mine — sometimes wonderful and sometimes terrible. Too much sweet plum pudding can cause a diabetic coma.

Reflections on Thirty-seven Years of Marriage

I GOT REALLY MAD the other day. I received a letter from a young man, in his mid-thirties, who told me he was getting married. He wrote, "Jenny and I have been living together very happily for five years. The only reason we're getting married is that we've decided we would like a child, and we think life is easier for children if their parents are married. But neither of us really wants to get married, and we worry a lot about whether or not marriage will ruin our relationship." I'm still so angry I'm afraid I may go into cardiac arrest unless I tell you how I feel — especially on my thirty-seventh wedding anniversary!

What makes me so angry is that young people have a choice to make about what they see and hear and believe, and often they turn toward the most negative facts instead of the positive ones. Peter, who wrote me this letter, is typical of this problem. His parents made a mess of their marriage, were never divorced, but imprisoned each other in misery. A couple of aunts and uncles got messy divorces, and, of course, Peter knows that in his age group divorce is almost as common as marriage. A jaundiced view of marriage is surely not impossible, if you feel inclined to search for the worst. On the other hand, Peter has known me and my husband for a long time. He knows we've been married for thirty-seven years and that, while we have struggled often and painfully, we have never given up on ourselves or each other. I know that Peter admires us a lot. How come he is so terrified of marriage, when there are role models that represent a positive side of marriage? A lot of his uncles and aunts are happily married, and, even in his own generation, if he wants to look in that direction, he can find plenty of couples knocking themselves out to understand each other, to make accommodations and adjustments, and to keep their marriages fresh and alive, growing and changing.

If Peter and Jenny are so full of misgivings, I'm worried about their getting married and having a child. Married life and parenthood are so tough and so demanding, and take so much courage, sensitivity, and patience, that it seems to me you have to want it desperately to make it work.

My husband and I are startled most of the time, these days. Neither of us really understands why we continue to find each other so mysterious, so fascinating, so unpredictable. It has suddenly occurred to me that our marriage is just about the same age as Peter is, and therein lies the secret. We have changed as dramatically and as purposefully as Peter has. He has gone from being a helpless infant to a grown man — the most remarkable process of growth and change we know about. When a marriage can grow and change with equal intensity, struggling from infancy to maturity, there's nothing better that can ever happen to human beings. I hope Peter and Jenny can learn that their growing up is just beginning.

Games the Unconscious Plays

THE OTHER MORNING, as I was putting my keys into my change purse, I thought to myself, "I really shouldn't keep so many keys on one key ring, because if I lose them, it will mean replacing about seven keys." The day was long and tiring; I had to stop at about five different stores, and I went to the dentist and the foot doctor. By that time I was so tired that I decided to splurge by taking a cab home, but before getting a cab I made one last stop at a cheese store to get my husband his favorite cheese. I'm sure you can anticipate what happened.

When I got into my apartment building, my keys, and the change purse they were in, were gone. My morning thoughts had been a self-fulfilling prophecy — and in that moment of truth, I knew I had to make a choice. I could either get hysterical and furious at myself for such stupidity, or I could try to figure out what message I was giving myself and learn from the experience. While I waited for the elevator man to let me into my apartment, I went over the events of the day, and it didn't take me too long to figure out that my unconscious was sending me a message, loud and clear: I had punished myself because I knew at some deeper level of consciousness that I was trying to do far too much, that I was refusing to acknowledge my fatigue, and that I was doing too many things for other people instead of meeting my own needs. Having realized in the morning that losing the key chain would be a real pain in the neck, I gave myself this punishment in the late afternoon.

There have been times when, for several days in a row, I have found myself tripping on the sidewalk. By the third pair of torn stockings I usually get the message: There's something wrong with the way I'm living, and I'm punishing myself in order to get my attention.

We are all victims of the games the unconscious can play on us. The flaming headache after we've been too polite to someone we can't stand. The car accident that occurs the day we had a knock-down, drag-out fight with a spouse or a boss.

The human mind is fascinating and mysterious, and it can be our teacher if we listen to what we are saying and doing. Recently my husband visited an army hospital where he had been stationed during World War II. After an hour there, he got back into the car and suddenly discovered that his foot was searching for a clutch — a reflex he couldn't control for several minutes. He hadn't driven a car with a clutch in twenty years. Memory and muscle had gone off on their own, sharpening the awareness of time passing.

Life is richer if we get into the games of the unconscious and discover more about ourselves.

Christmas Presents

BEFORE YOU START the usual exhausting round of shopping in crowded stores — before you start feeling that Christmas has become nothing but a commercial plot, I'd like to tell you a Christmas story about how we gave Aunt Lillie to my mother for Christmas.

It all happened about twenty-five years ago. My mother had been ill for several months and felt depressed about the coming holidays. The children in the family had all reached the age when all that mattered about our midwinter festival was presents, presents, presents. I was beginning to feel that the lovely traditions of most major religions, to try to bring some light and joy into the darkest days of the year, had been entirely forgotten. I felt betrayed.

Early in December I got a letter from Aunt Lillie. She wasn't really my aunt, but she and my mother had known each other since grade school, and I had adored her since she first taught me, at the age of one, to get down on all fours and bark like a doggie. She was one of my most favorite people all through my childhood, and it made me sad that she had moved to California and that my own child would not have the gift of Aunt Lillie's marvelous loving as she was growing up.

The letter said how sad and lonely Aunt Lillie was and how terribly she missed us all, especially my mother. That night my husband and I decided to give Lillie to my mother for Christmas. We borrowed part of the fare, got a round-trip ticket on the cheapest flight we could find, and Aunt Lillie arrived at our house a day or two before Christmas. At that time we lived in a house with two floors, and on Christmas Day we sat my mother on the couch and Aunt Lillie descended the stairs, wrapped from head to foot in white tissue paper with an enormous red ribbon tied around her middle. She stayed with my mother for about a week, and I guess it was the best and most memorable Christmas we ever had.

I hope it is a Christmas story which may make you think twice about getting into the shopping hassle. Whether you celebrate Christmas or Chanukah or any other kind of spiritual observance of the dark days of winter — whatever your own personal celebration may be — we need to remember that even the Druids decorated evergreens in the midst of winter and that in all of history there has been the need for human beings to huddle together in the dark and the cold. What we remember at such a time is that light and warmth come from loving, and that's the only present any of us really needs.

A Lifetime of Patchwork

MY MOUTH WAS WIDE OPEN, and my dentist was gazing unhappily at fifty-nine years of general deterioration, when he sighed in despair and said, "A lifetime of patchwork!" I nearly swallowed my removable bridge because he sure said a mouthful. This was a profound philosophical dental observation.

A lifetime of patchwork, indeed. Isn't that the story of our lives as we get closer and closer to old age? Not just the dental work in our mouths, but just about everything that has happened to us. We try to bring some order into each of our personal universes, but we never really succeed. As I look back on my life, it now seems to me that, because I could never know what the future held, the best that I could do was to fumble along, doing what I could to judge each crisis, each choice, each list of values and priorities as it came. By now I know I have to accept the fact that there is no clear line, no primary color, no simple design which emerges from the whole of life, but that patchwork is truly the name of the game.

Actually, I like this idea very much. The patchwork quilts that are part of American history are full of drama. When you look at an antique quilt that has been carefully preserved, you wonder how many women have savored this work of art and passed it on from generation to generation, together with the stories of its origin. That flowered, green material which keeps repeating itself was once the dress a great-great-grandmother wore to church every Sunday; that tiny square of pink was saved from a dress of the ancestor who died of smallpox in infancy; the triangles of brown corduroy came from the knickers great-uncle Ted wore playing some new-fangled game called baseball.

A patchwork quilt is the weaving together of life itself, the times of triumph and the memories of despair, the moments of ceremony and the fragments of routine — a history of the human condition.

When we try to make too many plans, to impose too much order in our lives, it seems to me that we are denying what is most essential about being human, and most miraculous: that we know we are mortal but that we cannot predict the future, and that somehow most of us develop the courage to take risks, to live through anguish, to celebrate love, and to stay truly glad we are alive. It doesn't make for a simple design, but a lifetime of patchwork sounds good to me.

The Birth of a Baby: Christmas

NO MATTER WHAT our particular religious connections and beliefs may be, all of us, Christians and non-Christians alike, are surely aware today of the sacredness of human life, the meaning of each new birth. As a matter of fact, all the midwinter festivals that I know about seem to emphasize children. There is a profound human recognition that a child can light up our lives even in the darkest days of winter. For me, the birth of a baby is the ultimate miracle of life — and I should know, having become a grandma for the first time very recently. Babies — children in general — are on most of our minds at Christmastime, and a most precious resource they surely are.

My husband was discussing the publication date of one of his books with a young woman editor. He had written the book, under great pressure from his publishers, in less than a year. Now his editor was telling him the book would not be published, after all, for another year and a half. "Good God!" he exploded. "You can make a *baby* in nine months. Why should it take a year and a half to publish a *book?*"

His editor looked him square in the eye and said, "When *we* publish a book, it is perfect. Which is more than you can say about a baby."

Poor woman! What she doesn't know about life! The perfect thing about babies is that they are not perfect, that they are so complicated and mysterious and unique that we can't review them or catalogue them in a library. They defy analysis and prediction. There is no way of measuring what misery or delight there will be in their lives, no way to assess what poetry there may be in their souls.

If you haven't been around one lately, I highly recommend a most refreshing outing. Find out what the visiting hours are in the maternity ward of the nearest hospital, and go and take a look at the babies in the nursery. For the time that you are looking, I guarantee that you will forget everything else — your headache, your unbalanced checkbook, your leaking roof, the dangers of war in the Mideast, the chemicals seeping into your drinking water, even the fact that your feet hurt. When we look at a baby, that's all there is in the whole world, and the reason for this is that in each baby there is an untold story. Nobody can tell how the story will turn out. Anything is possible. A tiny baby reminds us that, when all is said and done, we are human, we are a part of nature, and there is no machine that can match the miracle and the wonder of ourselves.

As the author of about fifteen mostly unknown books, I'm not knocking the publishing business; but one thing I'm sure about — no author will ever write, no editor will ever edit a book that is worth the little finger of any human child. I guess that's what we can all celebrate today.

Stuffed Animals

WELL, HALLELUJAH! There was an article in *The New York Times* announcing that a psychiatrist had discovered that stuffed animals are a great source of emotional comfort to children. Aren't you amazed? I know the thought never occurred to you before! But there's more to the story, so go get your teddy bear.

This psychiatrist actually did have an interesting point to make. For many years psychoanalysts took the attitude that while it was normal for a child to need a special blanket or toy until the age of about five, such an attachment was a sign of immaturity thereafter. What the good doctor was saying is that while we may get over needing to sleep with a teddy bear, there is nothing wrong at any age in enjoying personal possessions. He suggested that cars and paintings and other objects represent the adult's "special blanket."

The day after I read the article, I went to visit someone in the orthopedic ward of a hospital. A middle-aged woman with five kids, who had broken her back and was in great pain, lay on her bed with her eyes closed, clutching a toy duck that her children had brought her. In the next bed a young woman with a broken leg had a teddy bear and a unicorn, one on each side of her pillows. When I commented on this to a nurse, she said, "Oh, listen — we've realized for years that people never get over needing a stuffed animal!"

Paintings and cars may be substitutes for some people, but not me. I have two or three stuffed animals, and I do not accept the notion that I am in a state of regression — I just know what's good!

When my mother died, I happened to be alone in a hotel room three thousand miles from home. I'd bought a stuffed baby seal to give a niece, and in the middle of the night I unwrapped it, sat up in bed hugging it — singing a lullaby my mother used to sing — and sobbed my heart out. I was fifty-two years old at the time. A lady in California understood my feelings so well that when I wrote about this event in a magazine, she sent me a homemade Pooh, since she knew I'd given the seal to my niece.

If more people recognized just how comforting a stuffed animal can be at any stage, we might stop trying to accumulate so many other fancy, expensive things we don't really need.

When the mother of a little kid I know told him he'd been in a warm, safe place inside her body, he asked her if he'd had his special blanket before he was born. Something soft and furry is probably necessary to human well-being — perhaps a throwback to our ancestral homes in the trees! I for one wouldn't be without mine.

New Year's Eve

I HATE THOSE YELLOW SMILE BUTTONS for the same reason that I hate New Year's Eve. Both try to tell me when to be happy and when to have a good time, and both show a complete lack of understanding about the fact that smiling and having fun have to be spontaneous or it's all a fake. I'd like to assure you that you do *not* have to go out tonight and have a good time.

I can recall some New Year's Eves that were a lot of fun, and they were always times when we had no special plans. We'd meet a couple of friends for dinner or a movie, and we'd sort of wander around waiting for an adventure to overtake us; if it didn't, and we got tired, we went home and went to bed before twelve without guilt.

The worst New Year's Eves have been those involving going to a party and spending the evening trying to be gay, in the old-fashioned sense of the word. I don't think there is anything more depressing than feeling that you have to have a good time even if it kills you.

I hate the smile buttons because they deny a natural part of life — they suggest that there is a way to avoid being unhappy or angry if you just smile. If there have to be buttons at all, at least one half should be a grim face or a tear-stained one. It's so much easier to cope with life if we don't waste time and energy on pretending life can be beautiful all the time.

If you feel like putting on an old bathrobe and watching television, or if you want to wash your hair, or if you want to read a new mystery book tonight, go ahead and do it! If you feel like having a quiet dinner with some old friends — well, sure, why not — so long as you don't torture each other with having to be merry and waiting up for midnight. Instead of drinking too much in order to masquerade a conviviality you don't feel, call up a friend who's had an operation and listen to his or her miseries. There's nothing more cheering than to tell your troubles to someone, and you'll both feel better, because you've done a good deed.

And if you don't feel like calling anyone, and you're home alone and feeling sad and lonely, for heaven's sake, have some ice cream and go to sleep. There's no law that says you have to pay homage to the calendar. It hasn't been that great a year, so let it go in peace. Tomorrow morning, when everyone else has a hangover, you can greet the new day and meditate quietly over your breakfast about what you can do to help make the new year better.

Happy New Year!

One-Year Anniversary: A Summation

TODAY IS AN ANNIVERSARY for me, for it brings to an end one full year of my radio program, "Getting Along." In introducing myself one year ago, I promised no rose gardens, no simple answers to the complex problems of coping with the human condition. All I offered was my companionship in our mutual struggle to find better ways of getting along.

In the course of this year we have shared some tragedies and some joys. There have been some terrifying floods and earthquakes — and then there have been moments like the hostages returning from Iran. There have been discouraging evidences of human frailty, such as Abscam, and there have been moments of feeling deeply united in our horror at the attempted assassinations of President Reagan and Pope John Paul and at the murder of Anwar Sadat. There is a lifting of the spirit when one hears about the remarkable courage of the workers in Poland, and then a feeling of horror and despair at the brutality of countrymen toward each other in Iran and El Salvador. We hit a lot of highs and lows together, getting along.

None of us has gotten through this year unscathed in personal ways. The death of someone we loved; the pain of divorce; terror brought on by sudden unemployment; a debilitating chronic illness. The birthday of a grandchild was a day of joy; premenstrual tension and menopausal hot flashes brought some days of stress; feelings of depression for a while, and then a time of optimism and great energy. And then exhaustion — and times of anger at others, and guilt. Worries and nightmares, giggling over something silly, crying at one movie, practically having an accident from laughing too hard at another one. Periods of quiet serenity, and other times of trauma and crisis. There is no way around any of it.

But it does matter what we do about being mortal. It matters a lot. Have we tried to grow, to become more, through our life experiences? Did we learn from our frustrations? Are we wiser, more sensitive, and compassionate than we were a year ago? Are we absorbing the lessons life hands us, and do we use them for inner development?

A woman wrote me recently that sometimes she feels so guilty about the things she did wrong as a mother she could kill herself. But she said she was learning and getting better at it all the time. That's all we owe anyone; that's all we owe ourselves — that marvelous human potential for changing and growing. I'm still willing to settle for that. It's enough, and it's everything.

Index

Abortion, 80-81
Accident proneness, 119-20
Adolescence, 97-98, 128-29
Adoption, 157-60
Adulthood, 174-75. *See also* Middle age;
     Old age; Young adulthood
Aging, 54-55, 115-16, 180-81. *See also*
     Middle age; Old age
Agnosticism, 59-60
Airports, waiting in, 32-33
Alcoholism, 107
Ambivalence, 163-65
Anger, 2-3, 45, 70-71, 81-82, 104-05,
     161-62, 219-20
Anxiety, productive, 198-99
Automobiles
     accidents in, 119-20, 195-96
     drivers of, 118-19
Avenue of the Righteous (by Peter
     Hellman), 63

Babies, 29-30, 72, 239-40. *See also* Child
     raising; Children; Families
Backaches, 224-25
Baird, Bil, 217
Battering, in families, 227-28
Bigness, dangers of, 183-84
Binet, Alfred, 18
Birth control, 80-81
Birthdays, 5-6, 96-97, 98-100
Bisexuality, 133-34. *See also*
     Homosexuality
Blacks, 199-200
Books, 39-42
Born-again human beings, 84-85
Buchwald, Art, 44

Camps, children's, 114-15

Careers. *See* Work
Carrel, Alexis, 190-91
Celebration, 5-6, 34-35, 98-100, 232-33
Censorship, 39-42
Chanukah, 231, 237
Chauvinism, male, 48-49
Child raising, 72-73, 110, 155-56, 176-77
     and anger at children, 45, 176-77
     and children's camps, 114-15
     and day-care centers, 185-87
     and discipline, 187-88
     and exhaustion in children, 79-80
     fathers' role in, 112-13
     guilt about, 45, 114-15, 155, 161
     and nursery schools, 185-87
     by single parents, 165-71
     by stepparents, 170-71
     and teaching swimming, 12-21
     See also Babies; Children; Families
Children, 239-40
     adopted, 157-60
     battered, 227-28
     and death, exposure to, 63-64, 195-96
     exhaustion in, 79-80
     kidnapping of, by parents, 161-62
     and play, 61, 153
     protection of, 21-22, 80-81, 141-42,
          161-62, 181-82
     unwanted, 80-81
     See also Babies; Child raising; Families
Children of Jonestown, The (by Kenneth
     Wooden), 81
Choices, 1-4, 176-77
Christmas, 76, 221-22, 231, 233-34, 237-
     40
Citizenship, 111-12
Columbus Day, 182-83
Comforting, 162-63
Commitment, 225-26

Communication, 89-90, 147-48, 165-66. *See also* Families
Community centers, for teenagers, 84-85
Computer games, 12-13
Crying, 58-59, 179-80

Dating
    at a later age, 37-39
    services for, 88-89
Day-care centers, 185-86
Daydreaming, 7-8, 61, 86
Death, 63-64, 67-68, 201-02, 207, 232-33
Decisions. *See* Choices
Dependence, 100-01, 154-55
Depression, 9-12, 62-63, 76, 104-05, 148-49, 230-31. *See also* Grief
Dieting, 3-4, 77-78, 124-25, 221-22
Discipline, in child raising, 186-87
Divorce, 116-17, 148-49. *See also* Single parents
Dreams, 137-40
Drugs, 11, 107-08
Dunbar, Flanders, 119
Duncan, David Douglas (*The Fragile Miracle of Martin Gray*), 202

Education, 111-12, 173-74. *See also* Day-care centers; Nursery schools
Election Day, 205-06
Encounter groups. *See* Group therapy
Envy, 220-21. *See also* Jealousy
Exhaustion, children's, 79-80

Failure, 104-05
Families
    definitions of, 90-91
    extended, 66, 142-43
    fathers in, 112-13, 125-26, 165-71
    grandparents in, 66-67
    mothers in, 30-31, 75-76, 93-94, 191-94
    parents-in-law in, 101-02, 108-09
    physical abuse in, 227-28
    prejudice in, 94-95
    relationships in, 81-82, 101-02, 108-09, 125-26, 128-29, 151-52, 154-56, 177-78, 211-12

Families *(cont'd)*
    single parents in, 92-93, 165-71
    stepparents in, 170-71
    therapy in, 68-69, 227-28
    two careers or incomes in, 30-31, 93-94, 191-94
    See also Child raising; Marriage
Family Crucible, The (by Augustus Napier and Carl Whitaker), 69
Family therapy, 68-69, 227-28
Fathers, 112-13, 125-26, 165-71. *See also* Families
Father's Day, 112-13
For Those I Loved (by Martin Gray), 202
Forgetfulness, 35-37
Fragile Miracle of Martin Gray, The (by David Douglas Duncan), 202
Frank, Anne, 98-100
Frank, Fritzi, 98
Frank, Otto, 98-100
Freud, Sigmund, 72, 110
Friendship, 208-11
Fun, 152-53, 242. *See also* Play

Gassmann, Martha, 53
Generations, 54-55, 135-36, 162-63, 177-78, 211-12. *See also* Families
Glass, Joanna (*To Grandmother's House We Go*), 155
Glasser, Ronald (*365 Days*), 39-40
Grandparents, 66-67, 68. *See also* Families
Gray, Martin, 202
Grief, 35, 63-64, 148-49, 197-98, 201-02, 208-09, 232-33
Group therapy, 26-27, 55-56, 68-69
Growth, personal, 96-97, 137-40, 174-77, 243-44. *See also* Self-fulfillment
Grudges, 70-71
Guilt, 2-3
    about child raising, 45, 114-15, 155, 161
    and dieting, 3-4
    about men doing housework, 49
    about sex, 33-34
    in working mothers, 191-92
    See also Self-hatred

Hayes, Helen, 198-99

Healing
  holistic, 197-98
  psychic, 190-91
Hellman, Peter (*Avenue of the Righteous*),
  63
Heroism, 14-15, 63
Hitler, Adolf, 44
  Mein Kampf, author of, 41
Holidays, 221-23, 230-31. *See also*
  names of individual holidays
Holistic medicine, 197-98
Home pride, 47-48
Homemaking, 194-95
Homosexuality, 51-54. *See also*
  Bisexuality
Honesty, 26-27, 105-06
Hospices, 207
Hospitalization, 160-61
Hostility. *See* Anger
Hugging, 71-72
Human liberation, 132-33. *See also* Men's
  liberation; Women's liberation
Humor, 43-45, 164

Ideas, fear of, 41-42
Imagination, 153-54
Income taxes, 56-58
Inflation, 121-22
Insomnia, 134-35, 209-10
Intelligence tests, 16-19, 43

Jealousy, 102-03. *See also* Envy
Johnson, Virginia E., and William H.
  Masters, 33
Jonestown, Guyana, 81

Kaye, Danny, 44
Kazantzakis, Nikos, 180
Kidnapping of children, by parents, 161-
  62
King, Billie Jean, 133
King, Jr., Martin Luther, 14-15
Kinsey, Alfred Charles, 33, 53
Kukla, Fran, and Ollie, 153-54
Kuralt, Charles (*Sunday Morning*), 75

Labor Day, 171-72
Letters, 32, 126, 233-34
Lincoln, Abraham, 44

Living together, by unmarried couples,
  28-29
Loafing, 7-8. *See also* Daydreaming
Loneliness, 85-86
Love, 23-24, 109-10, 135-36, 146-47,
  164, 202-05, 208-09
Lying, 105-06

Macy Parade (Thanksgiving Day), 216-17
Male chauvinism, 48-49
Marriage, 28-29, 234-35
  communication in, 89-90
  martyr complex in, 50-51
  and parents-in-law, 108-09
  and prejudiced relatives, 94-95
  togetherness in, 6-7
  two careers or incomes in, 31, 93-94,
    191-94
  and vacations, 83-84
  and youth cult, 115-16
  See also Families
Martyr complex, in marriage, 50-51
Masters, William H., and Virginia E.
  Johnson, 33
Materialism, 121-22, 220-21
May, Rollo, 33-34
"Me generation," 135-36
Meditation, 156-57
Mein Kampf (by Adolf Hitler), 41
Men
  chauvinism of, 48-49
  and commitment, 225-26
  and crying, 58-59, 179-80
  liberation of, 130-32
  middle-aged, 179-80
  and relationships with women, 132,
    225-26
  traveling, 125-26
  See also Fathers
Men's liberation, 130-31. *See also* Human
  liberation
Mentally retarded, home for, 84-85
Miale, Florence, 83
Middle age, 96-98, 175, 179-80
Mistakes, 3-4
Money
  and income taxes, 56-57
  and inflation, 121-22
  lending of, 223-24

Money *(cont'd)*
in two-income families, 30-31
Morality, 126-27
Mortality, awareness of, 5-6, 54-55, 96-98, 180-81, 232-33
Mothers, 75-76
working, 30-31, 93-94, 191-94
See also Families
Mother's Day, 75-76
Mourning. *See* Grief

Names, importance of, 213
Napier, Augustus, and Carl Whitaker (*The Family Crucible*), 69
Nature, 74-75
New Year's Eve, 242-43
New Year's resolutions, 1-2
Nixon, Richard, 44
Nursery schools, 185-86
Nursing homes, 213-14. *See also* Old-age homes

Offices, windowless, 218-19
Old age, 54-55, 67-68, 175, 180-81, 238-39
children taking over in, 211-12
hospices in, 207
nursing homes in, 213-14
old-age homes in, 228-29
and senility, 206-07
and sex, 144-46, 228-29
Old-age homes, 228-29. *See also* Nursing homes
On Golden Pond (the play, by Ernest Thompson), 34
Overweight. *See* Dieting

Parapsychology, 189-90
Parent kidnappers, 161-62
Parenting. *See* Child raising
Parents. *See* Families
Parents-in-law, 101-02, 108-09
Physical abuse, in families, 227-28
Play, 61-62, 153-54. *See also* Fun
Prejudice, in families, 94-95
Privacy, 55-56, 143
Prostitutes, 87
Psychic healing, 190-91

Psychology, 42-43, 52, 53. *See also* Psychotherapy
Psychosomatic illness, 197-98
Psychotherapy, 24-26, 117, 137, 149-50, 197-98.
See also Family therapy; Group therapy; Psychology

Regression, 77
Religion, 59-60
Retirement, 143-44, 181
Ribble, Margaret, 72
Right to life, 80-81
Risks, 182-83
Rogers, Will, 44

St. Valentine's Day, 23-24
Sarton, May, 85
Satir, Virginia, 69
Self-fulfillment, 20-21, 117-18, 225-26.
See also Growth, personal
Self-hatred, 2-3, 53, 77-78, 102-03, 227-28. *See also* Guilt
Selye, Hans, 19, 143
Senility, 206-07
Sex, 33-34
bisexual, 133-34
education about, 86-87
guilt about, 33-34
homosexual, 51-54
in old age, 144-46, 228-29
Sex by Prescription (by Thomas Szasz), 33
Sharing workshops. *See* Group therapy
Shyness, 38-39
Siblings, 15-16, 41
Simon, Théodore, 18
Single parents, 92-93, 165-71. *See also* Families
Spitz, René, 72
Spock, Benjamin, 107, 110
Spring, 74-75
Stalin, Joseph, 44
Star Trek, 14
Stepparents, 170-71. *See also* Families
Stevenson, Adlai, 44
Stress, 19-20, 197-98, 219-20, 235-36
Stuffed animals, 240-41
Sunday (television program), 75

Swimming, by children, 120–21
Szasz, Thomas (*Sex by Prescription*), 33

Talking, 147–48, 165–66
Taxes, income, 56–57
Teachers, 173–74
Teenagers, 84–85, 128–29
Tell Me a Riddle (the movie), 67–68, 144–45
Thanksgiving Day, 215–17
Thanksgiving Day Macy Parade, 216–17
Thant, U, 182
Therapy. *See* Family therapy; Group therapy; Psychotherapy
365 Days (by Ronald Glasser), 39–40
Tillstrom, Burr (*Kukla, Fran, and Ollie*), 153–54
To Grandmother's House We Go (by Joanna Glass), 155
Touching, 71–72
Tragedy in life, 34–35, 124–25, 201–02. *See also* Death; Grief
Traumas, 104–05, 195–96
Travel, 32–33
    by working men, 125–26
    See also Vacations
Truman, Harry, 44

Unconscious, the, 235–36
Unemployment, 123–24

Vacations, 76–77, 229–30
    and marriage, 83–84
Voting, 205–06

Washington's Birthday, 26–27
Watson, John B., 110

Wertheimer, Max, 61
Whitaker, Carl, and Augustus Napier (*The Family Crucible*), 69
White House conferences on family, 90
Widowhood, 37–38, 63–65, 72. *See also* Death; Grief
Wills, 46–47
Women, 214–15
    middle-aged, 179–80
    and relationships with men, 132, 225–26
    single, 225–26
    working, 30–31, 93–94, 146–47, 191–94
Women's liberation, 146–47, 195, 214–15. *See also* Human liberation; Men's liberation
Wooden, Kenneth (*The Children of Jonestown*), 81
Words, fear of, 39–41
Work
    ethic of, 171–72
    loss of, 123–24
    men's and women's relationships in, 132
    and mothers, 30–31, 93–94, 191–94
    retirement from, 143–44
    and travel, 125–26
    and two-career or two-income families, 30–31, 93–94, 191–94
    and women, 30–31, 93–94, 146–47, 191–94
World Trade Center, New York, 183–84
Worrying, 129–30

Young adulthood, 154–55, 174–75
Youth cult, 115–16